Lecture Notes in Artificial Intelligence   7407

Subseries of Lecture Notes in Computer Science

LNAI Series Editors

Randy Goebel
   University of Alberta, Edmonton, Canada
Yuzuru Tanaka
   Hokkaido University, Sapporo, Japan
Wolfgang Wahlster
   DFKI and Saarland University, Saarbrücken, Germany

LNAI Founding Series Editor

Joerg Siekmann
   DFKI and Saarland University, Saarbrücken, Germany

Robert Trappl (Ed.)

Your Virtual Butler

The Making-of

 Springer

Series Editors

Randy Goebel, University of Alberta, Edmonton, Canada
Jörg Siekmann, University of Saarland, Saarbrücken, Germany
Wolfgang Wahlster, DFKI and University of Saarland, Saarbrücken, Germany

Volume Editor

Robert Trappl
Austrian Research Institute for Artificial Intelligence (OFAI) of the
Austrian Society for Cybernetic Studies (OSGK)
Freyung 6/6, 1010 Vienna, Austria
E-mail: robert.trappl@ofai.at
and
Center for Brain Research, Medical University of Vienna
Spitalgasse 4, 1090 Vienna, Austria
E-mail: robert.trappl@meduniwien.ac.at

ISSN 0302-9743   e-ISSN 1611-3349
ISBN 978-3-642-37345-9   e-ISBN 978-3-642-37346-6
DOI 10.1007/978-3-642-37346-6
Springer Heidelberg Dordrecht London New York

Library of Congress Control Number: 2013934225

CR Subject Classification (1998): I.2.0-1, I.2.9, I.2.11, H.5.3-4, K.4.1-2

LNCS Sublibrary: SL 7 – Artificial Intelligence

Typesetting: Camera-ready by author, data conversion by Scientific Publishing Services, Chennai, India

Printed on acid-free paper

Springer is part of Springer Science+Business Media (www.springer.com)

Preface

In most scenarios of the future, e.g., the one commissioned by the German Federal Ministry for Education and Research in their Vision "Living in a Networked World: Individually and Safely" and undertaken by the Institute of Future Studies and Technology Assessment named "Tina and Her Butler," there is a personalized virtual butler. This butler not only performs communication and coordination tasks, but also gives recommendations on how to handle everyday problems; the butler also knows some of the most intimate quirks of its owner. It clearly has to be trained by its mistress/master, but it also has to learn whether its assistance is welcome. This scenario is presented in Chap. 2.

The aim of this book is to explore the prerequisites of such a personalized virtual butler: What is known about the capacities and the needs of aging people; which methods of information and communication technologies have been used in assisting/conversing with persons, especially older ones, and with what results; what are the advantages/disadvantages of virtual butlers as mainly software programs compared to robots as butlers; and which methods, especially in artificial intelligence, have to be developed further and in which direction in order to realize a virtual butler in the foreseeable future?

When we planned this book, we first studied the literature in gerontopsychology and the experiences of persons working with aging people. Second, we considered the results of related projects in the EU Framework Programme for Research, e.g., COMPANIONS, LIREC, NETCARITY, HUMAINE, and RASCALLI. In HUMAINE, the Austrian Research Institute for Artificial Intelligence (OFAI) cooperated as a partner, in RASCALLI it even acted as a coordinator.

Through these sources, potential contributors to this book were identified, invited to submit position papers, preferably taking into consideration the scenario mentioned above, and then invited to participate in a two-day workshop at the OFAI to present and exchange their ideas. The workshop formed the basis for most of the chapters in this book.

The contributors to this book therefore come from, among others, the University of London, the Institute of Cognitive Science and Technology of the National Research Council of Italy, the University of British Columbia, the Westmont University in Santa Barbara, the Fraunhofer Institute of Production Technology and Automation, Stuttgart, and the University of Applied Sciences, Saarbrücken.

A book like this would not have been possible without the commitment of many persons.

First, I want to thank the authors, who took great pains to enhance their original position papers to book chapters by including new material and by considering the comments in and outside the discussions.

Second, I want to thank my colleagues at OFAI, who have been of great help, namely, Paolo Petta in establishing contact with potential contributors,

Sabine Payr for her support during the workshop and afterwards, and last but not least Karin Vorsteher for her great efforts in proofreading, formatting, preparing the index, and many other activities for which there is not enough space to list.

Third, I want to thank the editor of the LNAI series, Joerg Siekmann, for including this book in the series, and Springer for their support in the publication process, especially Christine Reiss, Ursula Barth, and Alfred Hofmann.

Finally, I want to thank the Austrian taxpayers whose money allowed us to develop the foundations for the workshop, to pay for the travel and hotel expenses of the participants of the workshop, and then to prepare this book. We received this money through the Austrian Federal Ministry of Transport, Innovation and Technology, with Doris Bures as Federal Minister, and its very supportive officers, Ingolf Schädler, Reinhard Goebl, Karl Supa, and Lisbeth Mosnik, to whom I offer my sincere gratitude for trusting that I would finally present a useful end product.

I hope you enjoy this book.

August 2012   Robert Trappl

Scenario - "Tina and Her Butler"

Robert Gassner and Karlheinz Steinmüller

"To live is to stay in touch", this could be the slogan of Tina S. She is quickly approaching the age of 70, but indeed still is — as many of the elderly in the year 2020 — enjoying a very active lifestyle: travels, honorary appointments, fitness, friends, relations, and the "part time office" with her son — no, you certainly could not say Tina is threatened with boredom.

Video-Conversations Only on Demand and . . .

Right now "James", the virtual butler, comes forward and announces an incoming call: granddaughter Victoria is getting in touch again. It is remarkable, though, that James is signalling a video-call: usually it is rather Tina who makes a point of getting a visual display even in short conversations with her grandchildren, the way otherwise only the family doctor does for virtual home visits.

Tina adjusts her posture in her chair. James interprets her movement correctly—a red blinking light indicates that James has turned on the tiny camera.

"Hello, Vicki, haunted by geometry assignments again?" Tina could hardly think of any other reason for a call with the optical channel.

"That was two years ago, grandma, in tenth grade, I now need you for something special," a rather dishevelled Victoria shows up on the small screen. "I need you, well, as contemporary witness. For a homework essay, with the topic 'When my grandparents were young'." Above all, Victoria would like to know how her ancestors managed to get by without the Evernet. And since the essay should be delivered with multimedia support, she needs original sound and pictures. "You don't mind, do you, grandma?"

. . . If Required with Electronic "Scenery"

No, that is not the issue. But Tina has to tidy herself up a bit, even if it is just for school homework: check the hair; optimise electronically the colour of the blouse; should she also have some jewellery composed into the picture? After all, she has not anticipated she would have to grant a TV interview today, so to say.

Insufficiencies of Communication Technology Are Overcome. . .

With her 17 years of age, Victoria still has a rather confused idea of the past. Of course cars and TV had long existed in Tina's youth, and appointments had also already been made by phone, only that you did not carry one around with you. "You ask about the biggest difference? Many things were simpler and for this very same reason more complicated: You have to imagine that way back then we had mostly to deal with lifeless devices, which would not talk to you, would not memorise anything, not even phone numbers. Later, roughly around the turn of the century, there was an upsurge of countless small appliances, of more or less practical value; but these did not have any exchanges among them yet. If you had entered a phone number in your cell phone, your laptop would still not know it by a long shot. You had to take care of everything yourself. — At that time, technology was often developed without enquiring accurately enough what the added value for the user could be or without having an eye on the social networks the technology was supposed to support. Imagine: even after the year 2000 we still had so-called multi-band phones and had to make elaborate decisions which network we wanted to communicate in ... One also had to decide for oneself whether and how to encode an email—or else to forget about it. It also was not straightforward to do, over a period one even had to send the so-called 'public keys' by oneself, — and at that time there was only just a single level of privacy. Today we have four levels of security—but you don't even notice, because your butler takes care of everything."

...By the Personalised Virtual Butler

No wonder Tina thinks highly of "her James": the personalised virtual butler takes on communication and coordination tasks, manages the calendar of appointments, "looks" after household technology and offers advice with many problems of daily life—from insurance to fitness; checks price tags; negotiates offers; and many things more. Furthermore, he is unconditionally "close-lipped", which is important insofar as he knows many of Tina's small quirks, for example, that she does not want to watch any movies on TV where spiders pop up. After all, she has been breaking in James for over five years now, and by now he already knows quite precisely when she wants to be approachable for whom, and at what time of the day it is the turn for what activities. Sometimes Tina even gets the impression that James already recognises her condition by the pitch of her voice and manages to guess whether she is up for a chat with one of her friends or not. —She simply has to ask maintenance service sometime, whether this is indeed possible, or whether she is just imagining it.

Users Are Recognised and Understood

"Back then," Tina continues, "devices did not know their users, and even if they had a speech module at all it would only babble some pre-recorded phrases— understanding and recognition being totally out of the question. At that time I had list of all kinds of passwords stuck to my screen—for the corporate workspace; for online-shopping; online-banking; etc. —they were all different, impossible to keep them all in mind.

Social Participation Thanks to Networked Worlds of Interaction

"But do you know, Victoria, perhaps the biggest difference is that for the elderly the scope of life kept shrinking; at first, they were not allowed to work any more; then, the body would not want to; sooner or later one was imprisoned within the house or in a single room and but for two, three close relatives or old acquaintances no-one would take care of you. Now there is an old gentleman in our condominium who is completely confined to his bed, care level 3.5, if that should mean anything to you, but he is still active in multiple associations and is even taking care of the net forum of his golf club. His body is giving up, but in some way he can still be a participant everywhere. That keeps him mentally in shape. — But now let's hear what your friend," — for a second she struggles for the name, then James prompts her, "what your friend Paul is doing".

But even as Victoria is still expanding about her current fad, James signals an incoming VoiceMail with an as decent as old-fashioned gong chime. In contrast to many young people Tina does not like to lead two conversations at once, but Victoria anyway states that she now will have to first process the information received: "I'll be back in touch, grandma."

The Virtual Butler as Mobility Agent

Tina's friend Gertrude announces she will be late for the agreed fitness training. She sounds somewhat irritated: the rain has upset her plans. In fact, her virtual butler had made re-arrangements in good time and looked up for her a connection by bus instead of the usual underground. But she held off too long with the accelerated departure and thus in spite of all caring mentoring she ended up catching only the back view of the bus. In her agitation, Gertrude does not disclose how long she now will have to shiver at the bus stop, but James already made his enquiries: she will arrive in a little over half an hour.

Virtual Travel Planning with "Farsightedness" and ... Agent Support

The "TV interview" has livened up Tina more than she would like to admit to herself. She runs to the window, as if Gertrude could already be coming, tinkers with the idea of going through the planning for summer vacation with James for yet another time. But she has already inspected her hotel room and the surrounding hiking goals twice. And whether any of the hotel guests would make for a dancing partner or a round of card games is better left for James to find out in advance.

"In the meantime, You could water the flowers for Dorothy, madam" James reminds her. "You promised to take care of the flowers until she gets back from her educational leave."

Mobile Communications "Almost as at Home"

Of course. This she had yet again—repressed. Tina is candid with herself. She had promised Dorry to do it, but she just does not fancy entering the alien flat. She pulls herself together, walks out into the small atrium of the semi-detached house. The lock clicks shut behind her; James is now "located" in her bracelet, which in addition to the communication interface also houses the VitalsMonitor.

Security as Required

Then Tina is standing in front of the neighbour's door. Why does not anybody open? "What's up, James?" With a thin "bracelet-voice" James explains that

Dorothy's apartment door is set to security level three and requires identification by voice in addition to the shake-hands of the virtual butler. "You will not quarrel with a door," Tina orders herself and utters her name.

Personalisation... According to Taste

Inside, Dorry's butler welcomes her with an altogether embarrassing confidentiality: "Hello Tina. How are you?"— She is here to take care of something, and not to small-talk with the software! But she knows, it is always awkward to deal with an alien butler. Already the fact that the "Djinn", as Dorry calls her Butler, is looking at her as an oriental bottle ghost from not one, but two screens does not match her sense of humour. James is reserved. Four years ago she invested the effort of having a tailored pictorial embodiment for James made up for her, it is true, but she hardly ever uses it. The voice, with a slightly posh twanging, emulating a famous actor from the century past, almost always does the trick for her.

Everything Automatic?

Dorry affords the luxury of having the flowers of her small winter garden not be watered by the domotics. What Tina delegated for herself to James (and the home technology controlled by him) with the aid of a few small pipes, Dorry prefers to keep in her own hands—"or else one could set up some leased or artificial plants as well!"

"Offnet" — Unavailability as Luxury

Some of the plants make an unwholesome impression—did they already look like this at the time of Dorry's departure? It would be Tina's preference to check back with Dorry, but Dorry is unreachable over her holidays—at least once a year "offNet", this is a bare minimum of luxury requirement. And this puppy of her Djinn declares himself not to be competent for this case, though otherwise he is paying so much heed to Dorry's preferences!

In all the hurry a flower pot overflows, an earthy broth drips onto the floor. Immediately the automatic vacuum cleaner comes snorkelling along, and steers around her shoes. "Djinn, why don't you do this once I'm away?" But the Djinn insists, "Dorry always wants wet dirt to be done away with before it starts to dry." In any case, Tina is jolly glad when the door closes behind her again.

Her mood brightens up instantly, as she sees Gertrude coming. Under Gertrude's umbrella they stroll to the community complex of the housing estate, where the exercise rooms are located.

Trust Is of the Essence

Gertrude, even though quite a few years Tina's elder, carries out the profession of a "personal secretary". She attends to several clients, mostly in financial matters. It is one of her most important tasks to maintain control for her clients over the multifarious electronic and unfortunately often too little considered payments in transportation, entertainment, or use of media, and thereby to prevent personal expenditure to get out of hand. Of course a virtual butler would also be able to do this, but, as Gertrude phrases it, "some people just want social control." In doing so, she leaves it open which client is placing too little trust in the payment system and who would rather want their own consumerism be controlled in a trustful manner.

Fitness Training for Body and Mind

Gertrude, as also Tina, is an ardent fan of VR-fitness. "Build the mind along with the body!" that already used to be the motto as this initially rather expensive technology was first introduced in commercial fitness studios. It is only a few years back that the operators of Tina's housing estate had their own fitness complex retrofitted with such a VR-Cave.

This time the two have chosen a walking unit through the Valley of the Kings. The run through actual sand, the treadmill underneath being almost imperceptible, the heat approximates the original weather conditions and the optical illusion is also sufficiently convincing. Of course they know that they cannot climb down into the tombs. And as they stamp along, a virtual guide refreshes their knowledge about the Old Empire. —- until James comes forward: the optimal training level has been reached. For next week, they book a virtual cross-country skiing track around an Inuit settlement in Greenland.

Expanded Participation in Political Life

A quick quarter of an hour later, Tina and Gertrude are cosily sitting together over a cup of coffee. Of course the coffee machine brew Gertrude's cup exactly to her liking: decaffeinated and with ample Crema. But whether it was James who still remembered Gertrude's taste or whether it was Gertrude's butler who took the initiative is of no concern to them. The only thing that matters is that the coffee tastes good and that they have the opportunity for an exchange over the next activities for the "party for social rejuvenation and generational balance". Tina and Gertrude share the view that the upcoming generation is being pushed to the fringes by being simply outnumbered by the seniors—and this cannot be good, neither for the old nor the young. Both first became members via the "electronic regional association", but by now have also already participated on site to a few events.

Work with Maximum Flexibility

They also agree that excluding the seniors from the labour market would not be of any help to anyone. Jointly with her son Karl, Tina herself operates a professional allocation service for volunteers and agency for honorary offices. Since Karl travels frequently in his second job as musician, they virtualised her office through and through. In this way, Tina and he can deal with almost everything at home or even from underway. This not only saves them the rent, but they can also stand in for each other in a most flexible manner.

Remote Servicing in the "Privacy Sphere"

Towards evening, Gertrude says good-bye. Tina cleans up. She is a little anxious: remote servicing of James is due tonight. There has never been any serious accident in this matter, and furthermore there is always a backup. And still...
Upon waking up, James will not be exactly the same any more. Perhaps react a tad differently from before in conversation. And even if there should be no perceivable changes: she will still be on the lookout herself, for an unusual stammer, a slip of the tongue... The first days after the inspection she always feels a bit eerie, most probably without any reason. And still... An inspection just is an uncomfortable thing, akin to a health check-up. You never know what the result will be.

Liability for Agents

In any case, James cannot get around having the check-up, since it is only by keeping up with the regular six-monthly inspections by certified personnel that the insurance protection against misconduct of the virtual butler will remain valid, e.g. taking on liability in case James should cause unwanted costs in his researches or negotiations or cause any other (intangible) damage. Furthermore, it is in Tina's best own interest to know whether James is still "clean", or for instance making superfluous suggestions due to infiltrated illegal client-binding software.

Trust Is Not a Matter of Luck

Of course Tina has exercised highest care in the selection of the servicing company: several offers, personal talks with personnel. Whoever thought to be able to fob her off with an electronic salesperson, a sales avatar, was already out. In principle she also does trust this Dr.-Ing. Mehlmann, who is going through James with a fine-tooth comb each time—she would not accept a service with changing or anonymous carers. The fact that this Dr.-Ing. once even advised against the update of a component speaks in his favour.

Levels of Realism

In the evening, Victoria calls up once more, this time only acoustically. With pride she reports about her good grades in a training program for employment applications, which is part of the school leaving exams. Unlike at Tina's times, the first round of applications (and accordingly also the training) always takes place in Cyberspace and is strictly carried out with gender-neutral avatars on both sides. "I would have gotten the job," Victoria is all enthused, after which she finally comes to the point. "Hey grandma, if you have the time,

I would perhaps stop by at your place sometime tomorrow. You have to show me the old family pictures once more, perhaps I can use something for my homework— 'Grandma with a change-of-the-century shlepptop' or some such. Why don't you finally have all the photos scanned in, anyway?"

Guess why. Tina has to smile. Would Victoria drop by, if all the photos were available on the Net?

Translated by Paolo Petta

Table of Contents

Introduction: From Jeeves to Jeannie to Siri, and Then?

Robert Trappl[1,2]

[1] Austrian Research Institute for Artificial Intelligence (OFAI), Freyung 6,
1010 Vienna, Austria
`robert.trappl@ofai.at`
[2] Center for Brain Research, Medical University of Vienna, Spitalgasse 4,
1090 Vienna, Austria

Abstract. Servants and butlers always have been playing an important role, not only in books of history but also in fiction, such as fairy tales, novels, plays, operas, and films. Three types of them are discussed: "Natural Servants", i.e. human ones, who understand the wishes of their masters well but, in any case, their mental and physical capabilities cannot exceed those of humans. "Ghost Servants" like genies with capabilities we humans can only dream of, and "Robotic Servants" that have a machine as a body and sensors and actuators controlled by complex, often smart programs. Several examples of each type are presented, relating them to the aims of a "virtual butler". Finally, the contribution of every chapter of this volume to the "making-of" is highlighted.

Probably the oldest information about an artificial butler was found in a tomb in Egypt, a figure about 4000 years old, bearing the inscription: "Hail, Shabti Figure! If by Osiris <name of the deceased> be decreed to do any of the work which is to be done in Khert-Nefer, let everything which stands in the way be removed from him – whether it be plough the fields, or to fill the channels with water, or to carry sand from the East to the West." The Shabti Figure replies, "I will do it, verily I am here when you call."

It is, evidently, unknown if this arrangement worked. Servants and butlers played a major role in the past, as is documented not only in history books but also in fiction, such as fairy tales, novels, and plays from ancient greek *tragoidia* to *commedia dell' arte*: characters like Truffaldino, Leporello, Figaro, Sancho Pansa, and many others are well-known.

Looking more closely at all these servants and butlers, one is tempted to distinguish between three types: 1. The "natural" servants, 2. the "ghost" servants, and 3. the "robotic" servants.

1. The "natural" servants are the human ones, even if they are fictional characters in a story or a play. Most of the servants mentioned above belong to this type. As an example, Jeeves may serve, in both meanings:

Jeeves and Wooster are fictional characters, presented in short stories and novels, written by G. P. Wodehouse, from 1915 to 1974, and, later, in a series of films, with actors Stephen Fry and Hugh Laurie. Bertie Wooster is a well-meaning but rather dim

R. Trappl (Ed.): Your Virtual Butler, LNAI 7407, pp. 1–8, 2013.

aristocrat and Jeeves his valet who is of unvaluable help with overbearing aunts, unbidden guests, friends in need, and romantic entanglements of Bertie. Several of these films already can be viewed on YouTube.

The difference between a "butler" and a "valet" is that the first is responsible for a person or a family and the household and therefore potentially also for other personnel while the second is responsible only for a single person. But clearly also a valet has to perform butler functions.

"Jeeves" has become a generic term for any useful and reliable person, at least in England. It is even to be found in the Oxford English Dictionary. An Internet search website had been named AskJeeves for ten years, when in 2006 its name was changed to Ask.com. Only recently Ask.com announced that Ask Jeeves Web Search is back, answering everyday questions. And in the computer game "The World of Warcraft" an engineer constructs a "Jeeves" robot to repair equipment, a "repbot".

Butlers may be knowledgeable, sometimes more than their masters, as it is the case with Jeeves who quotes Shakespeare and who reads in his free time Dostoyevsky and Spinoza. Butlers may be smarter and trickier than their masters, as not only Jeeves but also the majority of servants and butlers in plays by Nestroy, in the Commedia dell' Arte or in Mozart's Operas prove, and they may be strong, stronger than their masters, as Freitag compared with Robinson Crusoe or as Sancho Pansa compared with Don Quixotte.

But, in any case, their mental and physical capabilities cannot exceed those of humans.

2. Butlers or servants who are "ghosts" are, obviously, different: They have capabilities we humans can only dream of, like travelling faster than the speed of light, being present at two different places at the same time, reading thoughts, removing or even lifting heavy rocks, etc.

One of those ghost-servants is Alladin, in the story of "Alladin's Wonderful Lamp". This story is often believed to be part of the famous book "One Thousand and One Nights", a collection mainly of West and South Asian stories, compiled in Arabic during the Islamic Golden Age. However, the original contained "only" 282 stories, and the Alladin's story, together with many others, was added by Antoine Galland who made the first translation, actually a strong modification to accommodate French taste. The 12 volumes were published between 1704 and 1717 [1].

In this story, Alladin has a magic ring and when he rubs it, a "jinni" or "genie"— the Arabic word means "hidden (from sight)"—appears to fulfill his wishes. When Alladin's mother tries to clean an oil lamp that he has found during his first adventure, a second, far more powerful genie appears who is bound to the wishes of the person holding the lamp. Alladin, with the powers of this genie, becomes rich and powerful and marries the Emperor's daughter. The genie even builds him a wonderful palace, more magnificent than the one of the Emperor (for simplicity I have left out the evil sorcerer, his even more evil brother, etc., all of whom make the story even more thrilling).

A more contemporary version is Jeannie, a "2000-year-old-genie" in the sitcom/fantasy series "I Dream of Jeannie", with altogether 139 episodes broadcast between 1965 and 1970, and frequent reruns since then. In the pilot episode, the astronaut Captain Tony Nelson from the US Air Force lands (or waters?) in his capsule near a deserted island in the South Pacific.

When he sees a rolling bottle, he removes the stopper, accidentally rubs it and out comes an attractive woman, dressed in a harem costume. She feels very attracted to him and manages, unbeknown to Tony, to be taken back to his home. Most of the conflicts in the series arise from her desire to please him, fulfilling her mission as genie, but since she is not aware of the approved customs and habits in the USA, her actions thwart his intentions and plans. Anyway, since it is a TV-series from the Sixties, there had to be a happy ending, which was, at that time, marriage.

Two conclusions can be drawn from the behaviour of Jeannie: First, a servant or butler should not fall in love with his or her master or mistress, and second, s/he should have a good Theory of Mind of the person s/he is serving.

3. The "robotic" servant is different again: It has a physical body that is a machine which can be by far stronger than the master and it has a program that governs its actions.

A quite famous robot servant was the "Golem", invented, according to a "legend", by Rabbi Judah Loew ben Bezalel in Prague in the 16th Century. While golems, animated anthropomorphic beings made from inanimate matter, have populated Jewish religious and folk texts and traditions for almost two thousand years, it is strange that the first connection between Loew and a golem is mentioned in 1841 in a German article [2]. The story goes that Loew, for protecting the Jewish community from increasing assaults, made a strong servant out of clay. He animated it by writing a name of god or a magical formula, on a piece of paper that he put—here come two versions—either on his forehead or into his mouth. This paper was removed by him before every Sabbath. One Sabbath he forgot it, the Golem went berserk and destroyed houses and other property, but after the paper had been removed the Golem collapsed and became clay again. Another version is that Loew wrote the letters "emet", meaning "truth" or "reality" on his forehead, and when the Golem went berserk—there is also a version where he fell in love—the Rabbi removed the first "e". Thus the word read "met" which means "dead", the Golem collapsed, etc.

It is interesting to note that there is also a story of a female golem: Already in the 11th century the poet and philosopher Solomon ibn Gabirol is said to have created a female golem for his "domestic" needs. Ibn Gabirol was denounced to the authorities so that he had to deactivate her, to her original state of wood and hinges [2]. This seems to be the first account of both a female and a mechanical golem, thus a predecessor of Roxxxy, the first sex robot (as the company claims). Since this kind of servant will not be discussed in this book, we refer the interested reader to [3].

Let's jump ahead 1000 years: in 2011 Apple announced that the upcoming version of its iPhone, 4S, would have a new feature implemented in its operating system that could serve as a servant or butler: SIRI. SIRI originally was developed by Siri, Inc. This research was funded by the US DARPA via SRI's International's Artificial Intelligence Center through the "Personalized Assistant that Learns" and the "Cognitive Agent that Learns" Programs, in cooperation with six universities. The programs' titles make clear the aim of this development. Siri, Inc. was acquired by Apple in 2010 and a voice recognition system from Nuance was added. Brown and

Mohan see SIRI as a step towards a Virtual Personal Assistant that would serve a user like Jeeves served Bertie Wooster. Other companies have also presented their versions of virtual personal assistants, e.g. Jeannie (!) by Pannous as an app for Android platforms. The functionality of Siri, Jeannie, and others is demonstrated in several YouTube videos.

Now, is SIRI really a "robotic" servant? It is not obvious to think of smartphones as robots but on second thought it is plausible: There is a body, i.e. the hardware of the smartphone, and there are programs inside. Smartphones lack arms and legs but they have sensors and effectors that many robots lack. Among their sensors are a microphone for sound input, one or two cameras for visual input, plus position or magnetic field sensors but also, most important, a sensor for a special range of electromagnetic waves that it can analyse, e.g. information from the telephone company and, via this, from the Internet. As for effectors, it cannot only produce acoustic, visual or kinesthetic (vibrating) signals that its master or mistress comprehends (most of the time), it can also send signals to the telephone company and on to the Internet.

SIRI or the virtual personal assistants from other companies extend, in a qualitatively important way the possibilities of smartphones, more or less depending on the system: You can e.g. ask your assistant to make a call, send a message, find a business and get directions, request weather forecasts, schedule alarms or reminders, search the web, etc., etc. And it is personalized: If you ask, and this example is from a SIRI description, "Book a table at Il Fornaio in Novi for 7PM with my mom." SIRI assumes that Il Fornaio is a restaurant, "Novi" is a location, and "mom" is the mother of the speaker to be found in the contacts. However, you can continue with "Also send her an email reminder." and SIRI will know that with "her" refers to the mother of the speaker, using more than simple speech understanding, namely a complex natural language processing system from artificial intelligence research that can do anaphora resolution.

As an aside, it is interesting to note that all three, Jeeves, Jeannie and Siri, have at least one vowel that is pronounced "ee" in their names, two of them even two "ee"s, though their sex (or gender?) is different, namely male, female, and neuter. Do "ee"s happen to indicate servitude?

If we use "robotic" SIRI with its "ghostly" capabilities to contact and act over large distances in many parts of the world via Internet, what is still missing compared to a "natural" butler?

We need not look through the list of prerequisites of human butlers indicated in a butler academy, e.g. "By Royal Appointment The International Butler Academy" [4]--though this is both interesting and amusing—to see that what they still lack are capabilities that are considered essential for a long-term, satisfying cooperation with a human master/mistress.

This is where this book comes in: it is an attempt to elucidate in which respect we have to improve what is now state-of-the-art to develop the virtual butler into a welcome aid to a human being, the making-of.

The book therefore starts with a guiding vision, a scenario by Robert Gassner and Karlheinz Steinmüller: "Tina and her Butler" sub-titled "Living in the networked world: custom-made and safe". Tina is a lady quickly approaching the age of 70 while enjoying a very active lifestyle: she travels, has honorary appointments. Fitness, friends, and relations play an important role in her life, and she even runs a "part-time office" for her son. Living is made easier for her by a personalized butler, and this scenario shows many examples of how this is done.

This vision provides the framework for the following parts of the book: Part I shows in two chapters important psychological and social considerations, Part II demonstrates in six chapters experiences with/prerequisites for virtual or robotic companions, and Part III has three chapters on "Where and how do we go from here?", i.e. on further developments.

In the first chapter of Part I psychological experience and theories are discussed by Claudia Oppenauer-Meerskraut, a psychologist, within the scenario of "Tina and her Butler", in order to consider benefits and risks of a virtual assistant with artificial intelligence capabilities. Since social participation and maintenance of social contacts are necessary factors for well-being in old age these aspects are discussed regarding an increased use of virtual conversations instead of real visits.

It is interesting to note that recently a survey, though on a small and not representative sample, was undertaken to find out what kind of aid older persons would want and accept [5].

The second chapter of Part I by Kerstin Heuwinkel considers "trust" as an essential condition for a virtual butler. But trust has many meanings. People should not (only) be seen as rational problem solvers nor should human action be described as a chain of sequential and hierarchical step-by-step decisions, but emotional and social aspects have to be considered too. Trust should be seen as an integral part of interpersonal relationships that are shaped by cultural conditions. Therefore, in this chapter it is discussed if and how information and communication technologies, especially a virtual butler, can be framed in a way that trust is possible.

In the first chapter of Part II "Experiences with/Prerequisites for Virtual or Robotic Companions", Christina Conati attempts to answer the question what we can learn from adaptive user interfaces with regard to virtual butlers in general, and for the elderly in particular. Principles underlying the design of effective mixed-initiative interactions are listed that call for formal approaches to dealing both with the uncertainty on modeling relevant cognitive states of the user, as well as with the tradeoff between costs and benefits of the agent's actions under uncertainty. The author also discusses to what extent virtual butlers need to be transparent by providing means for their users to understand the rationale underlying their adaptive interventions.

In the second chapter of Part II, Ginevra Castellano and Peter W. McOwan investigate affect sensitivity as an important requirement for socially perceptive, successful long-term companions. The authors first review several studies to accomplish this difficult task and then describe Scherer's Component Process Model of Emotion in more detail, followed by a review of some challenges for building an affect recognition system. They require a multi-level approach, distinguishing between short-, medium- and long-range interaction. Finally, stressing the importance of empathy in human-human interaction, they present a framework for embedding empathy-enabling capabilities in socially perceptive companions.

In the third chapter Wayne Iba starts by describing our current understanding of the nature of service, consisting of a number of dimensions along which service may be measured and compared, and three modes in which service may be delivered. With these dimensions and modes the technical and social requirements for implementing artificial servants are considered. The author concludes that, while many prerequisites are either already available or could reasonably be developed, both technical and social challenges remain that may be difficult to overcome. The author then presents a brief overview of the experimental work of him and his group in which they attempt to generate and evaluate the fundamental elements of helpful assistance.

In the fourth chapter Massimo Zancanaro and his co-authors describe the responses of older persons to a virtual character in two contrasting settings. At first they list the difficulties in designing this study. Prior to the experiments, they undertook preparatory structured interviews, focus groups, and contextual enquiries. Two scenarios were therefore designed. In the first, an old lady living alone stumbles over a carpet and needs help. The virtual agent Alice is visualized on the wall and uses the phone to call for help and to unlock the door, and, if the old lady is conscious, consoles her. The interviews with the older persons led to descriptions of Alice as being annoying, because of observing the old lady, and not trustworthy. A professional interlocutor would have been preferred, even over a family member. In the second scenario, Alice was employed as an opponent in an Italian card game, installed as MPEG-based talking head in a table-top computer with a touch-screen. In this situation, Alice was found to be entertaining by a high majority of the older persons who joked with friends while playing and who would have liked to have this computer game available even after the end of the experiment.

In the fifth chapter David Benyon and Oli Mival see companions as they aim to change Human-Computer Interaction (HCI) into Human-Companion Relationships. Whilst the term "companion" is meant to invoke personification and anthropomorphism, the authors see companions as encompassing the widest possible range of devices and forms of interaction that, woven together, produce a relationship-building experience for people. Also a home equipped with ambient intelligence could be a companion. The authors present a model of the key components of companions that designers need to consider if they are to design for relationship building, then present some examples and scenarios for companions to illustrate the conceptualization, and proceed to a discussion about the development of near-companion technologies. They conclude that companions will have a lifetime, and perhaps an afterlife.

As an aside, it may also be rewarding to use the rich source of often long-term interactions between master/mistress-servant/maid in literature, theater and films to build the personalities requested for virtual or robot butlers [6].

In the sixth chapter, Ulrich Reiser and his co-authors promote the idea of a robot butler and investigate the advantages and disadvantages of embodiment for the scenario "Tina and her Butler". In order to make the discussion more tangible, they introduce Care-O-bot ® 3. It may be noted that, as the most prominent role of this robot, the researchers chose the butler. Several user studies provided inspiration during the design phase of this robot, in particular with respect to the robot's appearance and the user interaction concept. User interaction scenarios from research projects and, consequently, results of real-life trials conducted in an eldercare facility are presented and then used to discuss the pros and cons of embodiment.

In the first chapter of Part III "Where and how do we go from here?", Roger K. Moore begins with the observation that the quantity of training data required to improve state-of-the-art speech-based systems seems to be growing exponentially, and yet performance appears to be reaching an asymptote that is not only well short of human performance, but which may also be inadequate for many real-world applications. The author therefore steps outside the current approaches and draws inspiration from recent findings in the neurobiology of living systems. He highlights four areas: the growing evidence for an intimate relationship between sensor and motor behaviour, the power of negative feedback control to accommodate unpredictable disturbances in real-world environments, mechanisms for imitation and mental imagery for learning and modelling, and hierarchical models of temporal memory for predicting future behaviour and anticipating the outcome of events. The author shows that these results point towards a novel architecture for speech-based human-machine interaction, in which cooperative and communicative behaviour emerges as a by-product of a model of interaction where the system has in mind the needs and intentions of a user, and the user has in mind the needs and intentions of the system. The author concludes with a roadmap how to make, finally, voice-based interaction with a virtual butler a reality.

In the second chapter of Part III, Sabine Payr argues that it is already possible, with existing technologies, to go beyond fictional scenarios of virtual butlers or assistive robot companions, and that realistic, long-term studies of their use contribute much needed knowledge about user styles and hence design requirements. Such a study is reported, and the data collected are presented, compared, and discussed. The striking difference between idealized personae such as "Tina" and real users motivated a detailed case study about the frequently observed issue of initiative and floor management. The case study shows the considerable degree to which users shape human-robot interaction with their individual styles. Finally, the author outlines a few such user styles and on the basis of the data analysis in order to enrich future scenario descriptions with more realistic personae, stressing special design consequences.

In the third and final chapter of Part III, Stefan Rank first introduces the concept of scenario-based analysis for comparing agent-based technology design. Then he uses the characterization of the scenario "Tina and her Butler" to discuss several technological issues that arise from it. By disregarding non-technical issues, the author arrives at problems or, better, challenges of technology in a broad sense that could be steps in the direction of the virtual butler: language competence; synchronous operation at multiple locations; domain knowledge, including specialized knowledge; tightly integrated personalization across domains; affective interaction, empathy, politeness, relationship maintenance; real-time behaviour competence surpassing the average human; and autonomous coordination of the different competencies and multiple concerns. As the author stresses, the order of the presentation of these challenges is based on a subjective estimation of the complexity involved in arriving at the competence required for a virtual butler. –

The authors present a diversity of approaches for "and then", from the more technical point of view via the brain research oriented and psychological to the social one. The combined efforts are expected to lead to a virtual or a robot butler that will be welcomed as a long-term personal companion.

References

1. Tausendundeine Nacht. Nach der ältesten arabischen Handschrift in der Ausgabe von Muhsin Mahdi erstmals ins Deutsche übertragen und mit einem Anhang versehen von Claudia Ott. Deutscher Taschenbuch Verlag, München (2006)
2. Sherwin, B.L.: The Golem of Prague and His Ancestors. In: Putik, A. (ed.) Path of Life. Rabbi Judah Loew ben Bezalel ca. 1525-1609. Academia and Jewish Museum, Prague (2009)
3. The World's First Sex Robot, http://www.TrueCompanion.com (last checked August 12, 2012)
4. By Royal Appointment The International Butler Academy, http://www.butlerschool.com (last checked August 12, 2012)
5. Meyer, S.: Mein Freund der Roboter. Servicerobotik für ältere Menschen – eine Antwort auf den demographischen Wandel? VDE Verlag, Berlin (2011)
6. Trappl, R., Krajewski, M., Ruttkay, Z., Widrich, V.: Robots as Companions: What can we Learn from Servants and Companions in Literature, Theater, and Film? Procedia Computer Science 7, 96–98 (2011)

Part I
Psychological and Social Considerations

Would a Virtual Butler Do a Good Job for Old People? Psychological Considerations about Benefits and Risks of Technological Assistance

Claudia Oppenauer-Meerskraut[1,2]

[1] Center for Usability Research and Engineering (CURE), Modecenterstraße 17,
1110 Vienna, Austria
oppenauer@cure.at
[2] Institute of Clinical, Biological and Differential Psychology, Faculty of Psychology,
University Vienna, Liebiggasse 5, 1010 Vienna, Austria

Abstract. Psychological theories and knowledge are discussed within the scenario of "Tina and her butler" in order to consider benefits and risks of a virtual assistant with artificial intelligence. With the issue of cognitive functionality in old age learning and training aspects of daily life routine are argued to be diminished if too much assistance is offered. Since social participation and maintenance of social contacts are necessary factors for well-being in old age these aspects are discussed regarding an increased use of virtual conversations instead of real visits. Finally ethical considerations of the use of artificial intelligence and an outlook of future scientific research are given.

1   Introduction

The amount of research studies and funded national and international projects which deal with technological solutions for elderly people is amazing. Aging in place with support of technology has become a popular research field and produced products from various technology disciplines [1] with different technological impacts [2]. Improving the quality of life of older people is one of the most referred aim concerning the implementation of technology in old age. The growing population of the elderly in industrial countries and changes of family structures demand affordable solutions in order to encourage older people in their social participation and to satisfy their need of aging in place. Technology can be a significant resource for older people if the users perceive a device or system as helpful and not stigmatizing or too complex. Technology acceptance not only depends on needs and attitudes but also on age, gender, level of education and health, social, and cultural conditions [3]. Contrary to stereotypes, older people are willing to use new technologies but acceptance and use are only achieved if they receive adequate training and if they personally benefit from the technology [4].

Recently, particularly motivational factors awake interest in research studies. Findings suggest that perceived benefits and costs play a major role and highly correlate with

R. Trappl (Ed.): Your Virtual Butler, LNAI 7407, pp. 11–15, 2013.

usability [5, 6]. Nevertheless, there is a lack of literature about motivation and needs in old age. Consequently fundamental research in gerontology is required.

Modern technology is often discussed related to loneliness and specifically in old age a loss of social contacts is mentioned. On the other hand it is possible that technology enhances social life and encourages older people in their social participation. Thus, competences in using technology will become extremely relevant for successful aging and well-being [7]. Intelligent systems like a virtual assistance in the scenario of "Tina and her butler" are very complex and have a high impact on daily life because of the variety of functions and related possibilities. Which benefits and problems result from the use of a virtual butler are discussed below from a psychological point of view. First, cognitive theories and learning aspects are described. Furthermore the importance of social relationships is emphasized by the approach of successful aging. Finally ethical aspects are pointed out with regard to a more realistic view of older people and by illustrating the importance of needs and attitudes concerning technology use in old age.

2   Cognitive Functions and the Importance of Training in Old Age

Besides multimorbidity and fundamental health changes in old age, cognitive functions begin to decrease with age. Yerkes [8] showed a decline of cognitive functions in the age of 30 already. Although these results have to be interpreted in connection with selection criteria during military recruiting in the 1930s, this idea of aging continued. Aging is still seen as a physical, psychological and cognitive declension. Since a much more sophisticated view was needed, a different picture of intelligence and cognitive functions was generated and distinguished between *Crystallized* and *Fluid Intelligence*. Whereas the first one refers to knowledge and life experience of a person and takes until old age, Fluid Intelligence subsumes measurable cognitive functions such as reasoning, concentration or memory and tends to decline across the lifespan [9]. Nevertheless, cognitive functions as attention or memory have a certain amount of plasticity and need daily training for inhibiting a decline.

Further, it is well known that actions are unlearned if they are no longer exercised. Concerning the scenario of the virtual butler this approach is also linked with the theory of learned dependence [10]. The phenomenon of learned dependency was observed in health care settings and family systems. Claims of independency and autonomy as well as resources and competences of older persons are often ignored by caregivers and family members. If assistance and support is provided in situations although a person would be able to cope on his/her own it becomes redundant for the person to carry out an activity anymore. Due to missing training the person will unlearn certain activities and will loose more and more independence in this situation.

Despite this dilemma it remains unclear how many activities people would be willing to do independently and if too much support would be rejected by the users. Finally, the implementation of a virtual butler would maybe foster more than now the discussion of prevention and health promotion strategies in the future since training of cognitive or physical functions would no longer be implemented in daily life routine.

3   Successful Aging with a Virtual Butler

One of the most contradictory models of successful aging are the *Activity Theory* by Tartler [11] and the *Disengagement Theory* by Cumming and Henry [12]. Although both theories are already obsolete and replaced by more recent ones, they started a discussion about the influence of social contacts and role functions on well-being in old age. The Theory of Activity proposed that social relationships and role functions are essential for psychosocial well-being in old age. On the other hand Cumming and Henry argued that old people claim for social isolation. Retirement is seen as a natural process which is necessary in old age. Both theories have provoked intensive discussions in gerontology. Apart from the contrary point of view, these two theories dealt with the aspect of social relationships and networking. Carstensen [13] strengthens this aspect in her *Theory of Socio-emotional Selectivity* even more by differentiating two main goals of social relationships across the life span: Whereas information and knowledge seeking are main goals of social relationships in younger age, old people maintain their social relationships for emotional regulation and consequently have less but more intensive social contacts. Intimacy becomes more important than a high amount of different contacts in order to obtain relevant information.

Not only theories of aging deal with social contacts but also concepts of quality of life in old age. A Word Health Organization (WHO) working group developed a quality of life module for use with older adults [14]. By interviewing focus groups six aspects in addition to the main quality of life questionnaire could be found: changes in sensory abilities, autonomy, past, present and future activities, social participation, death and dying and intimacy. These results emphasize the importance of intensive social contacts and support the theory of Carstensen.

Whether a virtual butler could assist old people in maintaining their social contacts remains unclear since the market is far away from offering such a highly complex product. The scenario partly deals with the question of real and virtual contacts at the end of the description. Here Tina wonders if her granddaughter would visit her if she had no reason to come because a virtual visit would suffice. Even if the need for communication and exchange of information would be easy to fulfil, human contact and intimacy would be missing in a virtual world.

The mostly cited theory of successful aging is the concept of Baltes and Baltes [15] and their model of *Selective Optimization and Compensation*. Age related changes and losses make it necessary to select certain areas and activities of life in order to make optimization and compensation possible. The concept postulates that only a high effort allows continuing with certain activities in old age. According to this model technology could play a significant role for compensation of restricted functions and resources. A virtual butler could mainly compensate losses in instrumental activities of living (IADL) such as reminding of taking medicine, managing financial affairs or organizing meals by contacting delivery services. On the other hand the support of a virtual assistant would probably inhibit persons from managing things on their own and finally from training the brain.

4   Ethical Considerations

Artificial intelligence or virtual worlds always evoke a certain amount of scepticism and criticism. Most people only know about artificial intelligence or robotics from movies which discuss this theme in a critical and almost threatening way. However, these very general ethical dimensions of artificial intelligence cannot be discussed in this paper.

In the scenario an old man with a care level of 3.5 lives more or less in a virtual reality. He is still active in different societies and able to participate in meetings and decisions. Although social participation with the help of technology is definitely a benefit, there is a risk of neglecting real social contacts especially if persons have restrictions in mobility. The training of cognitive activity is obviously guaranteed but virtual communication will likely reduce intimate and real contacts because people will limit their communication to communication in the virtual world. On the other hand it remains unclear if this virtual communication will become normal and needs for real contacts will play a minor role. Finally needs of old people always have to be considered and technological assistance and support will only be accepted and used if old people perceive the technology as useful. If the use of a technology provides no benefits or creates new problems it will be rejected [16].

Above all, the image of older people which is described in the scenario does not correspond to the majority of older people. It has to be discussed if long life productivity and activity in old age are factors of success, which consequences such a classification would have and if such a distinction wouldn't be a discrimination of all people with limitations in cognitive or physical functions or people who have the need for retirement in old age.

5   Outlook

In spite of all discussed theoretical approaches it is necessary to ask old people about their attitudes and needs concerning the possibilities of a virtual butler. Needs and attitudes should not be ignored or neglected if both sides, technicians and users, want to benefit from technology. Ethical considerations have to be included in order to guarantee that needs are not only created by a technology market but technology is developed to support and assist in already known needs and problem scenarios which does not exclude that technology just satisfies the need for joy.

The short overview about psychological theories and models which could explain or predict acceptance of a virtual butler has certain limitations. From psychology simple interventions or guidelines are expected for a better understanding of technology use and acceptance. Indeed there are enough psychological approaches but as in every discipline specific questions and hypotheses acquire testing and evaluation of existing models. Although we already know a lot about human behaviour and experience, this knowledge has to be applied to new questions and scenarios. Thus, multidisciplinary research is needed in order to study technology acceptance with the help from different disciplines contributing scientific knowledge and methodology [17].

References

1. Bouma, H., Fozard, J.L., Bouwhuis, D.G., Taipale, V.: Gerontechnology in perspective. Gerontechnology 6(4), 190–216 (2007)
2. Van Bronswijk, J.E.M.H., Bouma, H., Fozard, J.L.: Technology for quality of life: an enriched taxonomy. Gerontechnology 2(2), 169–172 (2002)
3. Marcellini, F., Mollenkopf, H., Spazzafumo, L., Ruoppila, I.: Acceptance and use of technological solutions by the elderly in the outdoor environment: findings from a European survey. Z Gerontol Geriatr 33(3), 169–177 (2000)
4. Rogers, W.A., Mayhorn, C.B., Fisk, A.D.: Technology in Everyday Life for Older Adults. In: Burdick, D.C., Kwon, S. (eds.) Gerontechnology. Research and Practice in Technology and Aging, pp. 3–18. Springer, New York (2004)
5. Melenhorst, A.-S., Bouwhuis, D.-G.: When do older adults consider the internet? An exploratory study of benefit perception. Gerontechnology 3(2), 89–101 (2004)
6. Melenhorst, A.-S., Rogers, W.-A., Bouwhuis, D.-G.: Older Adults' Motivated Choice for Technological Innovation: Evidence for Benefit-Driven Selectivity. Psychology and Aging 21(1), 190–195 (2006)
7. Kaspar, R.: Technology and loneliness in old age. Gerontechnology 3(1), 42–48 (2004)
8. Yerkes, R.M.: Psychological examining in the United States Army. National Academy of Science, Washington (1921)
9. Lehr, U.: Psychologie des Alters. Quelle & Meyer, Wiebelsheim (2003)
10. Baltes, M.M.: Verlust der Selbständigkeit im Alter: Theoretische Überlegungen und empirische Befunde. Psychologische Rundschau 46, 159–170 (1995)
11. Tartler, R.: Das Alter in der modernen Gesellschaft. Enke, Stuttgart (1961)
12. Cumming, E., Henry, W.E.: Growing old – the process of disengagement. Basic Books Inc., New York (1961)
13. Carstensen, L.L.: Evidence for a life-span theory of socioemotional selectivity. In: Lewis, L.E., Haviland, M. (eds.) Handbook of Emotions, pp. 447–460. Guilford Press, New York (1995)
14. Power, M., Quinn, K., Schmidt, S., the WHOQOL-Old Group: Development of the WHOQOL-Old module. Quality of Life Research 14, 2197–2214 (2005)
15. Baltes, P.B., Baltes, M.M.: Successful aging: Perspectives from the behavioral sciences. Cambridge University Press, New York (1990)
16. McCreadie, C., Tinker, A.: The acceptability of assistive technology to older people. Ageing & Society 25, 91–110 (2005)
17. Oppenauer, C., Preschl, B., Kalteis, K., Kryspin-Exner, I.: Technology in Old Age from a Psychological Point of View. In: Holzinger, A. (ed.) USAB 2007. LNCS, vol. 4799, pp. 133–142. Springer, Heidelberg (2007)

Framing the Invisible – The Social Background of Trust

Kerstin Heuwinkel

University of Applied Sciences
Waldhausweg 14
66123 Saarbrücken, Germany
kerstin.heuwinkel@htw-saarland.de

Abstract. A butler is part of your personal surrounding – a person you can trust. If information and communication technology (ICT) shall become a virtual butler, trust is needed. But - trust has many meanings. Very often the focus is put on a cognitive model of trust. According to our studies, in healthcare and tourism this definition has to be broadened. People should not (only) be seen as rational problem solvers nor should human action be described as a chain of sequential and hierarchical step-by-step decisions. Emotional and social aspects have to be considered, too. Trust should be seen as integral part of interpersonal relationships that are shaped by cultural conditions. Referring to Goffman's frame analysis, we will discuss if and how ICT, especially the virtual butler, can be framed in a way that trust is possible.

1   Introduction

"Mr. B. needs a new hip. He uses the Internet in order to find the best hospital for this surgical treatment. A number of online services offer hospital rankings. He clicks through the websites. Some of them give a lot of medical information. Others show nice pictures of doctors, nurses, and rooms. Then, Mr. B. finds a hospital that offers "A new hip plus cultural and culinary highlights of Germany's most beautiful region." The package includes five nights in the hospital, the surgical treatment, five nights in a 4-star-hotel near the hospital, rooms are equipped with ambient assistant living applications to ensure continuous control, a daily check-up, three day-trips to interesting cultural attractions, lunch and dinner in at least 16 point Gault Millau ranked restaurants. A digital device is used in order to give actual information to the client and to send help in case of emergency."

This scenario will become real within the next year. In healthcare, a lot of approaches focus on the question how to support people during and after a medical treatment. The combination with tourism is only a next step. Healthcare and tourism are both said to be good application fields for information and communication technology (ICT)[1]. But on the other hand, patients and tourists are very sensitive clients, as they risk a lot. They have to rely on somebody else to a much higher degree

---

[1] For healthcare see [1], [2], [3], [4]. For the information based nature of tourism see [5], for ICT and tourism see [6], [7], [8]. For health tourism see [9], [10].

R. Trappl (Ed.): Your Virtual Butler, LNAI 7407, pp. 16–26, 2013.

than other customers. The patient's wellbeing depends on the abilities and performance of the medical staff. The tourist leaves his or her familiar surroundings and is confronted with unknown people and situations. Neither patients nor tourists can be sure that everything will be alright. If something goes wrong, they have to blame themselves to a certain degree. The use of ICT increases insecurity. The reason for this is the following paradox: People often overestimate the abilities of information and communication technology and are afraid of losing control and of being inferior.

The idea of humans depending on machines has ever since been related to diffuse fear and has been expressed in myths, such as the Golem, Frankenstein or Big Brother. On the other hand, people think that technology is defective and they are afraid of relying on it. Talking about "your virtual butler" makes it worse, as it implicates a personal relationship. If something goes wrong, it is not only a technological failure of the virtual butler. Instead, the person feels that an intimate part of life, perhaps even the whole person got hurt.

Thus, the virtual butler has to be designed in a way that it can be integrated in social relationships. The virtual butler needs something that can be defined as social sensitivity and intelligence. Erving Goffman's frame analysis will be used in order to identify requirements and to find out about necessary additional features of the virtual butler.

The structure of the paper is as follows: In the next chapter we will introduce the theoretical background. Bases for this are sociological and psychological theories. We will explain the terms "frames" and "framing". Furthermore, we will discuss the relevance of these theories with respect to ICT, especially the virtual butler. In section three empirical findings are presented. We finally conclude discussing some issues that seem to be crucial for developing the virtual butler.

2   Theoretical Background

Trust is fascinating. Although everybody seems to know what trust is, it is very difficult to give a definition. Trust has many meanings because it comprises cognitive, emotional, and behavioral factors [11]. Most often only cognitive factors are discussed, as they are easier to handle. Trust is seen as a game that is played between actors [12]. Actors who choose an action although it makes them vulnerable to others are said to trust. According to this approach, actors calculate outcomes and risks, possible benefits and costs. They think about the probability that their counterpart will act in a trusting way or not. Here, cognition is decisive. Measures that are said to increase this type of trust are contracts, security and data protection tools, control mechanisms, third parties and the like. All of them focus on single situations where actors have to decide about one single action. Every game is a new game.

However, social life is not like this. We all know this – the question is: What *is* the alternative to the cognitive concept of trust? The aim of this paper is to include emotions not on an individualistic but on an interpersonal or social level, i.e. feelings that arise from and are influenced by social forces. The underlying assumption is that human action follows certain social and cultural patterns [13]. A great part of the way how people act depends upon the accepted way of acting in the reference culture, i.e. the culture they identify with. Although every person has its own personality and individuality many actions are similar to a certain degree. Habits can be analyzed and described. This especially comes true in everyday life [14]. Thus, it depends to a great extent on social and cultural circumstances, if people trust or not. Trust as the willingness to make one-self vulnerable to others and their actions should be understood as an inter-subjective reality and social phenomenon [15]. We thereby emphasize the social character of trust.

In figure 1 trust is modeled as a relationship between two social actors: the person who trusts (often referred to as trustor) and the trusted person [16]. The figure shows that many factors determine the trustworthiness of a person. Trustworthiness as the description of a moral character results from both credibility and reliability. Credibility means that the trusted person will do what he or she announces to do. Reliability describes the ability to do what he or she announces to do [17]. It is very unlikely that the trustor calculates all these aspects and then decides what to do. Instead shared aims, values, and norms (including sanctions) allow a feeling of connectedness [18].

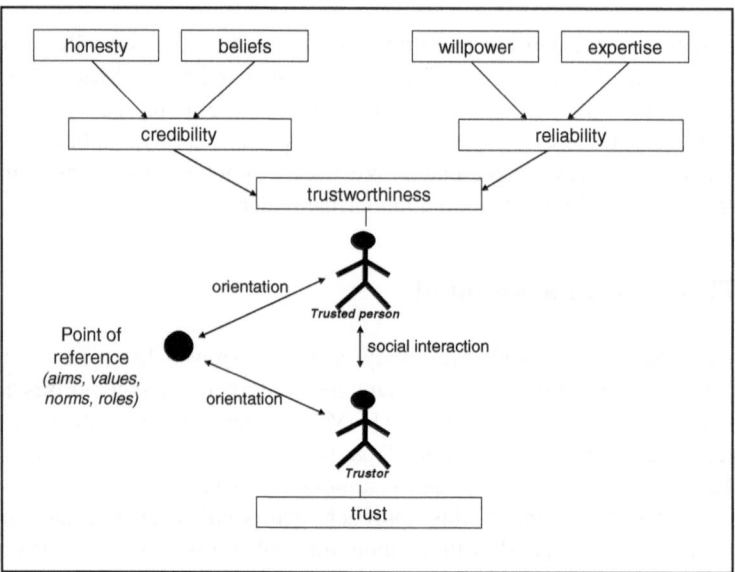

Fig. 1. Model of trust according to [19]

If we trust somebody, we feel an emotional connection. Our counterpart becomes part of us. If trust is broken, a part of *us* is broken. This is why trust diminishes risk, and, on the other hand, creates risk. Hence, the constellation is very complex. How can people handle this? How can they put all these little pieces together and attach meaning to this?

In order to explain how people get to know what is going on, Erving Goffman's theory of frames[2] is helpful [22]. Goffman wanted to explain how humans organize experience of everyday life. According to him, people use frames in order to structure and reduce the complexity of the world. By this, the facets of reality are arranged in a way that they make sense for a person. The concept of frames or framing, i.e. applying a frame to a certain situation, emphasizes the active process of perception and interpretation of a situation. In the next two sections, frames and framing will be explained.

2.1   Frames

According to Goffman, frames are models of social situations. They combine common social and cultural patterns that people learn during socialization, e.g. rules, values, goals, and positions, with individual attitudes and experiences. Frames are situated between the micro-level of the individual and the macro-level of society [23]. Frames help to understand what is going on. Social life is structured in a way that situation and frames are matching.

On the other hand, frames define possible actions and the willingness to do something. For example, the frame *booking a journey in a travel agency* includes defined roles (client and travel agent), the relationship between these roles, certain rules and behavior. Both travel agent and client know the frame and refer in their action to it. They share a common understanding of what, why, and how to act. Therefore, trusting the agent and the willingness to reveal intimate information only theoretically results in vulnerability, as according to the frame misuse is impossible. Thus, frames provide trust to a certain degree. Some frames include more trust than others. Examples for trusting frames are *surgery*; *confession*; *talk with friends*, and *announcement of the captain*.

Frames offer some benefits for individuals and societies. First, they determine the actor's perception of the situation. They define rules and goals that are valid for an actor in a certain situation. As a consequence, if a person trusts, he or she frames the counterpart in a positive way and will interpret actions according to this. But frames do not only help the individual. Furthermore, they have a social function, as people refer to frames. So frames facilitate mutual orientation, as well as communication and understanding. Finally, frames serve as a filter for information. Only the information that fits to the frame is accepted or, the other way round, information is interpreted according to the actual frame.

People are used to apply frames in order to manage everyday life and to act without rethinking each and everything. Every frame includes trust to a certain amount. As a result, frames should be integrated into information and communication systems in order to facilitate orientation for the individual and mutual understanding. They could be used as means for expression and communication with others, too. The

---

[2] Frames and framing are concepts that are used by a number of scholars from different areas, e.g. social sciences, politics, computer science and artificial intelligence [20], [21].

question is how to do so? In order to transfer frames to ICT and especially to the virtual butler a more detailed description of frames is needed.

According to our approach, frames can be characterized by at least seven factors [19]. In the following, we exemplify them by the virtual butler:

The *topic* of a frame classifies the frame. Examples are health, leisure time, work, family and so on. All other factors have to conform to the topic. The virtual butler should comply with the topic. But – which topic is the right one for the virtual butler? If the digital butler shall support a person in everyday life, many topics are relevant. So, perhaps we need a lot of specialized butlers for different topics and something like a meta-butler that manages and controls the other.

Locations can be compared to the stage where action takes place. The virtual butler should be connected to adequate locations. But, where can we locate the virtual butler – at the monitor, inside a mobile phone, or somewhere invisible in the infrastructures that surround us? It seems as if the virtual butler needs an adequate location to appear.

Equipment is a further specification of location and includes design, colors, accessories, and even smell. The virtual butler should fit to the equipment. That leads to the question of embodiment. Does the virtual butler need a body? The possibilities range from avatars to mobile devices and robots.

Time is the next factor. It is connected with topic and location. The virtual butler should be able to say "Goodnight"[3]. Although the ICT-world is proud of unlimited accessibility it should be discussed if limited hours of operation might be better.

The *role-set* describes the roles and the interplay between the roles. Well-known examples are patient and doctor, merchant and client, priest and believer. The virtual butler has to play a role – which one has to be discussed. Talking about a butler[4] already implicates a human-human-like relationship. Do we really want to establish a human-human interaction?

Others are persons who do not actively take part in the action. As humans are social beings, they need other persons for orientation. It is unspoken interaction in which someone observes others in order to decide what to do. The virtual butler should not isolate the person. Instead, it should make actions of persons visible who are in a similar situation.

In everyday life, *boundary-signs* signalize the change from one frame to another. Examples are sounds, phrases, appearance of new roles. The appearance of the virtual butler should be connected with boundary-signs.

Predecessor/successor emphasizes the aspect that frames refer to other frames and that frames are often arranged in a typical way, e.g. waiting room, lab, surgery, pharmacy. The virtual butler should know typical procedures.

---

[3] But in case of emergency he is by your side. In former days, butlers slept in the house and had to get up in the night, if the employer needed them.

[4] Due to the cultural and social background people have a different understanding of what a butler means. It should be discussed if other expressions such as servant, companion, or friend might be better. The same comes true for the description of the counterpart as user, client, operator, or master.

In table one, the factors are summarized. They are ordered as follows: factors that provide *factual orientation* (topic, location, equipment, and time), *social orientation* (role-set, others), or *procedural orientation* (boundary-signs, predecessor/successor).

Table 1. Missing frames in ICT

	Factors	Deficiencies in ICT	Solution for ICT
Factual	Topic	Missing symbols	Labeling, motives, colors
	Location	No location	Connection with real location
	Equipment	No equipment	Design, symbols
	Time	No time	Timely restricted offers
Social	Role-set	Missing roles, new roles	Labels, pictures, symbols
	Others	Others are invisible	Feedback, forums, blogs
Procedural	Boundary Signs	Mostly unplanned use	Click-through design
	Predecessor/ Successor	Missing routines	Integration of routines

All three types of orientation are necessary and closely connected with one another. Research in healthcare and tourism (see chapter 3) indicates that social orientation and interaction are the most important aspects [24], [25]. In the next section, the term framing will be explained.

2.2   Framing

Framing can be defined as the process in which a situation of everyday life is linked to one or more frames. According to our finding, framing comprises four components.

The first component is *recognition*. A person notices a situation and tries to find an appropriate frame. Here, "good" information is decisive. Good information means that information is available, simple, extensive, and congruent. Frame factors should be visible and information should flow smoothly. With respect to the virtual butler, in some cases a lot of information is hidden and in other cases too much information is offered. An intelligent information management is required in order to provide information that is needed to give the person the feeling that he/she is well-informed.

The second framing component is *calculation*. As situations differ, no situation will fit exactly to the frame. Deviations are normal to a certain degree and they are important, as they express liveliness, naturalness, and authenticity. Furthermore, the more people are used to situations, the more they are able to accept variations. In fact, they demand change. Thus, actions of the virtual butler may and should include deviation and variation. At the beginning, the virtual butler should comply fully with the frame. Later on, it is easier to accept variations. Until now, we do not know how to define the degree of deviation that will be accepted. In everyday life, people recognize if they are likely to misbehave and are able to adjust their behavior [26]. So, the virtual butler should be aware of the reactions of the counterpart and be able to correct the performance.

Recognition and calculation are individual activities. The person looks for information, selects frames, and calculates the deviation. *Integration* is the third component and emphasizes the social character of framing. People try to find out which frames are used by "relevant others". If others are relevant or not depends on the way the framing person sees it. While framing a situation, it should be visible how relevant others have framed the situation. If the frames fit together everything is fine. If not, communication should be possible in order to find out why different frames are used. Normally, the interaction between a person and the virtual butler is isolated. Others are not visible. Thus, a social application, e.g. a social media application, should be added to the virtual butler.

Continuity puts the emphasis on the aspect that frames are connected with other frames. The aspect was mentioned before, when the topic predecessor/successor was discussed. Additionally, continuity emphasizes that history and future are important aspects. People remember former actions and expect continuation. Thus, the virtual butler should have a memory and should somehow anticipate what will happen in the future.

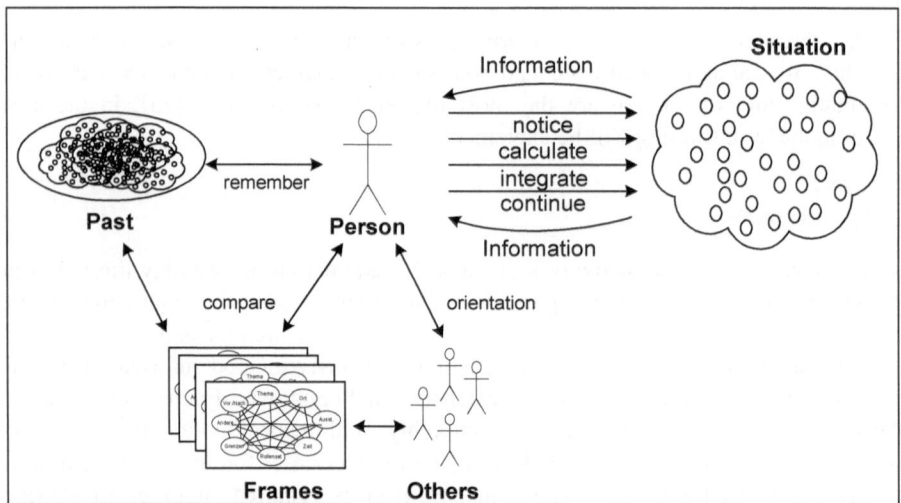

Fig. 2. Framing

Figure 2 illustrates the components and activities involved. The most important activities include information management and social network management. People need "good" information and the connection to other people in order to frame a situation successfully.

The analysis showed that a lot of activities that happen in everyday life are not supported by the virtual butler. Thus, additional applications are needed. In order to decide which applications might be the most efficient ones, the connection between frames, framing and trust will be discussed in the next section.

2.3   Frames, Framing and Trust

Frames and framing enable people to know what is going on in a situation. As a consequence, people feel better and safe. They think that they can manage the situation. Feeling good and safe and being able to manage a situation can be the first steps to trust. Next, frames connect a person and a situation. Feeling connected to somebody or something is – in the most cases – a positive emotion. Positive emotions have an enhancing impact on trust, too. Furthermore, frames influence the way how a person perceives a situation. If a positive frame is used, the whole situation is seen in a positive way.

To summarize, the virtual butler should be designed in a way that it easily can be framed. That means that user-friendly information should be given about the why, who, where, when, and how. Too many technological explanations should be avoided, unless a person asks for them. At the beginning, the virtual butler should not be responsible for everything. Instead, it should be a specialist for certain things and should gain more and more competence.

Next, different trustworthy frames can be defined. Frames that include sympathy are the first type of trustworthy frames. Those frames are most often connected with people who play an important role in life, e.g. mother, father, and friend. Professional frames can be trustworthy frames, too. Professional frames are needed when a person is not able to do something by one-self and needs help. Depending on the social and cultural background, certain occupational groups are more trustworthy than others. It is important that typical symbols and signs are visible, e.g. the doctor's white coat, certificates, and even typical sounds and smell.

Applied to the virtual butler, an interdisciplinary approach is needed in order to integrate the virtual butler into trustworthy frames. Starting point should be an analysis of the trustworthy frames that are relevant for a certain sector, e.g. the frames of a patient group and the frame of a doctor in the healthcare sector.

Trust as an emotional and social phenomenon can neither be planned nor guaranteed. The ability and willingness to trust always include individual aspects. Thus, frames and framing cannot guarantee trust. And, the absence of frames does not automatically lead to the absence of trust. But according to our findings – without frames it is much more unlikely that people trust than with frames. On the other hand, studies show that frames in combination with mechanisms that support framing activities increase the probability of trust. In the next section, some examples will be given.

3   Empirical Work

We started our research in 2002 and applied our findings to the following projects:

- 2002 – 2003: Smart-Wear: Wearable computing for journalists
- 2002 – 2003: Mobile solutions for salesmen
- 2003 – 2005: Digital Companion[5] for tourists
- 2004 – 2005: Digital Companion for patients
- starting 2006: Online promotion of industrial heritage
- starting 2008: ICT supported medical and health tourism

All these applications focus on ubiquitous computing where a person is accompanied or surrounded by information and communication technology. With respect to the devices in use, we worked with handhelds, smart phones, and ambient systems. We want to highlight the following findings:

- Finding 1: If technology invades a person's privacy, trust is needed. Here, it does not matter, if we talk about a website, a smart phone, or another device.
- Finding 2: The more invisible technology is, the more trust is needed. Embodiment – even the simplest form of using a mobile device - helps.
- Finding 3: The amount of trust that is needed increases with the perceived insecurity. The willingness to trust decreases correspondingly. But, if there is no other possibility the willingness to trust rises suddenly.

In order to make trust possible, we used already existing trusting relationships, e.g. a patient group, a well-known doctor, and tried to embed ICT. The Digital Companion was introduced during a group meeting in a hospital. It was presented as something that was designed to support the group by arranging meetings after their stay in the hospital. Furthermore, it should be a link to the hospital. The patients could decide about the content of the Digital Companion and how the bulletin board should work. Thus, the Digital Companion became part of the group and part of the person, as they could decide about the content.

In a project with patients suffering from obesity we learned a lot about the importance of (inter)active systems. Most of the applications tend to control the patient and to free him or her from obligations. According to our findings, people should not be seen as passive subjects. Instead, ICT should force patients to be active, to think, and to decide. Furthermore, change and surprise are important. Exhaustive system design seems to be outdated. Instead, little creative components should be combined by chance in order to give the feeling that the system is "alive". We discussed this topic with pediatrics and they put emphasize on this aspect, too. In order to interest children, applications should be surprising. Systematically and well-arranged content is boring, even if it is of a great variety. The experts said that less would be more. It would be enough to offer only one or two exercises per week, if they were changed regularly.

Another very important aspect is a step-by-step approach. Trust needs time to evolve. Because of this, one should start with applications that are on a low trust

---

[5] A Digital Companion is conceptualized as a personalized, mobile, and interactive application. From the user's point of view, the Digital Companion shall become a personal companion that accompanies the user in various situations – in professional life as well as in everyday life [27].

level. As time goes by a – hopefully trusting – relationship evolves. Then, other more trust requiring applications can be added. This step-by-step approach not only refers to the primary user, here the patient. Furthermore, all people involved, the doctors and nurses, need time in order to accept the structures and processes resulting from the new player. Here, trust was needed, too.

4   My Virtual Butler

To sum up, we have analyzed trust from a sociological point of view. We have defined major factors that are important for establishing trusting relationships. With respect to the virtual butler we have discussed many requirements. Some of them can be located on a technological level. Many others refer to organizational and methodological aspects. Thus, system design includes the core technological system and the surrounding social systems. On the one hand, this makes the aim of developing a virtual butler more difficult. On the other hand, we can use a lot of patterns of everyday life and enrich the – at least until now - still very poor technology.

As said before, a good strategy to make trust in technology possible is to take already existing trusting human-human relationships as anchor. A good butler has a lot of references. ICT needs references and social connections, too. We should not try to create a perfect technological entity. Instead, we should design technology in a way that it bridges the gaps that exist in an imperfect human world. And the other way round, we should organize human relationships in a way that they can bridge the gaps that exist in an imperfect technological world.

References

1. Eysenbach, G.: Consumer health informatics. BMJ 320, 1713–1716 (2000)
2. Ferguson, T.: Online patient-helpers and physicians working together: a new partnership for high quality health care. BMJ 321, 1129–1132 (2000)
3. Hall, et.al.: Measuring patients' trust in their primary care providers. Medical Care Research and Review 59(3), 293–318 (2002)
4. Thom, D., et al.: Patient trust in the physician: relationship to patient requests. Family Practice 19, 476–483 (2002)
5. Holloway, C.: The Business of Tourism. Prentice Hall (2006)
6. Fodness, D., Murray, B.: Tourist information search. Annals of Tourism Research 24, 502–523 (1997)
7. Buhalis, D.: E-Tourism: Information technology for strategic tourism management. Prentice Hall, London (2003)
8. Frew, A. (ed.): Information and Communication Technologies in Tourism. Springer, Wien (2005)
9. Smith, M., Puczko, L.: Health and Wellness Tourism. Elsevier/Butterworth Heinemann, Amsterdam, Boston (2008)
10. World Travel Organization. Tourism Highlights 2010. Madrid, World Travel Organization (2011)

11. Lewis, D., Weigert, A.: Trust as Social Reality. The University of California Press (1985)
12. Coleman, J.: Foundations of social theory. Harvard University Press (1990)
13. Bolton, G., Greiner, B., Ockenfels, A.: Engineering Trust - Reciprocity in the Production of Reputation Information. School of Economics Discussion Paper 2009/02, Sydney (2008)
14. Berger, P., Luckmann, T.: The Social Construction of Reality. Penguin Books, Harmondsworth (1975)
15. Lahno, B.: Institutional Trust: A Less Demanding Form of Trust? Revista Latinoamericana de Estudios Avanzados (RELEA) (Caracas) 16 (2002)
16. Gambetta, D.: Can We Trust Trust? In: Gambetta, D. (ed.) Trust: Making and Breaking Cooperative Relations. Blackwell, New York (1988)
17. Goffman, E.: Forms of Talk, Oxford (1981)
18. Elias, N.: The process of civilization. Blackwell (2000)
19. Heuwinkel, K.: Zwischen Heinzelmann und Frankenstein – Ansatz zur Etablierung digitaler Begleiter als moderne Vertraute des Menschen. Dissertation. Düsseldorf (2004)
20. Fisher, K.: Locating frames in the discursive universe. Sociological Research Online 2(3) (1997), http://www.socresonline.org.uk
21. Schank, R., Abelson, R.: Scripts, plans, goals, and understanding: an inquiry into human knowledge structures. Erlbaum, Hillsdale (1977)
22. Goffman, E.: Frame Analysis. Penguin Books, Harmondsworth (1974)
23. Giddens, A.: The Constitution of Society. Polity Press, Cambridge (1984)
24. Heuwinkel, K.: Nursing ICT: Methodological Approach to Analyse Patients' Needs and Expectations. In: Proceedings of ECEH 2006, Fribourg. Lecture Notes in Informatics (2006)
25. Heuwinkel, K.: eHealth and Tourism. In: Hein, A., Thoben, W., Appelrath, H., Jensch, P. (eds.) European Conference on eHealth 2007, Oldenburg. Lecture Notes in Informatics, vol. P-118 (2007)
26. Goffman, E.: The presentation of self in everyday life. Penguin Books, Harmondsworth (1971)
27. Heuwinkel, K., Königsmann, T.: Konzeption und Entwicklung mobiler Anwendungen, vol. 73. ISST-Bericht, Berlin (2004)

Part II
Experiences with/Prerequisites
for Virtual or Robotic Companions

Part II

Virtual Butler: What Can We Learn
from Adaptive User Interfaces?

Cristina Conati

University of British Columbia, Department of Computer Science,
2366 main Mall, Vancouver, BC, Canada
conati@cs.ubc.ca

Abstract. In this paper, we discuss approaches and results from the field of
User-Adaptive Interfaces that we believe can help advance the research on
virtual butlers in general, and for the elderly in particular. We list principles
underlying the design of effective mixed-initiative interactions that call for
formal approaches to dealing both with the uncertainty on modeling relevant
cognitive states of the user (e.g., goals, beliefs, preferences), as well as with the
tradeoff between costs and benefits of the agent's actions under uncertainty.
We also discuss the need for virtual butlers to understand the affective states of
their users, and to what extent they need to be transparent by providing means
for their users to understand the rationale underlying their adaptive
interventions.

1   Introduction

User-Adaptive interfaces (UAI) is an interdisciplinary field that integrates research in
Artificial Intelligence (AI), Human Computer Interaction (HCI) and Cognitive
Science to create user interfaces that *autonomously* and *intelligently* adapt to the
needs of individual users. Providing meaningful adaptation involves building a model
of user traits relevant to adequately tailoring the interaction, i.e., a *user model*.
Depending on the nature of the task and the extent of the support that the UAI aims to
provide, these traits may include simple performance measures (such as frequencies
of interface actions), domain-dependent cognitive traits (such as knowledge and
goals), meta-cognitive processes that cut across tasks and domains (such as reasoning
and learning skills), and affective states (such as moods and emotions).

The field of UAI has much in common with research on devising intelligent home
assistants, or virtual butlers. In this paper, we discuss how to apply ideas that have
been the focus of UAI research to the development and deployment of virtual butlers.
In particular, we introduce principles that were originally proposed as the basis for
successful mixed-initiative interactions with UAIs [1]. We then discuss a particular
form of user modeling, i.e., modeling of the user's affective states from causes and
effects, that can help virtual butlers create a long-term, comfortable relationship with
their users. Finally, we address an important issue that we believe is key for the
acceptance of technology designed to have a high impact on a user's everyday life,
especially if the users are elderly people who may be not comfortable with high-tech

R. Trappl (Ed.): Your Virtual Butler, LNAI 7407, pp. 29–41, 2013.

solutions. This is the issue of transparency/trust, or the degree to which the user needs/wants to understand the rationale underlying the behaviours of an intelligent assistant in order to trust its services.

2   Principles of Mixed-Initiative Interfaces

In the late 1990s', Microsoft research had already put forward the idea of a Virtual Butler for desktop assistance, as a result of lessons learned from the deployment of the Office Assistant for Microsoft Office. The principles underlying the design of this new form of desktop assistance where spelled out in a seminal paper [1]. The key point of the proposed paradigm was that adaptive interactions should be *mixed-initiative*. That is, the user and the adaptive component collaborate to achieve optimal personalization of service. We discuss here a subset of the twelve principles reported in that paper, that we believe are fundamental for the development of successful virtual butlers for the home.

(1) Developing significant value-added automation. Because automated services come with overheads due to their potential lack of transparency and reliability, they should be used only to support tasks that cannot be suitably aided through simpler solutions (see, for instance, the self-cleaning glass vs. glass-cleaning robot example in the chapter by Helmut Stesse).

(2) Considering uncertainty about a user's needs. Being able to provide automated services proactively often requires understanding user goals, beliefs, and preferences. There is bound to be uncertainty in assessing these elements, especially in a rather unconstrained environment like the home, where the user can engage in many different and possibly unrelated activities. This uncertainty should be explicitly taken into account with formal probabilistic techniques rather than by using ad hoc heuristics with less principled theoretical underpinnings.

(3) Employing dialog to resolve key uncertainties. One possible way for a virtual butler to reduce the uncertainty in assessing its user's needs is to ask the user directly. While this is an option that the agent should always consider, the decision of whether to engage in a dialogue with the user should be mediated by an awareness of the potential cost of needlessly bothering the user.

(4) Considering both the costs and benefits of each possible action when deciding what to do. Principle #3 above is an instance of the more general principle of weighing the potential costs and benefits of each possible course of action when deciding how the agent should act, given the uncertainty that permeates the agent's assessment of the user. For instance, if the agent is uncertain about how much a user needs a specific service now, it should evaluate both *costs* and *benefits* of interrupting the user to provide the service, vs. deferring the action to a time when it will be less intrusive, vs. asking the user for more information to help the agent with its decision. Similarly, considerations of potential costs and benefits of actions should help the agent scope the precision of service to match the uncertainty over user goals. That is, doing less but doing it correctly under uncertainty can be more useful that try to provide more specific help that may be unwanted. (related to notion of "useful incompetent helper" in Iba's chapter).

(5) Allowing efficient direct invocation and termination. It is crucial to provide efficient means for users to directly invoke or terminate automated services, to make up for poor decisions by the agents.

(6) Employing socially appropriate behaviours for agent–user interaction. An agent should be endowed with default behaviours and courtesies that match the social expectations for a benevolent assistant. In the context of this book, the expectations are those of the elderly users of virtual butlers.

(7) Continuing to improve over time. This capability can be achieved via two different strategies. The first entails giving the agent the capability to learn by observation, without requiring additional explicit information from the user. The second strategy entails providing mechanisms that allow users to provide explicit feedback to aid the system's learning (e.g., mechanisms to complete or refine inferences and doings of agent).

3   How Far Have UAI Gone?

Adaptive techniques have been investigated for many types of applications, including recommender systems, intelligent tutoring systems, e-games and e-tourism [2] for an overview. There has also been encouraging progress with mixed-initiative approaches, but most of the existing systems tend to be task and/or domain specific. Examples include the TRIPS system for mixed-initiative problem solving [3]; the DiamondHelp mixed-initiative system for task guidance [4]; the MapGen system for mixed-initiative planning, deployed to help with ground operations in the Mars Exploration Rover mission; the Support the Customer (STC) system to provide GE customers with support to diagnose faults in their appliances.

The initiative that so far has gotten closest to the idea of a more general-purpose mixed-initiative intelligent assistant is the CALO project (Cognitive Assistants that Learns and Organizes), sponsored by DARPA. The project involved over 30 institutions in the USA, with the goal of creating cognitive software systems that relieve the workload of knowledge workers by (i) engaging in and leading routine tasks (such as scheduling, task execution, meeting management, information management) and (ii) assisting when the unexpected happens. As stated in the project's official website, *"A CALO should be able to reason, learn from experience, be told what to do, explain what it is doing, reflect on its experience, and respond robustly to surprise."* These are capabilities that we may want in a house assistant, and the CALO project made substantial progress on the necessary machine learning aspects of this research [30, 31]. Less progress has been made on successfully applying the proposed technologies in practice, in a user-friendly, mixed-initiative fashion.

Why, then, despite the many years of research and the many resources devoted to adaptive and mixed-initiative systems, are we far from general-purpose intelligent assistants? The reason is that any form of virtual butler is "AI-complete"; that is, it requires dealing with all of the traditional AI challenges (knowledge representation, reasoning, planning, problem solving, natural language processing), with the additional complexity that these challenges need to be tackled for many different task domains and for interacting properly with the user. In the rest of the paper, we will focus on the latter problem (interaction with the user), specifically on two issues that we believe are especially relevant for supporting smooth interaction between an elderly user and a virtual butler: (i) enabling the virtual butler to model and respond to the user's affective states; (ii) enabling the user to understand the reasons behind the virtual butler's interventions.

4   Modeling User Affect from Causes and Effects

What should a virtual butler understand about its users? Certainly their goals, preferences and beliefs (which is challenging enough), but also their *moods* and *emotions* (e.g., *affect*), if we want an agent that can create a long-lasting, balanced and comfortable relationship with the user [5].

Recent years have seen a flourishing of research directed towards adding affective components to human–computer interactions, with the assumption that "affect-sensitive interfaces" can better meet users' needs by creating a more natural dialogue between humans and computers. One key element of this endeavour is the computer's capability to recognize the user's emotional states during the interaction, i.e., to have a model of the user's affect (or *affective user model*). Possible sources of information to assess user emotions include causal information on both context and the person's relevant traits, as well as diagnostic information on visible bodily reactions. However, the information provided by these sources is often ambiguous and even contradictory, making emotion assessment a task riddled with uncertainty, especially in situations that can give rise to multiple emotions, possibly overlapping and rapidly changing, as for instance during the course of an emotionally charged conversation.

Consistently with the second principle listed in Section 2 (*Considering uncertainty about a user's needs*), to handle this uncertainty we have proposed a probabilistic framework for modeling user affect that uses Dynamic Decision Network (DDN) [6] to leverage information on both the possible causes and the observable effects of the user's affective reaction [7, 33]. Most existing research in modeling user affect has focused on devising models that can capture *which* affective states a user is experience during a given interaction. [8, 10, 9, 11, 12, 32]. Our approach is designed to also provide insights on *why* a user is in a particular affective state, thus better enabling an interacting agent to adequately respond to the user's emotional reactions.

4.1   The Affect Modeling Framework

A DDN is a graph where nodes represent either stochastic variables of interest or points where an agent needs to make deliberate decisions. Arcs in the graph capture the direct probabilistic relationships between the nodes. Each node has an associated probability distribution representing the conditional probability of each of its possible values, given the values of its parent nodes. As evidence on one or more network variables becomes available, *ad hoc* algorithms update the posterior probabilities of all the other variables, given the observed values.

Fig. 1 shows a high-level representation of two time-slices in our DDN-based framework for affective modeling. Each time slice represents the model's variables at a particular point in time and, as the figure shows, the network can combine evidence on both the causes and effects of emotional reactions to assess the user's emotional state. The sub-network above the nodes *Emotional States* is the predictive component of the framework. It represents the relations between possible causes and emotional states as described in the OCC cognitive theory of emotions [15]. According to this theory, emotions derive from cognitive appraisal of the current situation, which consists of events, agents, and objects. The outcome of the appraisal depends on how the situation fits with the individual's goals and preferences. For instance, depending on whether the current event (e.g., the outcome of an interface agent's action) does or does not fit with the individual's goals, the person will feel either *joy* or *distress* toward the event. Correspondingly, if the current event is caused by a third-party agent, the person will feel *admiration* or *reproach* toward the agent; if the agent is oneself, the person will feel either *pride* or *shame*. Based on this structure, the OCC theory defines 22 different emotions, described in terms of their valence and the entity they relate to.

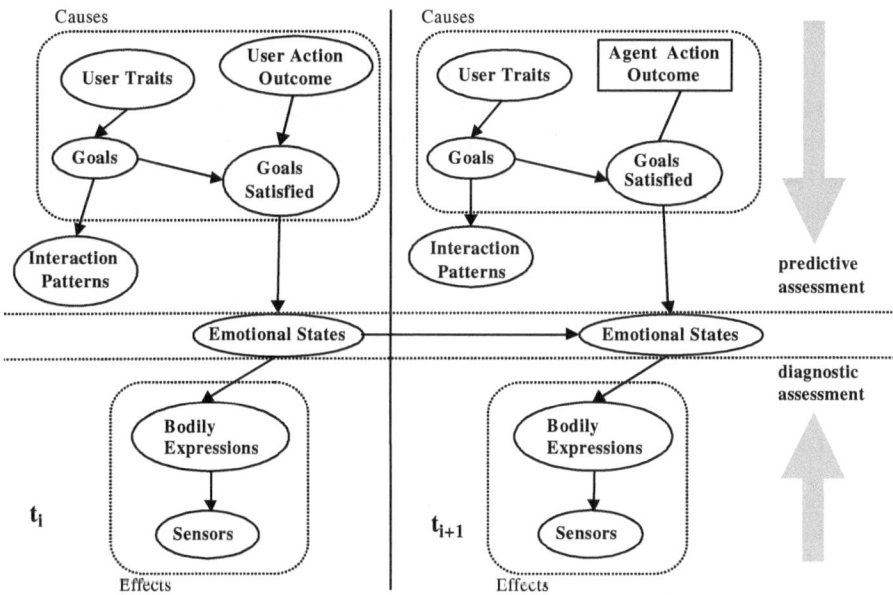

Fig. 1. High-level representation of the DDN for affective user modeling

We adopted this particular theory of emotion for our affective modeling framework, rather than alternative models that define emotions in terms of their level of valence and arousal [13], because its clear and intuitive representation of the causal nature of emotional reactions lends itself well to devising computational models that can assess *why* a user feels given emotions, as well as *what* these emotions are. This more fine-grained information enhances the capability of an interactive agent to adequately respond to user affect. For instance, if the agent can recognize that the user feels a negative emotion because of something wrong she has done (*shame* by OCC definition), it can decide to provide hints aimed at making the user feel better about herself. If the agent recognizes that the negative feelings are caused by its own behaviour (*reproach* by OCC definition) it may decide to take actions to make amends with the user. These specific interventions are not possible with approaches that detect emotions with no explicit knowledge of their causes [32].

Our OCC-based DDN for affective user modeling includes variables for goals that a user may have during the interaction with an autonomous agent, (nodes *Goals* in Fig. 1). The events subject to the user's appraisal are any outcomes generated by the user's or the agent's action (nodes *User Action Outcome* and *Agent Action Outcome* in Fig. 1). Agent action outcomes are represented as decision variables in the framework, indicating points where the agent decides how to intervene in the interaction. The desirability of an event in relation to the user's goals is represented by the node class *Goals Satisfied,* which in turn influences the user's *Emotional States* (we will call this part of the model *appraisal-subnetwork* from now on)

The user's goals are a key element of the OCC model, but assessing these goals is not trivial, especially when obtaining them directly from the user would be too intrusive. Thus, our DDN also includes nodes to infer user goals from indirect evidence (*goal-assessment subnetwork*). User goals can depend on *User Traits* such as personality and can influence user *Interaction Patterns*, which in turn can be inferred by observing the outcomes of individual user actions. Thus, both the relevant user traits and action outcomes can be used in the DDN as evidence for assessing user goals. The subnetwork below the nodes *Emotional States* is the diagnostic part of the affective modeling framework, representing the interaction between emotional states and their observable effects. *Emotional States* directly influence user *Bodily Expressions*, which in turn affect the output of *Sensors* that can detect them. Because in many situations a single sensor cannot reliably identify a specific emotional state, our framework is designed to modularly combine any available sensor information, and gracefully degrade in the presence of partial or noisy information.

4.2   Using the Framework for Affective User Modeling

We have instantiated the modeling framework described in the previous section to model user emotions during the interaction with PrimeClimb, an educational game designed to help students practice number factorization. The game includes a pedagogical agent that can provide individualized support when the student does not seem to be learning from the game [17]. Therefore, the affective model is designed to capture both feelings generated by the player's performance in the game (labeled as *pride/shame* in the OCC theory) as well as feelings generated by the agent's interventions (labeled as *admiration/reproach* in the OCC theory). The model also captures user's emotions towards game states (labeled as *joy/regret* in the OCC model).

As part of the iterative design and evaluation approach we adopted to build the affective model, we started by instantiating and evaluating the predictive part of our modeling framework. Creating the predictive part of the model required several user studies to identify common user goals during game playing, the probabilistic relationships between student personality traits, goals and interaction patterns to define the goal assessment network [17], and the probabilities that the outcomes of various student and agent actions satisfy each of the possible goals [18] for the appraisal network. We then experimented with adding to the model a diagnostic component that uses Electromigraphy (EMG) sensors placed on the user's forehead to detect frowns as signs of negative affect. Preliminary results show that with this model can achieve up to 73% accuracy in modeling emotions towards the agent [33].

4.3   Using the Framework for a Socially Intelligent Virtual Butler

The main advantage of the affective modeling approach described above is that, by explicitly modeling causes of affect, it gives an agent fine-grained information on how to respond to the affect. The second advantage is that it is flexible in taking advantage of the available sources of affective information, leveraging data on both causes and effects when available, but still being able to degrade gracefully when any of the potential information sources becomes unavailable or unreliable. This flexibility is enhanced if one adds to the model goals that explicitly represent lower level dimensions of affective reactions, i.e., valence and arousal. These dimensions are generally easier to assess than specific emotions, so the system has the chance to *"do less but do it more accurately"* in the presence of high level of uncertainty over a user's specific emotions, as suggested by the mixed-initiative principle #3 in Section 2. A third advantage is that the framework lends itself well to be used by an agent that takes both costs and benefits of its actions into account when deciding how to act. Dynamic decision networks are set up specifically to support a decision-theoretic approach to agent behaviour. In a decision-theoretic model [24], costs and benefits of agent behaviours are expressed as preferences over world states S (e.g., the possible affective states of a user for an affect-sensitive agent). In turn, these preferences are encoded via a utility function $U(S)$, which assigns a single number to express the desirability of each state S. Furthermore, for each action a available to the agent, and for each possible outcome state S' of that action, P(S'|E, a) represents the agent's belief that action a will result in state S', when the action is performed in a state identified by evidence E. The expected utility of an action a is then computed as

$$EU(A) = \Sigma_{S'} P(S'|E, a)U(S')$$

A decision-theoretic agent selects the action that maximizes this value when deciding how to act. DDNs allow modeling decision-theoretic behaviour via the inclusion of nodes that represent an agent's utilities, in addition to nodes representing probabilistic events in the world and the agent's decision points. By relying on propagation algorithms for Bayesian networks, DDNs allow computing the agent's action (or sequence of actions) with maximum expected utility given the available evidence on the current state of the world.

One potential drawback of our proposed approach is that it requires the detailed modeling of user goals and preferences, as well as how a user appraises different circumstances in the surrounding environment based on these goals and preferences. This modeling is bound to require a substantial amount of empirical data for each new user in order to be done accurately, but its cost is lessened by the fact that a virtual butler needs to understand user goals and preferences regardless of whether or not it includes an affective component. What is left then is the cost of modeling a user's appraisal criteria, and understanding how this cost compares with the gain in quality of the system's affective responses.

There are also two approach-independent issues that need to be investigated in order to devise emotionally intelligent virtual butlers. The first is deciding which emotions the virtual butler should be able to capture. The second is what should the virtual butler do to respond to those emotions.

The first issue requires, again, evaluating the cost of modeling each additional emotion against the value that can be gained in terms of usefulness/acceptance/impact of the virtual butler. The OCC model, for instance, accounts for twenty-two different emotions, including emotions related to feelings towards aspects of an entity (*liking, disliking, love, hatred*) and emotions related to appraising events in terms of their usefulness for others (*happy-for, resentment, gloating, pity*) or in terms of expected consequences for self *(hope, fear)*. While it is very possible that most users may encounter each of these emotions at one point or another, it is necessary to evaluate which ones are prominent enough to warrant attention, and among these which ones can/should be a concern for a virtual butler. For instance, the only reason to model a morally negative but positively valenced emotion such as *gloating* would be to try and discourage it, but this should hardly be a mission for the virtual butler for an elderly user.

Once the affective states that the virtual butler should recognize have been determined, the question becomes how they should affect the butler's behaviour. There are at least two levels at which affective information can be included in the agent's operation. One level, which we will define as *affect oriented*, involves having the agent respond to the user's affective state to directly influence it; for instance, one could envision a virtual butler that can detect its user's negative affective states and act specifically to help the user overcome them. A second level, which we will call *task oriented*, sees affective information as one of the factors that the agent must take into account to decide how to best accomplish a given task. Suppose, for instance, that a virtual butler needs to communicate to its user that her friend is cancelling a plan to go and see a movie the following evening, and that the agent has the choice to do it right away or wait until later in the day. While giving the news right away would give the user more time to make alternative arrangements if desired, the agent may decide to delay the action if it detects that the user is already in a negative state, especially if it thinks that the negative state is caused by feelings of being lonely.

Both these levels will require extensive investigations to define the impact of the agent's actions on an elderly user's affect. These investigations may be able to leverage existing theories on affective interventions from emotional psychology and existing knowledge on the effects of emotionally responsive artificial agents in domains other than domotics for the elderly [19, 21, 22, 20, 23, 34]. However, because there is very limited work on the dynamics of affective interactions between artificial agents and elderly users, ad-hoc empirical studies will need to be conducted to fill the theoretical gaps, especially given the focus on users who may be less familiar with artificial agents and perhaps less open to the idea of having empathic relations with one.

5   Enabling the User to Understand Its Butler

User modeling allows an adaptive agent to understand its user, but shouldn't the user also understand the system? The term "understand" here relates to comprehending the *rationale* underlying the agent's interventions and suggestions, and is connected to one of the main principles of good design in HCI: interface *transparency*, or the extent to which a user can understand system actions and/or has a clear picture of how the system works [2]. There are at least two reasons to believe that allowing an agent to expose the rationale underlying its behaviours to the user may improve its effectiveness. The first is that this capability would greatly improve the mixed-initiative aspect of the agent-user interaction, because the agent and the user can *discuss* the agent's decisions based on how well the agent can justify them, as opposed to having a one-shot mixed-initiative exchange where all the user can do is either accept or reject the agent's service. The second is that understanding the rationale underlying an agent's behaviour may increase the user's *trust* in the agent: the user may not be as put off by an agent's less-then-ideal action if the agent can show that it was suggested based on reasonable assumptions and sound reasoning.

There are numerous examples of adaptive or mixed-initiative systems that provide access to all or part of their rationale. For example, there are adaptive systems for education that include *inspectable student models*. These systems allow users to view and sometimes edit their student model, with the assumption that these operations give users a sense of what causes the particular adaptive behaviour to occur [25, 26]. Provision of rationale has also been explored in recommender systems [27], in expert systems [28] and in mixed-initiative approaches to interface customization [29] Evaluations provide encouraging evidence that the rationale can increase system transparency [26, 29], promote reflection [26], and improve users' reactions to system recommendations [27]. If not properly designed, however, rationale can be difficult to use [25, 29] and can even lead to less favourable responses towards the system [27]. [29] also showed that interest and willingness to look at the system rationale are strongly user dependent. In their work, rationale relates to describing to the user how MICA, an adaptive system that supports user customization of MS Word menus/toolbars, generates its customization suggestions.

MICA tries to identify the user's optimal personalized interface (PI from now on) by evaluating which menu and toolbar items should be included in the PI and which should reside solely in the full interface (FI), accessible via a button click in the PI. MICA then generates corresponding customization suggestions. To do so, MICA relies on a user model that assesses the user's *time performance* given a particular PI.

The performance assessment relies primarily on three factors: (1) *Usage Frequencies:* how often the user is expected to access each menu item; (2) *Expertise:* user's familiarity with the existing menus, to account for the fact that users with lower expertise are likely to be more negatively impacted by excess functionality; (3) *Interface Size:* detailed layout information on the FI and the PI under consideration, including the number of items present and where they are located.

MICA's rationale component describes why the system is making recommendations and the relevant user- and interface-specific factors influencing its decision-making process. Presenting this rationale has the potential to provide valuable insight into how the system works; however, effectively communicating the information to the average user is a challenging design task, particularly since MICA's algorithm is relatively complex. [29] dealt with the challenge via an iterative design and evaluation process that led to the rationale-explanation component shown in Figure 2.

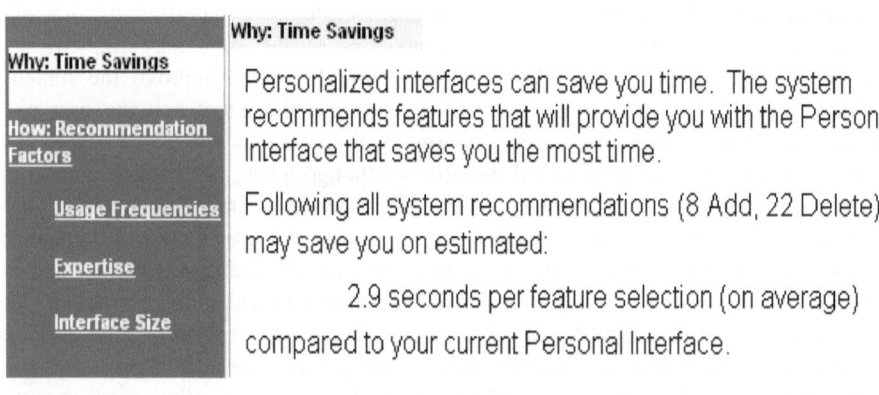

Fig. 2. "Why" component of MICA's rationale explanation

In this component, the user can access the rationale as soon as MICA generates a recommendation for customization. Once invoked, the dialogue box in Fig. 2 appears, including information on *why* and *how* the system makes recommendations. The "Why" component, displayed on the right of Fig. 2, indicates that the recommendations are based on time savings and provides an estimated savings per feature invocation (based on the user model's performance assessment) should the user choose to accept all recommendations.

The "How" component is a simplified explanation of MICA's decision-making. The first screen, "How: Recommendations Factors," explains that MICA balances the three factors described above (Usage Frequencies, Expertise, Interface Size). Next, three screens describe each factor in greater detail (two are shown in Fig. 3).

Findings from a formal qualitative study on the acceptance and impact of MICA's rationale functionality [29] indicate that the majority of users prefer to have the rationale present, but that a not-insignificant group of users do not need or want the information. For some users, the rationale led to increased trust, understanding, predictability, and motivation to accept recommendations. Others, however, felt that the rationale was just common sense, or was unnecessary in a mixed-initiative system or productivity application. Some users said that they did not need to see the rationale because they had an inherent trust in the system.

These findings suggest that, contrary to previously stated guidelines [2], system transparency may not, in fact, be important to all users in all contexts. But we should bear in mind that the tasks studied in [29] related to a productivity application, and were obtained in a laboratory setting with no serious consequences for having suboptimal task performance. These circumstances are likely to reduce the user's need to make sure that a system's suggestions are actually worth following, especially when weighed against the time and effort required to parse the system's explanations. Thus, there is a substantial amount of groundwork that needs to be done to assess how important system transparency is in the context of the interaction of elderly users with their virtual butler. If transparency turns out to be important, then researchers will need to focus their effort on understanding

- which level of understanding a virtual butler needs to promote (e.g., visualization of the system's user model vs. more explicit explanations of the inferences that generated the current model's predictions)
- How to best promote the chosen level(s) from an HCI point of view.

6   Discussion and Conclusions

In this paper, we have discussed approaches and results from the field of User-Adaptive Interfaces that we believe can help advance the research on virtual butlers in general, and for the elderly in particular. We have listed principles underlying the design of effective mixed-initiative interactions that call for formal approaches to dealing both with the uncertainty on modeling relevant cognitive states of the user (e.g., goals, beliefs, preferences), as well as with the tradeoff between costs and benefits of the agent's actions under uncertainty. We have also discussed the need for virtual butlers to understand the affective states of their users, and we have introduced a framework for affective user modeling that leverages both causes and effects of emotional reactions to assess the user's specific emotions, and why they arise. Finally, we have addressed the issue of system transparency, i.e., whether it is important/feasible that elderly users understand the rationale underlying the interventions of their butlers in order to make the most effective use of them.

What should emerge from this chapter, and from this book overall, is that there are still many more open questions than solutions along the road to devising Virtual Butlers for elderly citizens. Finding answers to these open questions should be a multidisciplinary endeavor, where psychologists and sociologists study the general principles underlying the interaction of elderly users with these kinds of advanced technologies, and IT experts use these principles to shape the technologies so that they can best suit this specific user population.

References

1. Horvitz, E.: Principles of Mixed-Initiative User Interfaces. In: Proceedings of CHI 1999, ACM SIGCHI Conference on Human Factors in Computing Systems, Pittsburgh, PA (1999)
2. Jameson, A.: Adaptive Interfaces and Agents. In: Sears, A., Jacko, J. (eds.) The Human-Computer Interaction Handbook: Fundamentals, Evolving Technologies and Emerging Applications, 2nd edn., pp. 433–458. CRC Press, Boca Raton (2008)
3. Ferguson, G., Allen, J.: Mixed-Initiative Dialogue Systems for Collaborative Problem-Solving. AI Magazine: Special Issue on Mixed-Initiative Assistants 28(2), 2–32 (2007)
4. Rich, C., Sidner, C.: DiamondHelp: A generic collaborative task guidance system. AI Magazine: Special Issue on Mixed-Initiative Assistants (2007)
5. Bickmore, T., Picard, R.: Establishing and maintaining long-term human-computer relationships. ACM Trans. Comput.-Hum. Interact. 12(2), 293–327 (2005)
6. Dean, T., Kanazawa, K.: A Model for Reasoning about Persistence and Causation. Computational Intelligence 5(3) (1989)
7. Conati, C.: Probabilistic Assessment of User's Emotions in Educational Games. Journal of Applied Artificial Intelligence, Special Issue on Merging Cognition and Affect in HCI 16(7-8), 555–575 (2002)
8. Healey, J.A., Picard, R.W.: Detecting Stress During Real-World Driving Tasks Using Physiological Sensors. IEEE Transactions on Intelligent Transportation Systems 6(2) (2005)
9. Prendinger, H., Mori, J., Ishizuka, M.: Recognizing, Modeling, and Responding to Users' Affective States. In: Ardissono, L., Brna, P., Mitrović, A. (eds.) UM 2005. LNCS (LNAI), vol. 3538, pp. 60–69. Springer, Heidelberg (2005)
10. Litman, D.J., Forbes-Riley, K.: Predicting Student Emotions in Computer-Human Tutoring Dialogues. In: 42nd Annual Meeting of the Association for Computational Linguistics, ACL (2004)
11. Mandryk, R.L., Inkpen, K.M., Calvert, T.W.: Using Psychophysiological Techniques to Measure User Experience with Entertainment Technologies. Journal of Behavior and Information Technology 25 (2006)
12. D'Mello, S.K., et al.: Automatic Detection of Learner's Affect from Conversational Cues. User Modeling and User-Adapted Interaction 18(1-2) (2008)
13. Lang, P.J.: The emotion probe: Studies of motivation and attention. American Psychologist 50 (1995)
14. D'Mello, S.K., Chipman, P., Graesser, A.C.: Posture as a predictor of learner's affective engagement. In: Proceedings of the 29th Annual Cognitive Science Society (2006)
15. Ortony, A., Clore, G.L., Collins, A.: The Cognitive Structure of Emotions. Cambridge University Press (1988)
16. Lang, P.J., et al.: Look at Pictures: Affective, Facial, Visceral, and Behavioral Reactions. Psychophysiology 30 (1993)
17. Zhou, X., Conati, C.: Inferring User Goals from Personality and Behavior in a Causal Model of User Affect. In: Proceedings of IUI 2003, International Conference on Intelligent User Interfaces, Miami, FL, U.S.A, pp. 211–218 (2003)
18. Conati, C., Maclaren, H.: Data-Driven Refinement of a Probabilistic Model of User Affect. In: Ardissono, L., Brna, P., Mitrović, A. (eds.) UM 2005. LNCS (LNAI), vol. 3538, pp. 40–49. Springer, Heidelberg (2005)
19. Klein, J., Moon, Y., Picard, R.: This Computer Responds to User Frustration: Theory, Design, Results, and Implications. Interacting with Computers 14(2), 119–140 (2002)

20. Burleson, W., Picard, R.W.: Gender-Specific Approaches to Developing Emotionally Intelligent Learning Companions. IEEE Intelligent Systems 22(4), 62–69 (2007)
21. Prendinger, H., Ishizuka, M.: The Empathic Companion: A Character-Based Interface That Addresses Users' Affective States. Applied Artificial Intelligence 19(3-4), 267–285 (2005)
22. Paiva, A., Dias, J., Sobral, D., Aylett, R., Woods, S., Hall, L.E., Zoll, C.: Learning By Feeling: Evoking Empathy With Synthetic Characters. Applied Artificial Intelligence 19(3-4), 235–266 (2005)
23. McQuiggan, S.W., Rowe, J.P., Lester, J.C.: The effects of empathetic virtual characters on presence in narrative-centered learning environments. In: CHI, pp. 1511–1520 (2008)
24. Howard, R.A., Matheson, J.E. (eds.): Readings in Decision Analysis. Decision Analysis Group, SRI International, Menlo Park, California (1977)
25. Czarkowski, M., Kay, J.: How to Give the User a Sense of Control over the Personalization of Adaptive Hypertext? In: Proc. of Adaptive Hypermedia and Adaptive Web-Based Systems (in Conjunction with UM 2003), pp. 121–131 (2003)
26. Zapata-Rivera, J.D., Greer, J.E.: Interacting with Inspectable Bayesian Student Models. International Journal of AI in Education 14 (2003)
27. Herlocker, J., Konstan, J.A., Riedl, J.: Explaining Collaborative Filtering Recommendations. In: Proc. of CSCW, pp. 241–250 (2000)
28. Horvitz, E., Breese, J., Henrion, M.: Decision Theory in Expert Systems and Artificial Intelligence. Journal of Approximate Reasoning 2, 247–302 (1988)
29. Bunt, A., McGrenere, J., Conati, C.: Understanding the Utility of Rationale in a Mixed-Initiative System for GUI Customization. In: Conati, C., McCoy, K., Paliouras, G. (eds.) UM 2007. LNCS (LNAI), vol. 4511, pp. 147–156. Springer, Heidelberg (2007)
30. Gervasio, M., Murdock, J.: What Were You Thinking? Filling in Missing Dataflow Through Inference in Learning from Demonstration. In: Proc. IUI 2009. ACM Press (2009)
31. Shen, J., Fitzhenry, E., Dietterich, T.G.: Discovering frequent work procedures from resource connections. In: IUI, pp. 277–286 (2009)
32. Arroyo, A., Cooper, D., Burleson, W., et al.: Emotion Sensors Go To School. In: AIED, pp. 17–24 (2009)
33. Conati, C.: Combining cognitive appraisal and sensors for affect detection in a framework for modeling user affect. In: Calvo, R.A., D'Mello, S.K. (eds.) New Perspectives on Affect and Learning Technologies. Springer, New York (in press)
34. D'Mello, S., Lehman, B., Sullins, J., Daigle, R., Combs, R., Vogt, K., Perkins, L., Graesser, A.: A Time for Emoting: When Affect-Sensitivity Is and Isn't Effective at Promoting Deep Learning. In: Aleven, V., Kay, J., Mostow, J. (eds.) ITS 2010, Part I. LNCS, vol. 6094, pp. 245–254. Springer, Heidelberg (2010)

Towards Affect Sensitive and Socially Perceptive Companions

Ginevra Castellano[1] and Peter W. McOwan[2]

[1] School of Electronic, Electrical and Computer Engineering,
University of Birmingham, UK
[2] School of Electronic Engineering and Computer Science,
Queen Mary University of London, UK
g.castellano@bham.ac.uk, pmco@eecs.qmul.ac.uk

Abstract. This chapter investigates affect sensitivity as an important requirement for socially perceptive companions. Challenges and issues arising in the design of an affect recognition framework for artificial companions are identified. A multi-level approach to the analysis of non-verbal affective expressions in human-companion interaction is also presented. The chapter ends with a discussion on the importance of affect recognition for the generation of empathic reactions and the establishment of long-term human-companion relationships.

1   Introduction

Machines endowed with social and emotional intelligence are becoming increasingly essential for many applications involving direct interaction with human users [1]. Artificial companions, whether as robots, graphical synthetic characters or socially interactive toys, are examples of artifacts that would benefit from the integration of social, affective capabilities into their underlying technology.

Artificial companions may be of crucial importance in many applications. As the average age of the population in many countries increases, health care for elderly people is becoming more problematic. Artificial companions may be able to provide additional functionalities that could assist primary and secondary users, e.g. carers, health care workers etc. Companions could also represent valuable tools for edutainment and therapy applications, as well as impact the entertainment industry (e.g., design of socially intelligent toys, intelligent interactive games, etc.). They could act as personal assistants in smart environments and be employed as interactive toys for therapy and rehabilitation purposes, for example by encouraging and mediating interactions between people affected by social, cognitive disabilities (e.g., people with autism [2]).

So far, existing prototypes of artificial companions have had only limited functionalities. While the possibilities opened up by digital technology are becoming larger and larger, computers and robots still lack many important social abilities and are not able yet to engage with humans in 'truly' natural interaction (as compared with human-human interaction). Establishing a relationship with human users requires an artificial companion that understands the way humans communicate, is able to

R. Trappl (Ed.): Your Virtual Butler, LNAI 7407, pp. 42–53, 2013.
© Springer-Verlag Berlin Heidelberg 2013

infer their mental and affective states based on their verbal and non-verbal behaviour [3], and to act in an appropriate way. For example, a socially intelligent companion acting as a personal assistant would not bore a human user by trying to help them to accomplish a specific task if they are not in a good mood or are planning to engage in some other activity (thus a companion should not interrupt you watching your favourite TV programme).

The design of an affect recognition and social perception module is the first step towards the generation of a socially acceptable behaviour. The human-computer and human-robot interaction communities have been dedicating increasing attention to the design of agents/robots capable of communicating with humans and interacting with them in a socially sensitive manner [4] [5]. These *socially perceptive companions* are endowed with communication channels and fundamental social skills taking inspiration from those characterising human beings. Nevertheless, while researchers have been increasingly investigating affect recognition [6], the design of such a module to be integrated in a human-computer or human-robot interaction framework has not been extensively addressed yet.

This chapter discusses some of the challenges in the design of affect sensitive and socially perceptive companions. An approach to affect recognition in human-companion interaction in which different non-verbal affective cues are analysed depending on the distance at which user and companion interact, is presented. Finally, the importance of affect recognition abilities is discussed with respect to the generation of empathic reactions and the establishment of an affective loop in human-companion interaction.

2   Background

A robot companion can be defined as a robot that (1) is useful, that is, is able to help, assist, entertain and motivate people, and (2) acts in a socially acceptable manner [4].

One of the main requirements for artificial companions is to be able to establish lasting relationship (i.e., over periods of weeks or months) with human users. Previous studies have shown that the novelty effect of artificial companions often quickly disappears [7] (see also [8] for an example of successful long-term companion). People tend to change their attitude and preferences towards the companions over time, and what they consider 'funny' or 'cool' initially may be perceived as 'boring' or 'annoying' at a later stage. Thus, artificial companions should be capable of adapting to the user's changes of attitude and state and behave accordingly in order to keep up the user's interest level. Current research conducted by the authors in the LIREC project [9] aims to endow companions with affect sensitivity and social perceptive abilities towards this aim.

There are examples of studies that have addressed the recognition of scenario-dependent, spontaneous affect-related states emerging during the interaction with a robot or virtual agent. Kapoor and Picard [10], for example, proposed an approach for the detection of interest in a learning environment by combining non verbal cues and information about the learner's task. Another example is the system proposed by Kapoor et al. [11], which allows for the automatic prediction of frustration of students interacting with a learning companion by using multimodal non-verbal cues such as facial expressions, head movement, posture, skin conductance and mouse pressure data. Peters et al. [12] modelled the user's interest and engagement with a virtual agent displaying shared attention behaviour, by using eye gaze and head direction information. Nakano and Ishii [13] proposed an approach to estimate the user's conversational engagement with a conversational agent based on analysis of gaze patterns. Kulic and Croft proposed an HMM-based system capable of estimating valence and arousal elicited by viewing robot motions using physiological data such as heart rate, skin conductance and corrugator muscle activity [14].

A few studies have proposed approaches for the detection of engagement with a robot. Rich and colleagues [15] proposed a computational model for the recognition of engagement between a human and a humanoid robot. Their model is based on the recognition of connection events such as directed gaze, mutual facial gaze, conversational adjacency pairs and backchannels. Castellano et al. [16] proposed a person-independent, Bayesian approach to detect children's engagement with an iCat robot acting as a game companion (see Figure 1) based on task and social interaction-based features. Within the same interaction scenario, automatic analysis and classification of affective body postures also proved successful for the discrimination of the user's engagement with the iCat robot [17].

Fig. 1. A child playing chess with the iCat robot. The iCat plays the role of a game companion in the MyFriend scenario [18] investigated in the LIREC project (from [17]).

3   Affect and Emotion

Emotions are described by Scherer [19] as "episodes of massive, synchronized recruitment of mental and semantic resources allowing to adapt to or cope with a stimulus event subjectively appraised as being highly pertinent to the needs, goals, and values of the individuals". According to this definition, emotions are phenomena consisting of coordinated changes in several components, occurring when a situation or event is considered as being relevant for an individual.

Scherer proposed a Component Process Model of Emotion (CPM) [20] [21] according to which emotion is defined as a sequence of state changes in five organismic subsystems: the cognitive system, the autonomic nervous system, the motor system, the motivational system and the monitor system. The processes occurring in these five subsystems represent, respectively, different components of an emotion:

1) *Cognitive processes*: this component refers to the appraisal processes that drive the changes in the other components. Emotional responses are generated as consequence of a subjective evaluation of internal or external stimulus events with respect to their relevance for individuals.

2) *Physiological arousal*: physiological arousal refers to all the changes activated by the autonomic nervous system, such as an increase or decrease in heart rate, breath rate, blood pressure, changes in skin conductance, temperature, muscles contractions, etc. These changes are usually related to the homeostatic regulation caused by the elicited emotion and the preparation of appropriate responses to the appraised stimulus [21].

3) *Motor expression*: motor expression consists of different forms of behavioural responses such as facial and vocal expressions, gesture and posture. Theorists of emotion often associated these behavioural responses with communicative functions necessary to inform other individuals of an individual's reaction and intentions [20].

4) *Action tendency*: this component refers to the behaviour preparation consequent to the elicitation of emotion. Action tendency allows individuals to be prompt to act depending on the context.

5) *Subjective feeling*: the subjective feeling can be considered as the result of all the changes in components during an emotional process, including the appraisal, the physiological responses, the motor expression and the action tendency. According to the CPM, a necessary condition for an emotional episode to occur is the synchronisation of all the processes described above, as a consequence of a situation/event appraised as highly relevant for an individual's well-being.

4   Affect Sensitivity

Affect sensitivity refers to the ability to analyse the verbal and non-verbal behaviour of users in order to understand their affective states.   The need for artificial companions to work in well defined, real-world scenarios, often in the user's own settings, requires research on affect recognition to be taken beyond the state of the art. In the following we review some of the challenges in the collection and analysis of representative data for building an affect recognition system for an artificial companion [3] [22] [23].

1) Spontaneous and non-prototypical affective expressions and states
Most previous studies focused primarily on the design of systems able to recognise basic emotions (e.g., joy, sadness, disgust, surprise, fear and anger), and were largely based on *acted* affective expressions [6]. While few studies have so far addressed the problem of finding methods for inferring more complex states, the design of artificial companions requires an affect sensitivity which goes beyond the ability to recognise prototypical emotions, and is able to capture more variegated affective signals conveying more subtle mental states and intentions including, for example, boredom, interest, frustration, agreement, willingness to interact, etc. Moreover, the design of an affect sensitive companion would benefit from the development of affect detectors which are trained and tested with spontaneous, real-life expressions. Although acted affective expressions collected in controlled environments present several advantages (e.g., precise definition, many expressions recorded from the same individual, very high quality of recordings, etc.), they are often exaggerated and decontextualised [24].

2) Sensitivity to multiple modalities of expression
While unimodal systems for affect recognition (mainly based on facial expression or voice analysis) have been deeply investigated, studies taking into account the multimodal nature of affective communication are still not numerous [6]. Humans can rely on different channels of information to understand the affective messages communicated by others. Similarly, it is expected an artificial companion to be able to analyse different channels of information in order to achieve a better understanding of the affective message communicated by the user. In this respect, an important issue to be addressed is the fusion of different modalities of expression, which must be designed by taking into account the relationship and correlation across different modalities.

3) *Dynamic account of affective expressions*
An important aspect to take into account is that affective expressions evolve over time and their dynamic changes communicate more than a static affect display. For an interactive companion to be able to interpret the user's state, the analysis of the dynamics of human behaviour is then a factor of crucial importance.

4) Robustness to real world scenarios
An affect recognition system for artificial companions has to be designed so as to be robust in real world applications. It must be built upon face and body detectors and facial and body features tracking systems that are robust to real environment conditions such as illumination changes, occlusions, dynamic backgrounds, etc.

5) Context sensitivity
In order to establish a truly natural interaction with the user, recognition abilities must be designed according to the context of interaction. A context sensitive affect recognition system must be sensitive to several types of contextual information, such as individual differences in expressing affect, personality of the person expressing affect, preferences, goals, underlying mood, task, environment, etc. Moreover, the design of an affect recognition system for an artificial companion

requires representative data: contextualised affective user expressions, i.e., expressions collected in the same scenario of the final application, are needed for system training and validation [25] [26].

5   A Multi-level Approach

Socially perceptive companions should be endowed with the ability to analyse different types of non-verbal affective cues emerging during the interaction with human users. These directly depend on the specific scenario of interaction.

In a given scenario, the distance between user and companion defines the level of interaction between them. This means that the distance impacts the ability and the need for the companion to perceive and interpret different affective cues and states. In the following sections we propose an approach that describes what type of analysis of affective expressions can be performed depending on the distance existing between user and companion.

5.1   Short Range Interaction

We refer to short-range interaction as the condition in which user and companion are face-to-face. Under these conditions, the cues that companions can base their prediction of affect on are those emerging in face-to-face interaction. With specific reference to non-verbal cues, examples are facial expressions, eye gaze, head gestures and orientation, posture, body expressivity [27]. An examplar work is the study by Kapoor et al. [11], described in Section 2. In the robotics domain, one of the most famous examples is the work by Breazeal and colleagues, who designed an attention system based on low-level perceptual stimuli for the Kismet robot [28]. An overview of other studies investigating analysis of affective cues in face-to-face interaction is provided in [6].

5.2   Medium-Range Interaction

In case of medium-range interaction, user and companion do not interact face-to-face, but the user is the range of the companion. When users are not too far and not too close to the companion, two examples of affective states/events that may be important for the companion to detect are the predisposition to interaction and the interaction initiation [29].

The assessment of such states/events does not necessarily require the high-level interpretation of complex cues and expressions. The main focus, at this level, is on global indicators, such as full-body movements and their qualities, for example the quantity of motion and the degree of contraction/expansion of movements and gestures, that are reported to be effective cues for affect discrimination (see, for example, [30] and [31]). Recognition of simple gestures and actions, such as waving, approach, or avoidance may also be relevant to infer some information about the user in interaction scenarios in which the user is not interacting face-to-face with the companion but at the same time is still in its proximity. A combination of low and high-level cues may be of help when the companion is required to assess an *interaction initiation* condition. As in such a condition it is expected that the user approaches the companion from a certain distance and then gets close to it, the combination of full-body movement analysis and recognition (e.g., amount of movement, motion direction, approach) and analysis of face-to-face cues, such as face direction and eye gaze (see the work by Peters [32] for an example of modelling an interaction initiation scenario in a multi-agent environment based on gaze) is envisioned to be included in a framework for affective and affect-related states recognition.

5.3   Long-Range Interaction

This section refers to interaction scenarios in which the user is in the same environment, but not in the range of the companion. Presence of people in the room, predisposition to interact, group affect are some of the affect-related states and expressions that a socially perceptive companion may be designed to detect. Coarse cues such as the amount of people present in the room and the frequency with which each person moves in proximity of the companion during an interaction session may be of help to the companion in determining whether it is required or not and from which user. Global indicators of movement are the main focus also for this type of scenario. Gross actions (such as walking towards the companion), expressivity of the single user [33] and group expressivity [34] are some of the indicators that a socially perceptive companion can analyse in order to assess an overall propension to interaction.

6   From Affect Recognition to Empathic Interaction

Affect sensitivity is a prerequisite for a companion to act socially and generate appropriate responses to the user's behaviour. Information about the user's affective behaviour can be used to influence the way a companion acts or communicates. For example, a companion can respond to low-level affective cues such as the way the user gestures (e.g., the expressivity of their movement) or to higher level data abstractions such as recognised facial expressions by exhibiting a low-level generated affective behavior (e.g., affective copying [35], mimicry [36], and establishing rapport [37]), or try to infer the user's affective state in order to plan a more complex response, e.g., an empathic reaction.

Empathy plays a key role in human-human communication. Accordingly, it is desirable that a companion is endowed with empathic behaviour, as this is likely to increase the chances of the establishment of long-term relationships with users [38]. Companions should be able to understand the user's affective state and react in a way that is appropriate given the context of the interaction. Empathy is the result of the interrelation and interaction of a variety of more elementary capabilities, relating to perception, memory, emotion, attention, theory of mind and social context. In order to create an empathic companion, these elements cannot be studied or modelled in isolation (see Figure 2).

Researchers in the social robots and virtual agents' community have started to study how to use information about the user's affective expressions and states to improve the affective loop [40]. The literature provides examples of agents and robots that can react to affective expressions of the user. Maatman and colleagues [41], for example, designed an agent capable of creating a sense of rapport in human speakers by providing real-time non-verbal listening feedback (e.g., head nods and shakes, changes in posture, etc.), including mimicry in response to the speaker's voice and body movements. Kopp et al. [42] endowed their agent Max with the ability to imitate natural gestures performed by humans. Reidsma and colleagues [43] designed a virtual rap dancer that invites users to join him in a dancing activity. Riek and Robinson [44] designed an expression-mimicking robot to support rapport in human-robot interaction. Other virtual agent systems infer affective information by perceiving and reasoning about higher level input provided by the user, such as the context of the interaction or the state of a game [45] [46].

Despite these efforts, the relation between affect sensitivity and empathy should be investigated further to provide additional insights on the factors behind the establishment of long-term human-companion relationships.

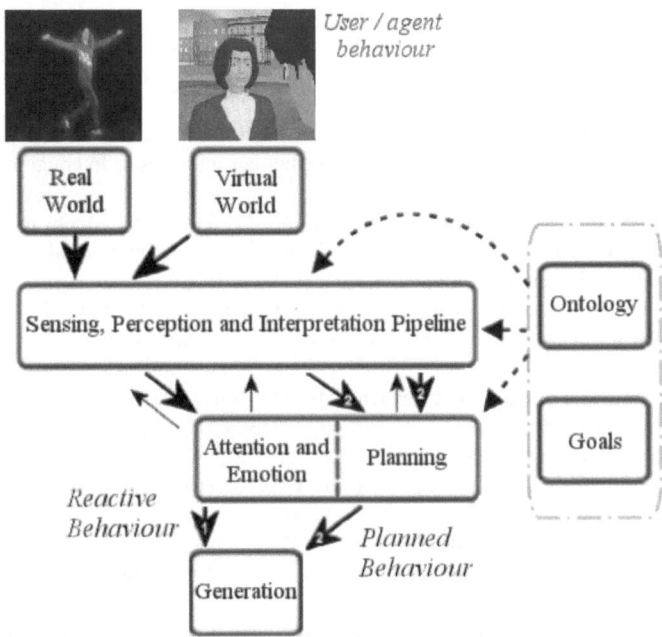

Fig. 2. Example of framework for embedding empathy-enabling capabilities in socially perceptive companions (from [39])

7   Conclusion

This chapter investigated affect sensitivity as an important requirement for socially perceptive companions. An overview of some of the issues and challenges in the design of an affect recognition framework for artificial companions is presented. Affect sensitivity is discussed with respect to issues such as the ability, for a companion, to perceive spontaneous and application-dependent affective states and to analyse multiple modalities of expression, the dynamic account of affective expressions, the robustness in real-world environment, and the sensitivity to context.

An approach to the analysis of different affective cues depending on the distance existing between user and companion in a given interaction scenario was also proposed. We claim that, in order to establish a truly natural and engaging interaction with the user, artificial companions should be endowed with recognition abilities that vary according to the context of interaction.

Finally, the generation of an affective loop based on affective sensitivity and appropriate empathic reactions was identified as a key requirement for the establishment of a long-term human-companion relationship.

Acknowledgements. This work was supported by the EU FP7 ICT-215554 project LIREC (LIving with Robots and Interactive Companions).

References

1. Picard, R.W.: Affective Computing. MIT Press (1997)
2. Robins, B., Dickerson, P., Stribling, P., Dautenhahn, K.: Robot-mediated joint attention in children with autism: A case study in robot-human interaction. Interaction Studies 5(2), 161–198 (2004)
3. Castellano, G., Leite, I., Pereira, A., Martinho, C., Paiva, A., McOwan, P.W.: Affect Recognition for Interactive Companions: Challenges and Design in Real World Scenarios. Journal on Multimodal User Interfaces 3(1), 89–98 (2010)
4. Dautenhahn, K.: Socially Intelligent Robots: Dimensions of Human-Robot Interaction. Philosophical Transactions of the Royal Society B: Biological Sciences 362(1480), 679–704 (2007)
5. Breazeal, C.: Role of expressive behaviour for robots that learn from people. Philosophical Transactions of the Royal Society B 364, 3527–3538 (2009)
6. Zeng, Z., Pantic, M., Roisman, G.I., Huang, T.S.: A Survey of Affect Recognition Methods: Audio, Visual, and Spontaneous Expressions. IEEE Transactions on Pattern Analysis and Machine Intelligence 31(1) (2009)
7. You, Z.-J., Shen, C.-Y., Chang, C.-W., Liu, B.-J., Chen, G.-D.: A Robot as a Teaching Assistant in an English Class. In: Proc. of the Sixth Int'l Conf. on Advanced Learning Technologies (2006)
8. Tanaka, F., Cicourel, A., Movellan, J.R.: Socialization between toddlers and robots at an early childhood education center. PNAS 104(46), 17954–17958 (2007)
9. http://www.lirec.eu
10. Kapoor, A., Picard, R.W.: Multimodal affect recognition in learning environments. In: Proceedings of the ACM International Conference on Multimedia, pp. 677–682 (2005)

11. Kapoor, A., Burleson, W., Picard, R.W.: Automatic Predictionof Frustration. International Journal of Human-Computer Studies 65(8), 724–736 (2007)
12. Peters, C., Asteriadis, S., Karpouzis, K.: Investigating shared attention with a virtual agent using a gaze-based interface. Journal on Multimodal User Interfaces 3(1-2), 119–130 (2010)
13. Nakano, Y.I., Ishii, R.: Estimating user's engagement from eye-gaze behaviors in human-agent conversations. In: Proceeding of the 14th International Conference on Intelligent User Interfaces, IUI 2010, pp. 139–148. ACM Press, New York (2010)
14. Kulic, D., Croft, E.A.: Affective state estimation for human-robot interaction. IEEE Transactions on Robotics 23(25), 991–1000 (2007)
15. Rich, C., Ponsler, B., Holroyd, A., Sidner, C.L.: Recognizing engagement in human-robot interaction. In: Proceeding of the 5th ACM/IEEE International Conference on Human-Robot Interaction, HRI 2010, pp. 375–382. ACM Press, New York (2010)
16. Castellano, G., Pereira, A., Leite, I., Paiva, A., McOwan, P.W.: Detecting user engagement with a robot companion using task and social interaction-based features. In: Proceedings of the International Conference on Multimodal Interfaces and Workshop on Machine Learning for Multimodal Interaction (ICMI-MLMI 2009), pp. 119–126. ACM Press, Cambridge (2009)
17. Sanghvi, J., Castellano, G., Leite, I., Pereira, A., McOwan, P.W., Paiva, A.: Automatic analysis of affective postures and body motion to detect engagement with a game companion. In: Proceedings of the ACM/IEEE International Conference on Human-Robot Interaction, Lausanne, Switzerland (2011)
18. Leite, I., Martinho, C., Pereira, A., Paiva, A.: iCat: An affective game buddy based on anticipatory mechanisms. In: Proceedings of the 7th International Joint Conference on Autonomous Agents and Multiagent Systems, vol. 3, pp. 1229–1232 (2008)
19. Scherer, K.R.: Subsystem synchronization and multimodal behavioural organization. In: Synchronization Workshop, HUMAINE/SCAS Summer School 2006, Genova (2006)
20. Scherer, K.R.: On the nature and function of emotion: A component process approach. In: Scherer, K.R., Ekman, P. (eds.) Approaches to Emotion, pp. 293–317. Erlbaum, Hillsdale (1984)
21. Scherer, K.R.: Which emotions can be induced by music? What are the underlying mechanisms? And how can we measure them? Journal of New Music Research 33(3), 239–251 (2004)
22. Castellano, G., Caridakis, G., Camurri, A., Karpouzis, K., Volpe, G., Kollias, S.: Body Gesture and Facial Expression Analysis for Automatic Affect Recognition. In: Scherer, K.R., Baenziger, T., Roesch, E.B. (eds.) Blueprint for Affective Computing: A Sourcebook. Oxford University Press, Oxford (2010)
23. Castellano, G., Peters, C.: Socially Perceptive Robots: Challenges and Concerns. Interaction Studies 11(2) (2010)
24. Scherer, K., Baenziger, T.: On the use of actor portrayals in research on emotional expression. In: Scherer, K.R., Baenziger, T., Roesch, E.B. (eds.) Blueprint for Affective Computing: A Sourcebook. Oxford University Press, Oxford (2010)
25. Afzal, S., Robinson, P.: Natural affect data – collection and annotation in learning context. In: Proceedings of the 3rd International Conference on Affective Computing and Intelligent Interaction (ACII 2009), pp. 22–28. IEEE (2009)
26. Castellano, G., Leite, I., Pereira, A., Martinho, C., Paiva, A., McOwan, P.W.: Inter-ACT: An affective and contextually rich multimodal video corpus for studying interaction with robots. In: Proceedings of the ACM International Conference on Multimedia, pp. 1031–1034. ACM (2010)

27. Vinciarelli, A., Pantic, M., Bourlard, H., Pentland, A.: Social signal processing: State-of-the-art and future perspectives of an emerging domain. In: Proceedings of the ACM International Conference on Multimedia (MM 2008), Vancouver, Canada, pp. 1061–1070 (2008)

28. Breazeal, C., Edsinger, A., Fitzpatrick, P., Scassellati, B.: Active vision for sociable robots. IEEE Transactions on Systems, Man and Cybernetics-Part A 31(5), 443–453 (2001)

29. Deshmukh, A., Castellano, G., Lim, M.Y., Aylett, R., McOwan, P.W.: Ubiquitous Social Perception Abilities for Interaction Initiation in Human-Robot Interaction. In: Proceedings of the 3rd International Workshop on Affect Interaction in Natural Environments, ACM Multimedia 2010, Florence, Italy (2010)

30. Camurri, A., Lagerlof, I., Volpe, G.: Recognizing emotion from dance movement: Comparison of spectator recognition and automated techniques. International Journal of Human-Computer Studies 59(1-2), 213–225 (2003)

31. Castellano, G., Mortillaro, M., Camurri, A., Volpe, G., Scherer, K.: Automated Analysis of Body Movement in Emotionally Expressive Piano Performances. Music Perception 26(2), 103–119 (2008)

32. Peters, C.: A perceptually-based theory of mind model for agent interaction initiation. International Journal of Humanoid Robotics (IJHR), Special issue on Achieving Human-Like Qualities in Interactive Virtual and Physical Humanoids 3(3), 321–340 (2006)

33. Castellano, G., Kessous, L., Caridakis, G.: Emotion Recognition through Multiple Modalities: Face, Body Gesture, Speech. In: Peter, C., Beale, R. (eds.) Affect and Emotion in HCI. LNCS, vol. 4868, pp. 92–103. Springer, Heidelberg (2008)

34. Bartel, C.A., Saavedra, R.: The collective construction of work group moods. Administrative Science Quarterly 45, 197–231 (2000)

35. Castellano, G., Mancini, M.: Analysis of Emotional Gestures for the Generation of Expressive Copying Behaviour in an Embodied Agent. In: Sales Dias, M., Gibet, S., Wanderley, M.M., Bastos, R. (eds.) GW 2007. LNCS (LNAI), vol. 5085, pp. 193–198. Springer, Heidelberg (2009)

36. Van Baaren, R., Holland, R., Kawakami, K., van Knippenberg, A.: Mimicry and prosocial behavior. Psychological Science 15(1), 71–74 (2004)

37. Gratch, J., Okhmatovskaia, A., Lamothe, F., Marsella, S.C., Morales, M., van der Werf, R.J., Morency, L.-P.: Virtual Rapport. In: Gratch, J., Young, M., Aylett, R.S., Ballin, D., Olivier, P. (eds.) IVA 2006. LNCS (LNAI), vol. 4133, pp. 14–27. Springer, Heidelberg (2006)

38. Leite, I., Pereira, A., Mascarenhas, S., Castellano, G., Martinho, C., Prada, R., Paiva, A.: Closing the Loop: from Affect Recognition to Empathic Interaction. In: Proceedings of the 3rd International Workshop on Affect Interaction in Natural Environments, ACM Multimedia 2010, Florence, Italy (2010)

39. Castellano, G.: Movement Expressivity Analysis in Affective Computers: From Recognition to Expression of Emotion, Ph.D.Thesis, Department of Communication, Computer and System Sciences, University of Genova, Italy (2008)

40. Conati, C., Marsella, S., Paiva, A.: Affective interactions: the computer in the affective loop. In: Proceedings of the 10th International Conference on Intelligent User Interfaces, IUI 2005, p. 7. ACM, New York (2005)

41. Maatman, R.M., Gratch, J., Marsella, S.C.: Natural Behavior of a Listening Agent. In: Panayiotopoulos, T., Gratch, J., Aylett, R.S., Ballin, D., Olivier, P., Rist, T. (eds.) IVA 2005. LNCS (LNAI), vol. 3661, pp. 25–36. Springer, Heidelberg (2005)

42. Kopp, S., Sowa, T., Wachsmuth, I.: Imitation Games with an Artificial Agent: From Mimicking to Understanding Shape-Related Iconic Gestures. In: Camurri, A., Volpe, G. (eds.) GW 2003. LNCS (LNAI), vol. 2915, pp. 436–447. Springer, Heidelberg (2004)

43. Reidsma, D., Nijholt, A., Poppe, R., Rienks, R., Hondorp, H.: Virtualrap dancer: Invitation to dance. In: CHI 2006 Extended Abstracts on Human Factors in Computing Systems, pp. 263–266. ACM (2006)

44. Riek, L., Paul, P., Robinson, P.: When my robot smiles at me: Enabling human-robot rapport via real-time head gesture mimicry. Journal on Multimodal User Interfaces 3(1), 99–108 (2010)

45. Lester, J.C., Towns, S.G., FitzGerald, P.J.: Achieving affective impact: visual emotive communication in lifelike pedagogical agents. The International Journal of Artificial Intelligence in Education 10, 278–291 (1999)

46. Bickmore, T., Picard, R.W.: Establishing and maintaining long-term human-computer relationships. ACM Transactions on Computer-Human Interaction 12(2), 293–327 (2004)

Before We Get There, Where Are We Going?

Wayne Iba

Westmont College 955 La Paz Road Santa Barbara CA 93108
iba@westmont.edu

Abstract. Fictional stories abound where artificial intelligence gives rise to man-made servants that make our lives a holiday (or a nightmare). Naturally, the optimist has a strong motive to ask: How might we design and implement an artificial servant? We regularly operate under the notion that one agent helps another by doing something for the other. However, the story behind this is much more complicated. In this position paper, we explore two questions: What is the nature of service that is helpful or "good"? and What will it take to design and implement agents that provide "good" service? We start by describing our current understanding of the nature of service, consisting of a number of dimensions along which service may be measured and compared, and three modes in which service may be delivered. With these dimensions and modes setting the stage, we consider the technical and social requirements for implementing artificial servants. We find that while many prerequisites are either already available or could reasonably be developed from the current state of the art, both technical and social challenges remain that are expected to be very difficult to overcome. Our experimental work attempts to generate and evaluate the fundamental elements of helpful assistance, and we provide a brief overview of our work. One surprising empirical result reminds us of a common understanding about help: providing assistance is a two-way street. Developing that two-way street may prove to be one of the most significant obstacles to realizing an artificial personal servant.

1 Introduction

Over the years, servants have come in many types and gone by many titles. Some of these names include: Chamberlain, valet, steward and butler. Often, the servant was responsible not only for some of the employer's immediate needs, but also for orchestrating an entire staff of other servants around the larger needs and wishes of the employer. Although the scope and details of responsibilities of these different types of servants varied, the common themes running through them all required acting on the behalf of the employer with his or her best interests at heart.

The butler has a storied past and tradition, but invariably embodies wit, efficiency, grace, tact, and intelligence that is often superior to the employer's. Those working on Germany's Ambient Assisted Living project have described a scenario where a software butler provides high quality assistance to an elderly woman, thereby enabling her to remain active, engaged and productive [5]. This imagined scenario represents a grand challenge for artificial intelligence. A much more modest goal (though still extremely challenging) would be a virtual secretary; see for example the CALO project [14]. Yet

R. Trappl (Ed.): Your Virtual Butler, LNAI 7407, pp. 54–69, 2013.

grand challenges have always helped focus effort on problems and toward solutions. Thus, it is indeed time for the Virtual Butler.

When initiating an expedition through uncharted territory, we face two strategic challenges apart from the many tactical problems to be overcome. One of these strategic problems is simply to construct a plan that will achieve the ultimate goal. But the prior question implicit in this challenge is actually determining what needs to be accomplished. In other words, what is the goal? For many expeditions that explore our physical world, the goal is obvious and the challenge is coming up with a feasible plan that accomplishes that goal. However, in the problem of designing an artificial servant – for example, a virtual butler – we may be facing the much more challenging task of determining what needs to be accomplished in order to have satisfied our goal. That is, how will we know when we get there? Since we want to implement an artificial servant, we need to understand what it means *to serve.*

If we want to help someone, how do we know what action on our part will be of the greatest assistance? From the other perspective, how can we ask for help in situations where we do not even know what we need? We need answers to these and other questions if we hope to design intelligent assistants that will help users accomplish tasks that humans find challenging.

Much of the work in artificial intelligence addresses problems that, when solved, could reasonably be expected to make a difference in people's lives [4,13]. The problem is that these targets of opportunity are sometimes selected without a vision for what would be most needed or most helpful. For example, the automation of a particular task may not provide maximal benefit to the user. Or even worse, over-eager helpers may automate an activity that users actually enjoy doing.

One approach to this problem is to respond directly to user requests. This strategy takes a conservative stance in the assumption that a user's explicit request indicates value to that user and a desire to have the task completed by the servant. However, this leads to two additional problems. First, although the user's needs can be easily anticipated in many situations, requiring an explicit request reduces the overall benefit [6]. Second, often the user does not even know for which particular help to ask. This commonly occurs in help-desk trouble shooting contexts [3].

These problems are further complicated when we realize that competence alone is not sufficient nor even necessary to provide helpful assistance [15,8]. Consequently, the ability to accomplish a task on behalf of another is not a reliable indicator that the task should be performed. In some settings, a partial solution to one of the tasks may be more helpful than a complete solution to a different task. For example, a would-be helper can either partially complete task A or completely perform task B. As it turns out, the person needing help can also perform task B but has no clue how to approach task A. In this case, it would be better for the helper to partially solve task A.

In this chapter, We claim that our hypothetical virtual butler must embody a set of qualities or virtues that we collectively associate with any servant worthy of the name. We present these qualities as a set of *service dimensions* that are fundamental to "helpful" assistance. We also describe three different *modes* in which service may be delivered. For each dimension of service and each mode of service, we consider how the scenario of Tina and her Butler, James, addresses the issue in question [5]. After describing our understanding of the nature of service, we turn to the prerequisites – both technical and social – for implementing an assistant along the lines of the virtual butlers in the scenario. Finally, we describe how some of these qualities of service have been or could be implemented within a primitive simulated world. We close by considering some of the implications that may follow from the realization of the types of artificial servants envisioned here.

2   Understanding the Nature of Helpfulness

Providing assistance can be one of those activities that is performed for the benefit of another agent without sufficient reflection. Helpfulness, like *trust* [7], is one of those ineffable qualities that we recognize when we see it but are unable to define in terms of necessary and sufficient features. We want to better understand the nature of assistance that is truly helpful.

At one point or another, everyone has experienced service that was exceptional or memorable – either because it was unusually good or unusually bad. Either at a restaurant, an auto mechanic, or a health clinic, we have been "assisted" by someone who was inattentive, incompetent, unscrupulous, or even all three at the same time. Likewise, most of us have encountered situations where the service provider anticipated our needs, took care of those needs efficiently, or treated us with genuine respect and courtesy. This common experience forms the basis of our primary claim, which we consider to be self-evident:

ASSUMPTION 1:*Not all assistance is actually helpful*
If we are willing to grant this assumption, then at least two questions should immediately spring to mind: How can we evaluate the quality of assistance? and How can we construct agents that are truly helpful? Both questions have implicitly been at the core of essentially all work in the area of intelligent assistants. However, the implicit answers to the first question are sometimes overly narrow.

2.1   Dimensions of Service

QUESTION 1:*How can we evaluate the quality or goodness of assistance?*
A traditional answer to this first question focuses on the assistant alone and amounts to specifying a task that needs to be done and then measuring how often or how completely an assistant accomplishes the given task. Essentially, this approach measures the *competence* of a service provider's assistance in a given encounter. Unfortunately, this addresses only a single facet of assistance. We identify at least five other dimensions that influence the positive or negative assessment of an interaction. Other dimensions along which we can view an assistant include: attention, anticipation, persistence, deference, and integrity. Briefly, each of these other dimensions allow us to describe characteristics of assistance that contribute to our assessment of a particular engagement as being helpful or not.

It is not surprising that competence is so frequently the focus when evaluating the quality of service. When we design systems with the intent of providing assistance, we go to great lengths to ensure that the system performs as well as can be arranged in advance. Indeed, the virtual butlers in the scenario are exceptionally competent [5]. But as we argue, competence is not a necessary nor sufficient feature. Rather it is but one of a set of factors which combine to determine the overall quality of service. It might be helpful to imagine virtual butlers that do not provide expert assistance yet still prove to be quite helpful.

In addition to competent action, we expect an assistant to pay *attention* to our current situation and track changes in our needs over time. For example, a good waiter in a restaurant will attend to the water glass, refilling as necessary. Furthermore, the good waiter should attend to patrons who are drinking more water over the course of their meals and check their water level more frequently so that the glass is not empty longer than necessary. In the scenario, James attends to the conversation Tina has with her granddaughter, Victoria; when it notices Tina struggling to recall the name of Victoria's friend, James reminds Tina that the name is Paul.

We would also hope that our assistant can *anticipate* our needs and satisfy those needs or perform tasks that contribute to our goals in a timely fashion and perhaps without being asked.[1] In the scenario, James anticipates Tina's desire to know when to expect her friend after a disruption in Gertrude's plans; based on this anticipation, James makes inquiries and reports the revised time of arrival.

Once given a task, we hope that an assistant will be *persistent* in completing the task. In the scenario, James reminds Tina that she needs to water her friend's plants. We have no way of knowing, but perhaps this was the fifth reminder – the risk of upsetting or pestering Tina must certainly be considered. However, if James is accurately recognizing when Tina becomes sidetracked and if Tina values her friend and her friend's plants, she will ultimately appreciate James' persistence.

Also, an assistant should operate with some *deference* toward those it is intending to assist; this might amount to giving the goals of the client a higher priority than the goals of the assistant itself. Perhaps we might think that artificial servants would have no goals of their own. But certainly a system as sophisticated as James will set for itself goals to research various topics in order to better serve Tina in the future. Thus, if a direct request from Tina interferes with these self-initiated goals, deference would suggest the immediate request be completed first. This would not necessarily be a hard and fast consequence, but there should be an inclination in that direction. Dorothy's butler displays an explicit instance of deference (to Dorothy) when it insists on cleaning up the spilled water despite Tina's request that it wait until she leaves.

Finally, an assistant should operate with *integrity*; that is, information and services must not be misrepresented and payments charged for the assistance should be fair. Integrity is especially important when servants are provided by a third party who may be responsible or liable for the actions of the servant. In the scenario, James' integrity and trustworthiness is taken as a starting point and liability policies, mandatory inspections, and independent service companies are introduced to sustain and safeguard that baseline.

---

[1] In this context, we do not wish to address the thorny issue of autonomy or initiative; this certainly requires additional consideration. Considerable work is ongoing in mixed-initiative planning and scheduling. Minimally, we can say that accurate anticipation is better than faulty anticipation whether or not the assistant is able to act independently on that anticipation.

Each of these, together with the *competence* of an assistant, combine to determine the overall helpfulness of a given service interaction. However, we do not claim that this list is exhaustive. Other factors that may represent distinct dimensions might include *timeliness* and *discretion*. An act of service may need to be situated appropriately in time in order to be genuinely helpful. That is, acting too early or too late may be useless to the recipient. Notice, the act is the same and may arise from all of the same forces representing the other dimensions, but time would seem to be a dimension along which the resulting level of helpfulness varies. Note however, that the previous dimensions increase helpfulness in one direction and decrease in the other. With time, we have a decrease in helpfulness in both directions as one moves away from the "just right" point.

Additionally, discretion may be a distinct dimension in its own right. Here, we want to do more than measure the servant's ability to act only in the right situation. If that were the only concern, a combination of attentiveness, competence, and anticipation might suffice. Instead, discretion should measure the ability and success at avoiding the unnecessary release of information about the client that should instead be kept private. For example, search queries may reveal the client's interest in goods and services; even worse, they might reveal how much she is willing to pay for them. The information stored in the virtual servant must not be shared unnecessarily.

2.2 Modes of Service

The dimensions of service described above move us towards a set of metrics with which we can evaluate a particular servant according to *what* it does. Orthogonally, we can distinguish three modes of service that address *how* assistance is delivered. These modes include: responsive, anticipatory, and instructive.

The simplest and most primitive form of assistance we call *responsive*. This type of assistance occurs when a servant responds to an explicit request that the servant perform some specific task. Note that while we consider this the first and most simple mode of service, the tasks itself may be far from trivial. What is simple in this case is the element of service that is necessary. Compare the requests, "bring me that pitcher" and "plan a dinner party for my ten closest friends." The two tasks differ significantly in terms of their respective complexity along multiple lines. However, the service task is fundamentally the same and reasonably straight-forward in both cases: perform the specified task as requested by the client.

The scenario of Tina and her Butler does not provide any examples of responsive service. This is not surprising, as a virtual butler with James' overall capabilities makes this mode of service rather uninteresting. Of course, we should assume that numerous such exchanges take place on a regular basis. But it is interesting to note that the scenario provides no such examples. The broader skills reported in the scenario serve to subsume responsive service events, which simply go without mention.

The next mode, *anticipatory service*, delivers assistance without the need for explicit requests. Anticipatory assistance requires a helper to infer another agent's goals and plans, so as to perform a task at the appropriate time without needing to be asked to do so. This mode of service comes in two sub-varieties: mimicry and invention.

Anticipatory assistance has been reasonably well studied [2] and some of our earlier work addressed this very problem [11]. However, most previous work has focused on predicting and accomplishing actions that would be, or were about to be performed anyway. We may call this *anticipatory-mimicry* assistance. In addition to such predictions, anticipatory assistance also includes the identification of superior alternatives that would not necessarily have been selected otherwise. We can call this type *anticipatory-invention*.

We can imagine artificial assistants using a classification paradigm in order to provide anticipatory-mimicry assistance. Given a problem solving situation, the assistant must classify the situation as one that is appropriate for a particular action with respect to the agent being helped. That is, using an acquired model of the client's patterns of behavior, the helper predicts what she would want done in the present situation. If the action is one that the helper can accomplish itself, then it has an opportunity for providing anticipatory-mimicry.

For anticipatory-invention, we can employ the same classification strategy except the appropriateness of the action is determined with respect to the helper itself. That is, the helper must put itself in the situation of the other agent and then determine what it would do in that situation. So we have separate models for each agent and a helper must be able to apply them flexibly[2].

Anticipatory-invention creates the opportunity for introducing significantly more effective solutions than considered by the client alone. However, we know that this can create problems for the client with respect to their ability or willingness to accept the such assistance [15]. While working at NASA Ames Research Center, we collaborated on the development of advanced technology for air-traffic control. In that lab among both retired and active air-traffic controllers, it was a universally accepted doctrine that any solution other than what the human controller would have done was unacceptable; it did not matter if the alternative was provably both safer and more efficient. While this state of affairs is both distressing and understandable, the example points to the challenge of getting users to think outside their conceptual boxes. Further, this problem is amplified in the instructive assistance context.

Instructive assistance requires the client receiving assistance to change its behavior so as to obviate assistance in similar situations in the future. In essence, this requires both teaching on the part of the servant and learning on the part of the client.

Perhaps we can continue to employ a classification strategy for instructive assistance – where the client changes its goals and beliefs so as to subsequently alter its behavior in similar future situations. In this case, the agent receiving help needs to acquire a model of the helper and then apply that model to its own situation. This seems to be a straightforward inversion of the strategy employed by the helper in anticipatory assistance.

While we suppose this approach will prove somewhat effective, it is not without reason for caution. First note what is required for the client to acquire a useful model of the helper; the helper must behave in view of the client and behave in a manner that leads to the intended model. Of course, we would want helpers to be able to instruct through communication rather than demonstration. Next also consider that what the client might be missing is an appropriate link between the consequences of an action

---

[2] This suggests *empathy* as another candidate dimension of service. Empathy, the ability to reason within another agent's set of beliefs, values and goals, would be a distinct dimension from deference, which reflects a prioritization between goals.

and a goal which the action satisfies. Thus, what is needed is a learning mechanism that lets agents form models of their actions and their effects, and not just models of when certain actions are appropriate. Further complicating this matter, we ultimately want to provide assistance to humans over whom we do not have the ability to inject learning mechanisms. Clearly, continued conceptual work needs to be done.

2.3 Implications for Evaluation and Design

Reflection on the dimensions and modes above suggests at least two corollary assumptions to our central claim. These assumptions may provide further constraints on the design of assistants.

ASSUMPTION 1.1:*Competent helpers are not enough*
Good assistance requires more than simply performing a task for another agent. This is true even when the task in question really needs to be done. For example, if two sub-tasks must be completed in a specific sequence, then an assistant that arbitrarily does one task may not be helping. Or two sub-tasks may have significantly different difficulties and help is needed with the most difficult one; in this case, an assistant that completes the easier task may not be as helpful as the one that makes partial progress on the more difficult task. Again, performing a task may bring a user enjoyment and having the task completed by an assistant could deprive the user of that satisfaction. Thus, we have several examples where an assistant may be competent, anticipatory, and persistent, yet may fail to be helpful. Note then that these features – competence, anticipation, and persistence – are not sufficient for helpful assistance.

But if the examples above are not helpful, what is missing? In each case, an assistant that was attentive to the goals of the one receiving the help would have avoided the problems identified. That is not to say that attention is then the key to good service; other examples involving attentive but incompetent assistants would demonstrate the non-sufficiency of attention. To sharpen this point, let us consider situations where we might be surprised to find helpful assistance.

ASSUMPTION 1.2:*Incompetent helpers can be helpful*
The long tradition of apprenticeship provides adequate evidence that assistants with less than masterful skills can provide helpful service while they are developing their expertise. A child helping its parent on a project around the house can also provide real help by fetching tools or parts. Together with the previous assumption, this suggests that competence is neither a necessary nor sufficient feature of good assistance.

We claim that there are no set of necessary and sufficient features that define "good" assistance. If we want to carefully and fully evaluate the quality of service delivered by our intelligent assistants, then we need to consider all of these dimensions. Note that this is true regardless of the service mode; the measurement with respect to the dimensions applies whether the service being evaluated is a response to an explicit request, an act taken by the servant in anticipation of a need, or a teaching moment. However, in addition to providing a strategy for evaluating assistants, these dimensions also suggest behaviors or inclinations that assistants should display, and thus contribute to an answer to our second question.

QUESTION 2:*How do we design agents that can deliver "good" assistance?*
Of course, we ultimately want to design and implement assistants that can be truly helpful. The dimensions identified above may be generally useful for evaluating the assistance provided by a given agent compared to that of another. They may also suggest designs for how to implement assistants. Most simply, an assistant design should respond to each of the six dimensions. Because they are neither necessary nor sufficient, assistants without one or more of these capabilities may still prove helpful. Holding all other things equal, an improvement along one dimension leads to an overall improvement in helpfulness.

3   Prerequisites for a Virtual Butler

This collection of papers attempts to shed light on the variety of prerequisites needed to implement a virtual butler along the lines of Tina's James [5]. For these prerequisites, we want to consider how far along we are toward delivering their respective functions. Some of the papers focus on technical requirements [16], while others look more to social factors. [1].

In this paper, we propose a framework within which we can understand service and classify and evaluate systems that provide service. Nevertheless, some prerequisites need to be considered, if only in passing.

3.1   Technical Prerequisites

The technical prerequisites for a virtual butler on the order of Tina's James may be grouped into three categories: perception, analysis, and effectors.

3.1.1   Perception
Certainly, a servant needs to have sensory access to the environment. Several of the dimensions of service introduced earlier depend directly on the ability to monitor the situation. Most obviously, attention implies a continuous sampling of the setting. In addition, persistence requires that the servant can determine when a task is completed or no longer relevant, anticipation requires some cues to trigger the expected need, deference depends on the recognition of the current goals of the client, and even competence tends to require feedback from the environment.

More specifically, service agents need to sense and recognize a range of features in the environment. Perhaps most importantly, the servant must have the ability to perceive the goals of the client. Complicating matters, this effectively means that the helper must perceive the client's actions from which her goals must be inferred.

From the scenario, it is difficult to determine James' level of embodiment. It seems that James has access to an extensive sensor network, including a portal (complete with sensory capabilities of its own) carried by Tina. Fortunately, the relevant actions from which James takes cues are mostly taking place over electronic communication media. Thus, James has ready access to much of the information needed to fulfill our expectations. Nevertheless, there is the need to understand language and speech – no small feat!

Furthermore, perhaps an information source equally important to the actions of clients is their emotional states. The scenario does not address mood directly but we can easily imagine that our butler should perceive our emotions and act accordingly. It is not clear whether this ability is an optional add-on or if it will prove to be necessary. We suspect that it will prove to be indispensable.

3.1.2   Analysis

An agent's perceptual faculties provide the information on which actions may be based. In order to settle on the appropriate actions in a given set of circumstances, an effective servant must be able to reason. This reasoning must take into account not only the information from the current setting but also stored information about the client and how the world works generally.

The virtual servant needs to be able to acquire and utilize models of habits. These models may have to be acquired for both the client and her close friends (again underlining the perceptual need to recognize individuals). But beyond models of habits, the servant also needs to acquire models of actions. Note, our virtual butler may come with considerable knowledge built-in, but it must be able to adjust and augment this knowledge based on the behaviors of those in the servant's milieu. Specifically, a model is needed for the consequences of particular actions taken by the client, and for the consequences of actions taken by the servant. Furthermore, how do consequences vary with conditions (e.g., mood)? Even if we suppose the servant has an accurate perception of mood, this is not enough – it needs to know how its actions will shape the client's response in the context of a given mood.

3.1.3   Effectors

When all is said and done, our servant needs to do something to benefit us. This requires that it be able to manipulate the world in some way. The scenario depends significantly on communication via natural language, but also alludes to miscellaneous devices such as coffee machines, watering systems, and door locks. Additionally, it seems virtual butlers can (or should) query the network, make purchases, and move electronic resources. Fortunately, many of these are already practicable for automated or autonomous systems. Unfortunately, the most critical ability – to communicate with the human client – is also the most difficult and most remote at this time.

3.2   Social Prerequisites

In addition to the technical prerequisites identified above, there are a number of requirements at the social and political level that will be necessary before Tina's butler James can become a reality. Here we will consider only liability, privacy and general acceptance. However, this is by no means intended as a comprehensive list.

The scenario addresses the issue of liability. If one implements their own virtual butler and it does something self-disadvantageous or even damaging to another, the responsibility clearly rests with the developer. And as corporations provide "servants for hire" they will bear responsibility for misconduct of their "agents." This should not prove to be too difficult as we already have very similar models with hired cleaning services that employ humans who occasionally break things or even steal things.

A more serious and problematic issue concerns privacy. Again, the scenario identifies this as an issue, but in this case, we do not think it will be as easily addressed. The attenuation of privacy associated with service is unavoidable. One of the largely unaddressed issues in providing service is the participation of the client in the manifestation of quality service. In earlier work, we established the commitment of the client as a significant contributing factor in the provision of service [10]. This topic will certainly need much more exploration, but it is safe to say that society must come to accept some loss of privacy in exchange for the services imagined in the scenario.

On a related theme, people desiring these services will need to adapt to and come to accept the oversight of virtual servants. Although we might think that people will gladly welcome the help afforded by such agents, this adjustment will not be as simple as it might seem. Consider the impact on some people of being reminded, corrected, and coached to do things they do not want to do but which are genuinely in their best interests. Naturally, some will welcome these interactions and be truly grateful. However, many people will need significant growth before they would avail themselves of the benefits virtual servants represent.

And finally, if we implement a virtual butler of James' sophistication, we will confront the standard ethical issues that have up to this point been only academic concerns. These issues include: What does it mean to be a person? Do rights attach to persons or humans? What is a fair wage for such service? and How do we resolve ownership of information gathered by a virtual butler? An argument could be made that answering these issues is more pressing than any other technical or social issue. If we find ourselves in the future relying on James' services, it might be too late to think about these ethical problems.

4   Empirical Progress

In the preceding discussion, we consider the modes of service and the dimensions by which service may be evaluated. This treatment of the nature of service should yield insight toward the design and implementation of artificial servants along the lines of Tina's butler, James. As stated earlier, implementing a virtual servant at that level depends on a natural language understanding capability far beyond the current state of the art. Yet desiring to explore the provision of service, we have simplified the problem and lowered our expectations significantly.

We have conducted our work within the context of the MÆDEN simulated environment [9,10]. This multi-agent environment supports basic tasks (two-dimensional navigation, search and retrieval) over a variety of difficulties, as well as being agnostic with respect to agent architectures and communication protocols. Using the GARCIA agent framework [12], we have implemented agents that ask for and deliver assistance (clients and servants respectively) in the midst of problem solving tasks. Within this framework, we can view agents according to all of the dimensions discussed above and can instantiate servants with varying levels of some dimensions. We have run numerous experiments evaluating the behavior of GARCIA agents solving problem-worlds

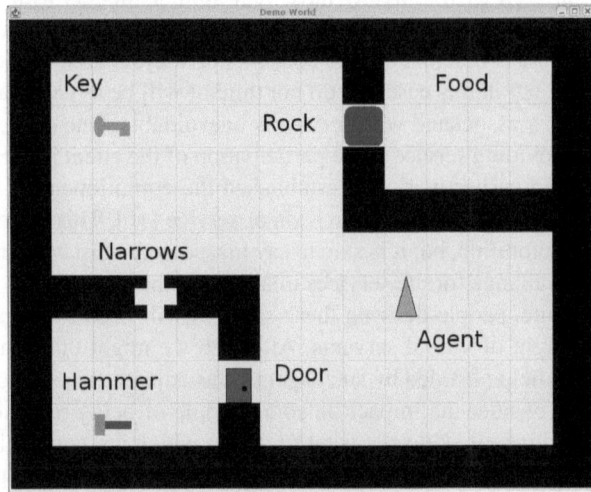

Fig. 1. A screen shot of MÆDEN's display showing most types of objects in a particular world problem. To solve this world, the agent must: get the key, open the door, get the hammer, break the rock, and finally get and eat the food.

of varying difficulty within the MÆDEN environment. Later, we will consider whether our simplified environment and agent framework adequately supports the need for and provision of service in ways that tell us anything about service in general or the implementation of a virtual butler in particular. In this section, we briefly describe the MÆDEN simulator, our GARCIA framework, and several of our experiments and their results.

4.1 Simulating Worlds with MÆDEN

We can best describe the simulator in terms of the objects in the world and how they interact, the senses and actions available to an agent, and problems that an agent must solve.

The MÆDEN simulator represents grid-based worlds consisting of obstacles and artifacts. Artifacts include agents, tools (hammers and keys), and food (the goal). Different types of obstacles (walls, rocks, doors, narrows and quicksand) impose different constraints. For example, walls are impassable but rocks and doors may be removed by hammers and keys respectively. The agent may pass through a narrows only if it is not holding an item (hammer, key or food). Quicksand can be crossed even while carrying a tool, but the agent cannot turn or do other actions (e.g., use a tool or talk with another agent) without sinking (dying). Figure 1 presents a screen shot of a world containing most of the item types; the items have been labeled for demonstration.

Agents sense the world around them, move about in the world, and manipulate the world. The default senses include smell and sight. An agent can smell the general direction of the food (in terms of forward, back, right or left) regardless of distance. The

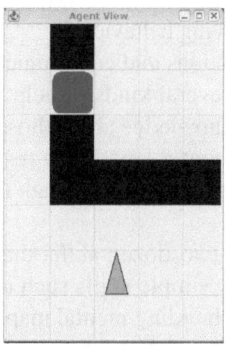

Fig. 2. This screen shot shows the visual field that an agent perceives for the situation portrayed in Figure 1. Note that from just this view, the agent knows where the food is located but does not yet know if there is a direct path to the food around one of the ends of the visible wall.

agent also has a visual map of the local surroundings; it can see a total of seven rows, each one of which is five grid-cells wide. For the agent in Figure 1, Figure 2 shows the visible surroundings. If this was the initial configuration of the world, the agent would have no knowledge of the key or the room containing a hammer behind a door, all off to the agent's left. For that matter, it doesn't know that the food is inaccessible without breaking the rock that is visible. As the agent moves about and observes more of the world, it may piece together a map of the world but that is a matter of the agent design.

A MÆDEN problem consists of a world specification that defines the initial config-uration of the environment. In its current form, there is one task that an agent must complete – to move from its initial position to the location of the food item, and then pick up and consume it. Solving this task may involve simple movement, perhaps avoid-ing obstacles. But it may also involve opening doors, or digging through walls. Opening doors requires the agent to obtain a key and digging through a wall (only certain walls may be dug through) requires the possession of a hammer. Hammers and keys may be initially positioned such that interacting sequences of subgoals are required to solve the problem. For example, the agent in Figure 1 will need to find the key in order to remove the hammer from the lower-left room. (Recall that the agent could enter the room through the narrows but could not remove the hammer until the door is opened.) Only after removing the hammer can the agent break the rock that prevents access to the food.

4.2   Building Agents in GARCIA

Our focus has been on teasing apart the elements that enable or inhibit "helpful" assis-tance. As such, optimal problem-solving ability is not the primary objective, rather, our goal is to explore the ways helpful assistance occurs when agents with differing skills or competencies communicate and work together toward a problem solution. Thus, in our architecture, GARCIA, an agent's primary characteristics consist of communication between agents, independent and layered skills, and parameters that influence the communication and problem-solving behaviors.

Currently, agents can ask questions and communicate knowledge about items in the world, and can ask directly for several kinds of help. The vocabulary is limited to the items in the world and states of knowledge about those objects. For example, one agent might ask another if it knows about a key. If the response is positive, the first might followup to determine if the second knows of a path to the item or if it already has the item in its possession.

We have implemented about two dozen skills that may be independently granted to agents. These range from very simple skills such as following the smell toward the food, to more complex ones like building mental maps, opening doors, breaking rocks, and searching for the shortest path to a location. When an agent instance is created, we specify the subset of skills that it may use.

This approach to instantiating agents using a menu checklist of skills, together with parameters that regulate the application of those skills and the willingness of agents to communicate, allow us to vary GARCIA agents along several of the dimensions of helpful assistance. Competence is addressed directly by the skills an agent may employ and is varied by selecting larger or smaller sets of skills. An agent's knowledge has an associated time-stamp that determines how strongly the knowledge is held. We model a servant's level of attention according to the length of time after which the agent will check with the client to determine if the knowledge is still valid. For example, while helping another agent find an item, if the helper's sense of the client's need for the item becomes stale, it may query the other agent as to its current needs. Agents do not currently implement anticipation although this is a topic of ongoing development. Persistence is modeled for both the helper and the client using a parameter that controls how readily a helper will abandon the looked-for help and how long an agent will wait for the desired help. Deference and persistence partially overlap; we think of deference as the willingness of the helper to take on a task whereas persistence reflects the helper's willingness to complete a task once started. We currently model only a high level of deference, as our agents will always attempt to help when asked. The integrity of GARCIA agents reflects the degree to which help given corresponds appropriately to the expectations of the agent making the request. We have modeled integrity by having a payment exchange with help requests and a parameter for the helper that controls what proportion of the payment is applied to providing help.

Our goal for GARCIA is to have sample agents that vary across all six dimensions allowing us to model and better understand the full range of assistance from helpful to unhelpful.

4.3   Previous Experiments

Our previous experiments have addressed competence, persistence, and integrity. We evaluated problem solving success rates and efficiency while varying the skills that an assistant possessed. As expected, our dependent measures (number of problems solved and average cost to solve them) improved with increasing skills. We also varied parameters that control persistence and integrity with the obvious anticipated results.

So far, we have mostly focused on an incompetent client seeking help from an assistant that is more skilled to varying degrees. More recent experiments have varied the collections of skills possessed by the client and servant respectively. Not surprisingly, experimental settings where the full set of skills are available between the two agents yielded the best results.

5 Discussion

In this paper, we have presented our current understanding of the nature of service. Consisting of a set of dimensions that support evaluation and three modes of delivering service, we can apply this understanding to the scenario of Tina and her Butler, James. We see that James manifests many of the dimensions that signify good or helpful service. For example, we have seen that virtual butlers in the imagined scenario are competent, attentive, anticipatory, honest, deferent, and possibly persistent.

In presenting the dimensions and modes of service, we stated that these were independent of each other. In the scenario, we see James providing service primarily in the anticipatory mode. However, we assumed that responsive service events are occurring regularly. Further, we speculate that when reminding Tina to water her friend's plants, James is acting partially in the instructive mode of service. In this case, James is attempting to get Tina to adjust the priorities over her set of goals so as to execute the plant-watering task as she had originally promised her friend, Dorothy.

We also summarized our implementation of a simulated world, MÆDEN, and agent architecture, GARCIA. When we consider and compare the properties of our simulated environment to the real world, we want to know if the necessary conditions for service have been simplified away or not. We have all the elements of the real world – sensory perception, reasoning, action, communication – without the real world's complexity. But will this simplified setting move us toward a virtual butler like James? That is the critical question and one which is part of our ongoing work.

In the mean time, an encouraging result that emerged from our empirical work highlights the role of the client in the exchange of assistance. A client may request help but later, based on a level of persistence, give up on the assistant and continue trying to solve the problem on its own (possibly asking for help again later). We observed that the client's commitment to the assistant positively influenced the overall success rate and efficiency. Although it is commonly understood that unteachable students cannot be effectively served, we were not expecting to encounter this effect in our tests. In our consideration of social prerequisites, we identified the importance of the client's participation in service exchanges; in that context, involvement took the form of willingness to adapt. It is surprising to us that empirical results obtained from our simplified world pointed to the same general conclusion.

5.1 Next Steps

In future work, we will continue exploring the nature of service and extending our world and agent framework. To dig deeper into the dimensions and modes of service, we will be proposing dimensions that pertain to characteristics or qualities of the client. At the very least, we can say the quality of the assistance provided will depend on the client's willingness to accept and integrate the assistant's work. However, we suspect that there are other dimensions that pertain to the client that need to be identified.

Currently, the client's only goal is to eat the food, and the servant's only goal is to assist the client. Most recently, we have extended the MÆDEN simulator to support multiple competing goals; these include gathering gold tokens and stockpiling caches of food pieces harvested from a food-source. These and other ongoing extensions to MÆDEN will allow us to examine a broader range of behaviors with respect to deference and integrity.

Using GARCIA, we have implemented agents that in addition to forming models of the world, form models of other agents and what the other agents know. We still need to evaluate the efficacy of these models with respect to the responsive service that we have been exercising.

Of course, a more exciting goal entails using these models to predict other agents' goals and then provide anticipatory service. Because we are already acquiring models of other agents, mimicking what the client would do in a given situation should be relatively straight-forward. Next, because we have regularly been working with incompetent clients, it should be another small step for helper agents to find and propose solutions that are more efficient than those the client would come up with on its own, thus providing anticipatory-invention service.

5.2 Conclusion

In order to be confident that we are making small steps toward a virtual butler, we need to first understand what we want. Exploring the nature of service should help us articulate the reasons we consider James to be an excellent virtual butler while we would judge some other implementation as less desirable. We also hope that implementing and testing an artificial servant in a simplified environment will shed light on the path we need to follow in order get to where we want to go. However, we also noted that we have significant ethical dilemmas to resolve before we reach the point that James is making our coffee and managing our investments.

References

1. Benyon, D., Mival, O.: Scenarios for Companions. In: Trappl, R. (ed.) Your Virtual Butler. LNCS (LNAI), vol. 7407, pp. 71–88. Springer, Heidelberg (2013)
2. Billsus, D., Pazzani, M.J.: A hybrid user model for news story classification. In: Proceedings of the Seventh International Conference on User Modeling, UM 1999, pp. 99–108. Springer-Verlag New York, Inc., Secaucus (1999)
3. Delisle, S., Moulin, B.: User interfaces and help systems: From helplessness to intelligent assistance. Artificial Intelligence Review 18(2), 117–151 (2002), doi: http://dx.doi.org/10.1023/A:1015179704819
4. Faulring, A., Mohnkern, K., Steinfeld, A., Myers, B.A.: Successful user interfaces for radar. In: CHI 2008 Workshop on Usable Artificial Intelligence (2008)
5. Gassner, R., Steinmüller, K.: Tina and Her Butler. In: Trappl, R. (ed.) Your Virtual Butler. LNCS (LNAI), vol. 7407. Springer, Heidelberg (2013)

6. Gervasio, M.T., Iba, W., Langley, P.: Learning user evaluation functions for adaptive scheduling assistance. In: Proceedings of the Sixteenth International Conference on Machine Learning, ICML 1999, pp. 152–161. Morgan Kaufmann Publishers Inc., San Francisco (1999)

7. Heuwinkel, K.: Framing the Invisible - The Social Background of Trust. In: Trappl, R. (ed.) Your Virtual Butler. LNCS (LNAI), vol. 7407, pp. 8–18. Springer, Heidelberg (2013)

8. Iba, W.: When is assistance really helpful? In: Interaction Challenges for Intelligent Assistants: Papers from the AAAI Spring Symposium. AAAI Press, Menlo Park (2007)

9. Iba, W., Burwell, N.: Building a testbed for studying service. In: Proceedings of the Stanford Spring Symposium on Persistent Assistants: Living and Working with Artificial Intelligence. AAAI Press, Palo Alto (2005)

10. Iba, W., Burwell, N.: Studying service: An exploration of the costs and benefits of assistance. In: Proceedings of the 18th International FLAIRS Conference. AAAI Press, Menlo Park (2005)

11. Iba, W., Gervasio, M.: Adapting to user preferences in crisis response. In: Proceedings of the 4th International Conference on Intelligent User Interfaces, IUI 1999, pp. 87–90. ACM, New York (1999), doi: http://doi.acm.org/10.1145/291080.291095

12. Iba, W., Holm, J.: Assistance: Is it better to receive than to give? In: Proceedings of the 2006 International Conference on Artificial Intelligence, pp. 84–87. CSREA Press, Las Vegas (2006)

13. Langley, P.: User modeling in adaptive interfaces. In: User Modeling: Proceedings of the Seventh International Conference, UM 1999. SpringWien (1999)

14. Meyers, K., Berry, P., Blythe, J., Conley, K., Gervasio, M., McGuinness, D., Morley, D., Pfeffer, A., Pollack, M., Tambe, M.: An intelligent personal assistant for task and time management. AI Magazine 28(2), 47–61 (2007)

15. Myers, K.L., Yorke-Smith, N.: Proactive behavior of a personal assistive agent. In: Proceedings of the AAMAS Workshop on Metareasoning in Agent-Based Systems, Honolulu, HI, pp. 31–45 (2007)

16. Rank, S.: What Issue Should Your Virtual Butler Solve Next? In: Trappl, R. (ed.) Your Virtual Butler. LNCS (LNAI), vol. 7407, pp. 171–178. Springer, Heidelberg (2013)

Virtual Helper or Virtual Card Player?
Contrasting Responses of Older Users

Massimo Zancanaro[1], Silvia Gabrielli[2], Anthony Jameson[3], Chiara Leonardi[1],
Elena Not[1], and Fabio Pianesi[1]

[1] FBK, Trento, Italy
[2] Create-Net, Trento, Italy
[3] DFKI, Saarbrücken, Germany

Abstract. In the NETCARITY project, we conducted several complementary
investigation activities with elderly people revolving around the design of
technology for the home environment. In this paper, we investigate the potential
impact of virtual characters in making the interaction with the technology-
enhanced home more effective and engaging. We briefly discuss two
experiences in using a virtual agent as an interface metaphor for a computer
system targeted to elderly people with very low computer skill. The lesson that
can be learned from those experiences is that a virtual agent may sometimes be
effectively used to improve the acceptance of new technologies for this class of
users. In particular, in settings characterized by a social interaction, where
emotional stress is low (as with entertainment applications), the presence of a
virtual character facilitates the acceptance of the technology by helping it to fit
into the social environment. In the opposite case, in contexts where trust is an
important factor or in life-threatening situations, a virtual agent is less likely to
be credible.

1 Introduction

Ambient Assisted Living (AAL) technology can play a crucial role in enhancing the
feeling of confidence in elderly by assuring the basic support of everyday activities
and the detection of health critical situations, as well as by stimulating the social and
psychological engagement that fosters the emotional well-being, crucial for dignity
and quality of life [1]. Although older adults have a difficult relationship with
technology [3], the conviction that age-related "technophobia" represents the main
obstacle to technology usage is progressively disappearing. On the contrary, one of
the main reasons for the scarce use of technology by elderly people is that hardware
and software design, and in particular interfaces, simply have not been conceived to
suit them [13].

For the definition of appropriate AAL services in the context of the European
project NETCARITY, we adopted a User-Centered Design approach which advocates
a strict interaction with end users and other relevant stakeholders to guarantee that
users' needs, preferences and contextual factors are properly taken into account
during the design and the implementation of technology. However, involving older

R. Trappl (Ed.): Your Virtual Butler, LNAI 7407, pp. 70–78, 2013.

people greatly challenges the applicability and validity of traditional research tools (e.g., questionnaires, focus groups, interviews, practical workshops, shadowing, cultural probes, etc.), because of physiological, psychological, and ethical issues that come into play.

A number of factors associated with old age need to be taken into account during the design study. For example, distress of travelling, unfamiliar environments, or meeting unfamiliar people: These may be problems when organizing focus groups [10], because the psychological discomfort might hamper the willingness to participate and contribute frankly to the discussion. For this reason, it is important to choose a familiar environment, possibly letting already known care givers or social assistants contact people for making appointments; to spend some time to let people get used to discussion partners and researchers; and possibly to offer refreshments and leisure activities afterwards [4].

Another aspect concerns sensory and cognitive impairments, which may be a problem too for focus groups involving visual/oral presentations and practical activities [10]. All the material, research questions, and style of a focus group with older users need to be carefully adjusted to the actual people who take part in the discussion.

Then, elderly people often feel low confidence in discussing technological issues: This feeling impacts on the quality of answers in questionnaires, where older people are more likely to use 'don't know' options [11]. The subjects may hesitate to express certain opinions (e.g., concerning intrusiveness, uselessness, or complexity) to a researcher associated with the technology [4].

Finally, interviews in public or neutral places often do not reveal complete or correct information. In-home observations are valuable, as they allow researchers to notice things that are not explicitly mentioned [4], yet it is often difficult to get consent for a visit. When this is granted, special care needs to be devoted to planning and performing the visit. Older people may have expectations about the behaviour of guests entering their home (e.g., having coffee, having a conversation, providing feedback on the outcome of the visit): Appropriate and ethical behaviour of the observer is essential to establish friendliness and trust, and at the same time to avoid unrealistic or inaccurate expectations which will be disappointed [4].

In the NETCARITY project, we conducted several complementary investigation activities with elderly people revolving around the design of technology for the home environment. We performed 6 preparatory structured interviews with social workers working with elderly people, followed by 8 focus groups, 3 structured interviews, and 7 contextual inquires with a group of 26 elderly people from 65 to 85 years old. Initially, general focus groups and preliminary interviews asked the elders about: daily routines and difficulties in performing activities of daily life; perceived needs and risky situations, both outside and inside home; social network and free-time activities, performed both outside and inside the home; use of the domestic space and affective relationship with objects and rooms; use of traditional technology; attitudes towards modern technology (cell phone, video, computer, internet, etc.); impact of aging process on life style; activities aimed at the preservation of good health; use of, and attitude towards, existing social and health services; use of, and attitude towards, computers; desiderata for new services supporting a better quality of life. In more structured focus groups, we then presented the participants with scenarios of daily life at home where technology could be helpful, asking them to imagine potential pros and cons. In contextual inquiries, we tried to access the domestic environment of elderly people to observe the actual use of technology, and we investigated more in detail: (i) how elderly people approach technological artifacts, (ii) which technologies they most often use, (iii) in which ways they use them, and (iv) which values they associate with these interactions (for a more detailed description of these activities and the outcomes, see [8,9]).

Among other technologies, we decided to investigate the potential impact of virtual characters in making the interaction with the technology-enhanced home more effective and engaging. For the scenarios and the actual prototypes, we used Alice, an MPEG-based talking head, that acts as a conversational character and is controlled by means of an XML language [2].

2   Familiarity-Driven Design

From our initial interviews, two major factors appeared to have a high impact. First of all, lack of engagement: for a large part of the older population, technology is perceived as unfamiliar and "alien" and is associated with feelings of hostility and anxiety. Second, even when elderly people perceive the potentials of technologies, they consider the investment of personal resources needed to use a new artifact to be too high. This is a matter of accountability and acceptability, because technology is not sufficiently transparent to communicate its uses and objectives, and a matter of accessibility and usability, because elderly people cannot take the high step necessary to learn how to reach their own objectives by using a technology. Drawing from this analysis, it clearly appears that a major role in the liaison between elderly people and technology is played by the familiarity of the language used by the technology to tell about its usage, objectives and meanings, and emotional values.

Current applications and products for elderly people typically handle accessibility, but they often fail on familiarity. For example, a web site built to be accessible is surely more readable and simpler, but remains an artifact distant from the culture and knowledge of a senior person. In other words, such a technology is grammatically legible for a senior, but it is based on an unknown semantics.

Familiarity is defined by Heiddeger as "the readiness to cope with an entity" [7]. Coping with an entity means understanding it, previewing it, and sharing knowledge with it. By extension, a familiar technology is something that the user is ready to face on the base of a common ground of concepts, meanings and practices that are not conscious or intended, but that are rather present in a nonprominent way [12].

Appealing stimulus material, like dramatized stories of technology use, turns out to be particularly effective in initiating the discussion on unfamiliar computer-based solutions with elderly people. During the services definition phase, we conducted 5 focus groups based on personas and narrative scenarios presented through comics. Personas are invented characters with personal features, life stories, goals and tasks [6]. They are introduced to users to favor empathy and identification, and to encourage the production of personal interpretations (see a sample persona profile used in NETCARITY in Figure 1). All the stimulus material was validated in advance with stakeholders to maximize efficacy.

RITA

ha 80 anni e vive col suo gatto
a Gardolo da 15 anni

Rita is 80 years old. She lives with her cat in a suburb of Trento. She has a bad back so she cannot go out every time she wants. She feels a little lonely, especially during the evening, and her days drag by.

Fig. 1. Sample persona profile

Participants were stimulated to discuss the verisimilitude of personas and the plausibility of the presented situation, and they were encouraged to freely envisage possible solutions (technological and nontechnological) to the presented problematic situation and to express their fears, needs, and preferences. At this stage of the discussion, many personal stories emerged, and the focus group facilitator had the challenging role of containing the emotional involvement of participants. Later on, a technological scenario was presented, suggesting a possible role of technology in solving the problem, and elders were again encouraged to express their opinions, doubts, and suggestions (see the pictures in Figure 2).

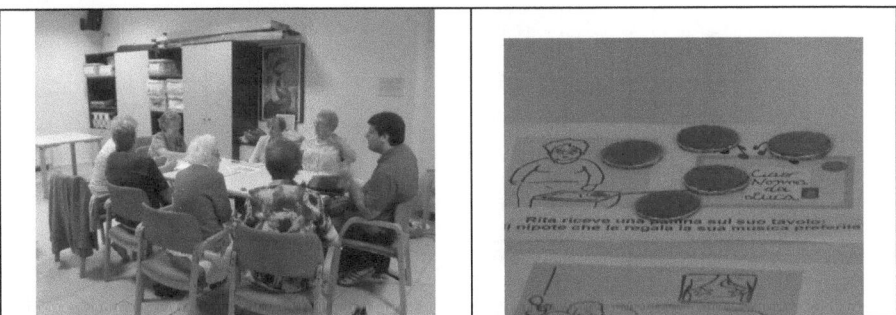

Fig. 2. Discussion in a focus group (left); coloured tokens to vote on scenarios (right)

3   Alice as an Assistant

Two specific scenarios were conceived to investigate the potential impact of using of a virtual character to support an older person in emergency situations and for protection. The scenarios depicted a virtual character acting as a front end for a fall detection system and as a mediator for a smart door. The persona involved in these scenarios is Miss Nina, a 73-year-old lady living alone in Trento. She is an active person, she likes to go out, and she loves to keep some spare time, to cultivate her interests and hobbies.

In the first scenario, Nina is walking in her house pensively, and she stumbles on a carpet. She falls down. She is conscious, but she cannot get up. The house door is locked, and nobody can access the house to help her. The system recognizes her body lying on the floor, the absence of any acoustical event, and the absence of movement. It triggers an alarm and visualizes the Alice virtual agent on the wall. Alice calls to Nina in order to check her state. In the absence of any answer, the system tries to contact a list of phone numbers previously provided (near and dear phone numbers). The system sends a recorded message to these numbers, asking for an intervention (if there is a call center or an operator assigned to this service, the warning message will be delivered to them by means of a warning on their console). In the meantime, Alice soothes Nina by telling her that someone is going to arrive (in case she can hear even if she cannot talk; see Figure 3). Otherwise, if Nina is able to talk and asks for help, the system starts the emergency procedure described above and Alice appears on the wall to reassure Nina until somebody on the contact list answers the call and the system activates the speakerphone function in order to allow Nina talk with a relative or a friend directly.

Fig. 3. A portion of the emergency scenario

In the second scenario that we discussed with users, the monitoring system recognizes a potentially risky situation and activates the virtual assistant Alice. Alice asks Nina if she is all right, or if she needs some help. Nina asks for help. Alice contacts a call center operator, who sends a medical assistant to help Nina. The assistant receives on her personal cell phone a code to unlock Nina's door. This code will work only in this emergency situation and does not grant the access to the house in other moments. Using the code, the assistant can enter Nina's house.

The goal of these scenarios was to evaluate the acceptability of the monitoring functionalities and the mediation role of Alice. We were also interested in understanding to what extent the elderly people would let the system take the initiative, such as automatically calling for help or unlocking the door. The scenarios were evaluated by means of focus groups as described above.

Overall, the monitoring system was perceived as a useful service: The perceived usefulness was evaluated as more important than the concerns about having video cameras in the house. Of course, privacy was mentioned as a critical issue, but our user groups were willing to accept monitoring technologies if they are understood as useful and important for maintaining an independent life.

There was a good agreement on the proposition that this kind of service might improve the feeling of being safe at home, much more than commercial wearable systems whose efficacy depends on whether the user wears them all the time. The installed cameras were feared to be expensive and intrusive.

The general attitude toward Alice was not positive. In particular, a virtual agent was considered less trustworthy than a real person in planning an intervention. Most of the subjects expressed the need for a sort of filter between the elderly person and the rescuers: a professional operator is preferred not only over the virtual agent but also over a family member.

Many subjects expressed concern about the feeling of being "observed" by a stranger, even if it is an inanimate being. They also suggested that in such a sensitive situation, a simpler vocal interaction would be more acceptable. The final outcome of the scenario evaluation with our user group is that the remote interaction with a real person would be preferred, as it is regarded as more trustworthy for planning an appropriate intervention. It is worth noting that, when it comes to an emergency situation, a professional operator as interlocutor is preferred even over a family member, to avoid disturbing or upsetting loved ones at inconvenient times.

4   Alice as Playmate

While virtual agents may be annoying or not trustworthy in a domestic setting in the case of an emergency, we found that in a different type of situation they serve a useful social function.

In another study [5], Alice was employed as an opponent for the computer version of a very common card game in Italy called Briscola. The fundamental aspect of the Briscola card game is the high level of sociality: Lively and spirited interaction with opponents is an essential part of the game itself.

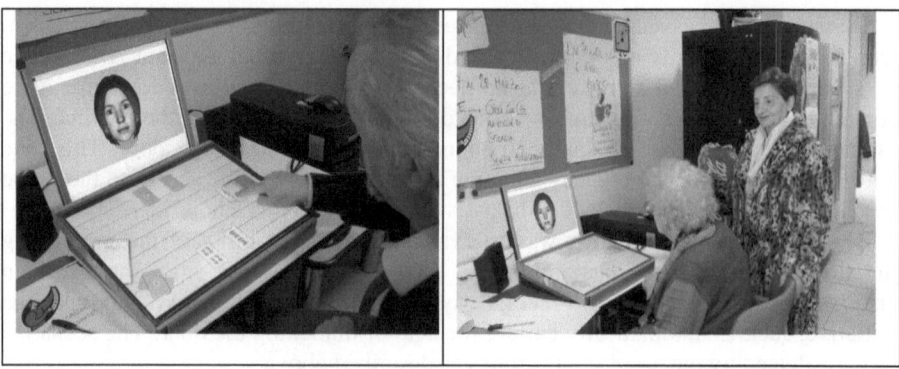

Fig. 4. Alice challenging an experienced Briscola player (left) and social interaction during a Briscola game (right)

The computer version of the game was implemented on a touch-based tabletop system (see Figure 4). A careful use of animations helped the player focus her attention on what was happening on the board. Each user played individually against the conversational agent Alice by sitting in front of the horizontal tabletop surface (40×25 cm) and the associated vertical display, interacting with the tabletop using one finger. The user performed drag-and-drop actions on cards displayed on the tabletop, while the system's card movements were implemented as slow Flash animations. In order to support a form of socialization during a game, the virtual character Alice was programmed to comment regularly on the user's moves and on other events of the game, using colloquial formulations and in some cases the local dialect. For example, after an ill-considered move by the user, Alice might say "You may live to regret that!". The system's level of Briscola skill was kept in the medium-to-low range.

The system was regularly used by 42 regular visitors of a local senior citizens' center (55% females), in the age range 55–91 (mean= 75.5) who on the whole possessed very limited computer skills, if any. The study lasted for 4 weeks, and most of the players played several times during this period.

The quantitative and qualitative data (see [5] for a more extensive description) show that participants quickly reached a point where they found the playing on the touchscreen easy. The generally good usability and acceptance of the tabletop system is confirmed by the number of matches that participants played spontaneously during the second and third weeks of the study, despite being able to choose freely between that system and other activities at the center (including the playing of Briscola in the traditional way): 22 players played a total of 67 games. During the final week, all but 5 of the 27 respondents gave a positive response to the question as to whether they would continue to play with this system if it remained available at the center.

Regarding the responses to the virtual character, the results showed that Alice was positively accepted by all the users. Indeed, they generally found Alice to be entertaining rather than distracting, and although participants were regularly offered the opportunity to turn off the display of Alice before the game began, this offer was never accepted.

Furthermore, the presence of a virtual agent made the computer's Briscola algorithm appear less trivial than it actually was: Several players interpreted clumsy moves by the computer as steps in longer-term smart strategies.

Alice played an interesting role in helping users to switch their attention between the game and their friends. In the normal Briscola game, players often pause to converse and have to be reminded when it is their turn to play. Similarly, while playing with the system, users would often enjoy conversation with their friends and Alice would remind them, in an amusing way, that it was their turn to play.

An unexpected positive function of Alice was that she seemed to make it socially acceptable for a visitor to play Briscola with the computer even when – as was usually the case – friends were nearby. Playing a computer game in the midst of one's friends would normally project a rather self-centered and unsociable impression. But Alice's social interaction was just human-like enough to make it natural for players to talk back at her and make jokes while their friends watched with amusement. This experience illustrates how a simple virtual character can serve as a sort of social "packaging" of a computer application that enables it to fit better into a social environment.

5   Conclusions

We briefly discussed two experiences in using (or proposing) a virtual agent as an interface metaphor for a computer system targeted to elderly people with very low computer skill. The lesson that can be learned from those experiences is that a virtual agent may sometimes be effectively used to improve the acceptance of new technologies for this class of users. In particular, in settings characterized by a social interaction, where emotional stress is low (as with entertainment applications), the presence of a virtual character facilitates the acceptance of the technology by helping it to fit into the social environment. In the opposite case, in contexts where trust is an important factor or in life-threatening situations, a virtual agent is less likely to be credible. Far from conveying the idea of artificial intelligence, it may foster the idea (or the fear) of the computer as a dumb and annoying machine.

Acknowledgments. The research described in this paper was supported by the European project NETCARITY (VI FP, IST2005-045508) and the targeted research unit PREVOLUTION (code PsychMM) funded by the Provincia Autonoma di Trento. We would like to thank the staff and the guests of the Centro Belenzani, Trento for their participation in the focus groups and in the Briscola study.

References

1. Abeles, R.P., Gif, H., Candory, M.G.: Aging and quality of life. Springer Publishing Company, New York (1994)
2. Balci, K., Not, E., Zancanaro, M., Pianesi, F.: Xface open source project and smil-agent scripting language for creating and animating embodied conversational agents. In: Proceedings of the 15th international Conference on Multimedia, Augsburg (September 2007)

3. Deets, H.B.: Aging and Technology: The Convergence of Two Revolutions. Cyber Psychology & Behavior 2(6), 501–503 (1999)
4. Dickinson, A., Goodman, J., Syme, A., Eisma, R., Tiwari, L., Mival, O., Newell, A.: Domesticating Technology: In-home requirements gathering with frail older people. In: Proc. of 10th International Conference on Human - Computer Interaction HCI, pp. 827–831 (2003)
5. Gabrielli, S., Bellutti, S., Jameson, A., Leonardi, C., Zancanaro, M.: A Single-User Tabletop Card Game System for Older Persons: General Lessons Learned From an In-Situ Study. In: Proceedings of the 3rd IEEE Tabletops and Interaction Surfaces 2008, Amsterdam, Netherlands, October 1-3, pp. 91–94 (2008)
6. Grudin, J., Pruitt, J.: Participatory design and product development: An infrastructure for engagement. In: Proceedings of of Participatory Design Conference, PDC 2002, pp. 144–16 (2002)
7. Heidegger, M.: Being and Time. Harper Collins, New York (1927)
8. Leonardi, C., Mennecozzi, C., Not, E., Pianesi, F., Zancanaro, M.: Getting older people involved in the process of Ambient Assisted Living research and development. In: Proceedings of the 6th International Conference of the International Society for Gerontechnology, ISG 2008, Pisa, Italy, June 4-7 (2008)
9. Leonardi, C., Mennecozzi, C., Not, E., Pianesi, F., Zancanaro, M.: Designing a familiar technology for elderly people. In: Proceedings of the 6th International Conference of the International Society for Gerontechnology, ISG 2008, Pisa, Italy, June 4-7 (2008)
10. Lines, L., Hone, K.S.: Research methods for older adults. In: Proc. of Workshop: A New Research Agenda For Older Adults, held at BCS HCI 2002, pp. 36–37 (2002)
11. Park, D., Schwarz, N. (eds.): Cognitive Aging: A Primer Aging. Taylor & Francis, Philadelphia (2000)
12. Turner, P., Van de Walle, G.: Familiarity As A Basis of Universal Design. Journal of Gerontechnology 5(3), 150–159 (2006)
13. Zimmer, Z., Chappell, N.L.: Receptivity to new technology among older adults. Disability and Rehabilitation 21(5/6), 222–230 (1999)

Scenarios for Companions

David Benyon and Oli Mival

Centre for Interaction Design
Edinburgh Napier University
Edinburgh, EH10 5DT
{d.benyon,o.mival}@napier.ac.uk

Abstract. This paper is concerned with understanding the needs of Companion owners (the people formerly known as 'users'). The problem with developing technologies such as companions is in knowing what the requirements are. People cannot really be expected to express their needs for companions before the technology that will drive the idea has been invented. Yet we know that the technology that will provide the sort of personalised, persistent interactions that characterise companions is coming, the question we are interested in is how requirements for companions can be generated. We are concerned with the whole interaction design, not just the speech recognition and language understanding, the gestures, or the inferences the companion can make. We are interested in how the companion will learn, or be instructed, so that the interaction can evolve and develop with the individual. We are concerned with the whole interaction experience and with how the different components fit together. In this chapter we present a conceptualisation of the companion idea and then illustrate how the development of personas and scenarios in the context of companion technologies can help us generate the requirements for these technologies. Finally we comment on some of today's technologies that already starting to demonstrate the characteristics of companions.

1   Introduction

Over the last nine years we have been investigating new forms of human-computer interaction (HCI) based around the concept of 'companions'. In the context of a three-year project looking at technologies for older people we explored the ideas of artificial companions that could move across devices and that were 'personality rich' [1], [2]. A two-week summer school explored the idea of a companion that accompanied people to a large arts festival. During a four-year EC-funded project called Companions, we developed a number of companion concepts and prototypes [3]. We have also referred to this idea under the term 'personification technologies' [4]. [5] because the aim of these new forms of interaction (as we characterize it) is to encourage people to personify the technology and to attribute human-like characteristics to it.

Wilks [6] has also characterised the companion concept. He sees it an intelligent, personalised, persistent, multimodal interface to the Internet. Drawing upon recent

R. Trappl (Ed.): Your Virtual Butler, LNAI 7407, pp. 79–96, 2013.
© Springer-Verlag Berlin Heidelberg 2013

advances in Human Language Technology (HLT), inference and knowledge representation, he sees a companion as a humane conversational partner. Others are now using the term 'companion' in the HCI and computing literature without it having a formal definition. The EC-funded LIREC project [7] uses the term in a natural sense. Both the SERA project [8] and the Semaine project [9] similarly use the term, generally referring to an agent that engages in non task-specific activities such as chatting about general events, or asking 'How was your day?'[10].

Our view of companions is that they aim to change Human-Computer Interaction (HCI) into Human-Companion Relationships. We see companions as a natural development of HCI. Companions may be represented as a 'virtual human' on-screen character or as an embodied conversational agent (ECA), but they do not have to be. Whilst the term 'companion' is meant to invoke personification, and anthropomorphism, we see companions as encompassing the widest possible range of devices and forms of interaction that woven together produce a relationship-building experience for people. A home embedded with ambient intelligence could be a companion. A character that moves across devices and domains, and understands its owner's needs and wishes could be a companion.

In this paper we will explore the concept further. We start in section 2 with our model of the key components of companions that designers need to consider if they are to design for relationship building, [3], [4]. Section 3 presents some examples and scenarios for companions to illustrate the conceptualization. A discussion about the conceptualization and the development of near-companion technologies is provided in section 4 and section 5 offers some conclusions.

It would be wrong to think of companions as simple devices. Companions represent the next generation of people's interactions with information and with each other. If they are to be successful companions will require new services and service providers. They will have a lifetime, and perhaps an afterlife.

2   Characteristics of Companions

Companions are a development of agents, a concept that has a history going back to the early 1990s. Agents appear in the literature as software agents, interface agents or embodied conversational agents (ECA). ECAs have typically been more concerned with behaviours of on-screen characters [11]. ECAs can vary from simplistic task-orientated agents that just deal with focused activities such as booking cinema or railway tickets to more complex systems that aim to build relationships with people. The work on relational agents by Bickmore is most prominent here with their real estate agent, REA [12]. Other work on relational agents includes Pelachaud's work with GRETA [11].

Interface agents have focused on dealing with some specific aspects of HCI. Some early thoughts on interacting with interface agents highlighted speech as a key element [13], but there was much more general work that now appears in the personalization literature such as UMUAI journal and the IUI conferences. The ideas of interface agents have led to quite heated debates about their suitability. Shneidermann's discussion with Pattie Maes is probably the most famous [14].

In software the traditional model of agents is that they have beliefs, desires and intentions, sometimes referred to as BDI agents. Drawing on a model of action that is popular in artificial intelligence circles, BDI agents seek to represent cognitive processes. Software agents also appear as a software engineering paradigm associated with distributed and parallel ways of solving problems.

Companions draw upon aspects of all these, and on spoken natural language technologies. Agents are proactive, seeking to achieve their goals as well as being reactive to events. They will have character and be helpful. It is this combination (elaborated below) that we believe will shift interactions into relationships.

In their discussion of relational agents, Bickmore and Picard [12] argue that maintaining relationships involves managing expectations, attitudes and intentions. They emphasise that relationships are long-term built up over time through many interactions. Relationships are fundamentally social and emotional, persistent and personalised. Relationships demonstrate interdependence between two parties – a change in one results in a change to the other. Relationships demonstrate unique patterns of interaction for a particular dyad, a sense of 'reliable alliance'.

The art of HCI will need to change if designers are to create experiences that allow people to build relationships with their companions. We do not accept that it is possible to design relationships per se, but it is possible to design artefacts and systems that will enable people to develop relationships with them. We summarise our approach as a 'star model' of designing for relationships (Figure 1).

It is these characteristics of relationships as rich and extended forms of affective and social interaction that we are trying to tease apart so that we can provide advice for people designing companions. Digesting all our experience to date we describe companions by looking at the characteristics of companions in terms of utility, form, personality, emotion, social aspects and trust.

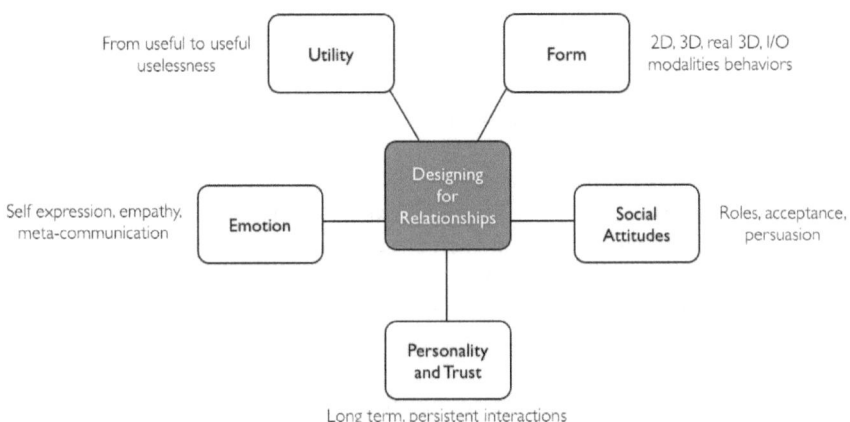

Fig. 1. The star model of designing for relationships

2.1   Utility

The issue of the utility of companions is a good place to start as there is a spectrum of usefulness for companions. At one end is non-specific purpose (i.e. companions that serve no specific function) whilst at the other is specific purpose. A cat has no specific function other than to be a cat, while a care assistant undertakes specific tasks such as distributing medication, monitoring health and supervising exercise; but both may be considered companions. A companion can be concerned with entertainment and having fun resulting in pleasure, or it can be about providing assistance and support. Somewhere in the middle are companions that aim to provide basic functionality for people who find undertaking some activity difficult, but which also provide a less purposeful facility — for casual conversation perhaps.

Utility is also concerned with the allocation of function between the two participants in a relationship. For example, one of the scenarios described below, PhotoPal, could automatically discard blurred pictures, adjust for 'red-eye' and remove pictures that were much too dark. But we would not want our PhotoPal companion to decide which pictures should be lightened a little. This sort of judgment should rightly come from the human in this relationship. Leave PhotoPal to perform the function of lightening the picture, but leave the human to judge which pictures to lighten.

The 'instrumental support' [12] provided by a companion is a key part of relationship building and so companions need to be helpful, but not pushy. They need to be proactive, but let the human make decisions. There can be great utility in not being useful.

2.2   Form

The form that a companion takes refers to all the issues of interaction such as dialogues, gestures, behaviours and the other operational aspects of the interaction. It also refers to the representational aspects such as whether it is 2D, graphical 3D or true 3D, whether it has a humanoid, abstract or animal form, and the modalities for interaction that it makes use of. The many aesthetic issues are also considered under this heading. The form and the behaviours of the companion are likely to vary widely between different owners. We observed in an older people's focus group that although the detailed behaviours of Sony's AIBO [15] were noted, they were not fore-grounded. Utility was the big issue and the details were secondary. This represents a utilitarian view of technology that we might expect of the older generation. Younger people tend to be more relaxed about usefulness and more focused on design details.

Certainly the attention that Sony paid to the behaviours of AIBO lead to a stronger emotional attachment. In a number of informal evaluations of AIBO, people would regularly comment on 'him' being upset, enjoying something, being grumpy and so on. The attribution of beliefs, desires and intentions to an essentially inanimate object is an important aspect of designing for relationships. For example people say that AIBO likes having his ears stroked, when there are no sensors in his ears. The careful construction of a mixture of interface characteristics — sound, ear movement and lights on the head in this case – result in people enjoying the interaction and attributing intelligence and emotion to the product.

Much of the work in the ECA literature concentrates on the form of the agent and on achieving realistic behaviours that suggest non-verbal communication. Ensuring that speech is coordinated correctly with head movement and facial expression is critical. A well-known problem in designing on-screen avatars is the 'uncanny valley' [16]. People are willing to accept unrealistic movements and people are willing to accept realistic movements, but in between is the uncanny valley where people feel quite uncomfortable having almost natural movements that are just not quite right.

2.3   Emotion

Designing for pleasure and design for affect are key issues for companions. Norman [17] discusses the three types of pleasure that need to be considered; visceral, behavioural and reflective. Attractive things make people feel good which makes them more creative and more able. Emotional integration and stability are key aspects of relationships [12]. There should be opportunities for each partner to talk about themselves to help self-disclose and to help with self-expression. Relationships provide reassurance of worth and value and emotional interchange will help increasing familiarity. Interactions should establish common ground and overall be polite. Politeness is a key attribute of the media equation described by Reeves and Nass [18].

Emotional aspects of the interaction also come through meta-relational communication, such as checking that everything is all right, use of humour and talking about the past and future. Another key aspect of an interaction if it is to become a relationship is empathy; empathy leads to emotional support and provides foundations for relationship-enhancing behaviours.

These aspects emphasize the personalised nature of relationships – as only in highly personalised interactions can empathy occur.

2.4   Personality and Trust

Personality is treated as a key aspect of the media equation [18], where Reeves and Nass develop the computer as social actor (CASA) theory. They undertook a number of studies that showed how assertive people prefer to interact with an assertive computer and submissive people prefer interacting with submissive devices. As soon as interaction moves from the utilitarian to the complexity of a relationship, people will want to interact with personalities that they like. Their point is that computers could not really be more unlike people and yet people treat computers as if they were human, demonstrating many of the ingrained social attitudes that characterize thoughtless human-human interaction. There is already evidence for the 'persona effect' [19] in some human-computer interaction where the interface includes an on-screen avatar. We can expect much more anthropomorphism the more human-like companions become.

Trust is "A positive belief about the perceived reliability of, dependability of, and confidence in a person, object or process" according to Fogg [20]. Trust is a key relationship that develops over time through small talk, getting acquainted talk and through acceptable 'continuity' behaviours. Routine behaviours and interactions contribute to developing a relationship where they are emphasizing commonalities and shared values. Fogg's notion of 'persuasive technologies' [20] is based on getting people to do things they would not otherwise do. In the context of companions, though, this is exactly what you would hope a companion would do — providing it was ultimately for the good. A Health and Fitness companion for example (see below) should try to persuade its owner to run harder, or train more energetically. It is for their own good after all.

2.5   Social Attitudes

Bickmore and Picard [12] emphasise appraisal support as a key aspect of relationship building and the importance of other social ties such as group belonging, opportunities to nurture, autonomy support and social network support. None of our investigations have involved opportunities to nurture, but of course the Tamagotchi, the 'loveable egg' that children need to feed to keep alive demonstrates this clearly. In the summer school studies that we undertook, overcoming loneliness and acting as a social lubricant were two important principles that the designs sought to achieve.

These social attitudes are central to relationship building. Reeves and Nass [18] identify specialists and team mates as different social roles that people play in relationships. They discuss many examples of how people like to engage with people who share their values, background and culture. These are the issue that create the media equation; 'media equal real life'.

2.6   Summary

These five areas that contribute to relationship building between people and companions help us to focus on the key issues that need to be designed. They should not be considered to be the only issues that matter in developing companions, however. For example, learning is a key issue for relationship building that is not addressed under these headings. Neither is remembering, yet a companion must be able to relate current interactions to past interactions, preferences and interests. Companions need to have an architecture along the lie of any intelligent interface technology [21] where keywords are usually used to constitute a companion's knowledge. However, with companions we want to go further than simple key-word tags.

Companions have extended conversations with their owners as part of their multimodal interactions. To help with relationship building we want to associate objects from a domain of application with whole conversations in natural language that have happened between a person and a companion. These conversations will be highly domain specific, at least to start with, but will grow over time. Already we have effective spoken natural language interactions in domains characterised by structures tasks such as buying cinema tickets and train tickets. What we do not have is ways of joining up these natural language interactions, learning about individuals or engaging in less structured activities.

The dialogues (consisting of many modalities) of companions will need to embrace a whole new set of concepts if relationships are to be formed. Persuasion is one of them and pro-activity another. The dialogues will need politeness and humour. They will also need explanation, rationale, discussion, disagreement and argumentation.

Interaction design will need to understand and develop a new set of techniques that will enable people to work at this level. And interaction design must do this as the inter-networked world becomes increasingly complex. New methodologies and new attitudes to design will be needed. Designing for relationships is very different than designing for function. Companions demand a further step to deal with the characteristics of, and to design for relationships.

Besides the change in interaction design and a richer understanding of domains through richer description of domain objects are the other characteristics of the content that companions deliver. It is not obvious that discussions such as 'how was your day' [10], or general chit-chat as with the Semaine agent [8] are what people want, or need. Finding the right content to provide through companion technologies is central to their success as forms of HCI.

3   Scenarios for Companions

Scenarios are narratives describing what people do when engaged in particular activities [22], although how scenarios are actually used varies widely. Scenarios might be based on in-depth ethnographic studies or on brief collaborative sessions with potential stakeholders for some new system. Carroll [22] develops the principles of scenarios and how they can be used throughout systems development. The power of using scenarios (and personas, the people in the scenarios) is recognised across design methodologies and domains. They are helpful in grounding the design process and act as a shared point of reference, not only for the design team but also for the people who will interact with the result of the design. Scenarios can be both conceptual and concrete depending on their purpose of use, for example the same artefact may provide a conceptual overview of what something does to a potential user whilst providing concrete aesthetic guidelines to an interface designer or programmer. These artefacts take several forms from simple text based outlines, to mood boards, to storyboards, to short movies.

In this section we present some scenarios of use for companions, illustrating the range of issues that need to be considered in design.

3.1   PhotoPal

Wilks [6] introduces the idea of a companion to help older people sort out their photos and life memories. With many of us now having thousands and thousands of digital photos, sorting them, classifying them and organizing them becomes a huge issue. How could the average person with no classification or editing skills even begin to make a coherent shape of such a mass of data? It is with this question, against the background of a lot of interest in 'photoware' that the concept of the PhotoPal has been examined.

We have implemented a prototype PhotoPal and used this with forty people (see figure 2). The PhotoPal concept can be considered a digital photo editing, sorting and sharing companion. The owner interacts through natural language dialogue with the companion, represented by an on-screen avatar. Through the process of talking about the quality of their photos ("that's a little dark"), the location where they were taken ("oh, I took this picture this in my garden"), the time it was taken ("this was on my birthday") and the content ("on the right is my brother, he's holding his daughter in his arms"), the companion is able to fix quality issues, organize folders by content location and date, and most importantly develop a rich amount of metadata. This interaction – where rich descriptions in natural language are used to identify the semantics and affective aspects of the photos is being called "Talk2Tag". Furthermore, the PhotoPal companion can then use the social and familial networking knowledge structure that the Talk2Tag process has generated to engage in smart sharing. For example, pictures from a family gathering can be sent to the interactive smart photo frames of the family members who were there, or perhaps those that were not. Having the photos tagged in this way will also facilitate the owner reminiscing with the companion and hence allowing PhotoPal to gather even more information about the details and relationships depicted in the photographs.

Fig. 2. Screenshot of the COMPANIONS project PhotoPal

3.2   GoPal, a Mobile Companion for the Older User

GoPal is a scenario (shown in Figure 3) concerning a mobile, characterful user interface supported by a cross platform software architecture. In the scenario, an older user, William (72), is reminded by Harvey whilst out and about that his favourite team is playing a football match that is on TV. GoPal asks if William would like it recorded. After vocal or touch based confirmation, GoPal then moves to William's home PVR (Personal Video Recorder) and interacts with the functions on William's behalf. When William returns home GoPal moves onto the TV and reminds William that he can watch the game.

GoPal is more than a reminder service or simple interface front end. The nature of the technology is to shift what would otherwise be a fairly traditional interaction into the realms of a relationship. This is achieved through the emotional investment of the user, in this case William. Much in the way that people, and older people in particular, attribute personality to their pets (for example, a cat is cool, smart and sophisticated, a dog is loyal, playful and so on) it may be possible to harness this mechanism to attribute personality and subsequent emotional investment to GoPal.

An expansion of this scenario may look at how GoPal could integrate alongside other home technologies. For example in a smart kitchen GoPal could monitor William's blood pressure and pulse unobtrusively through a simple strip sensor on the handle of his kettle. As such, GoPal is a technology that could have a significant impact on an older person independent living whilst providing companionship and functionality through a supportive relationship rather than an interaction.

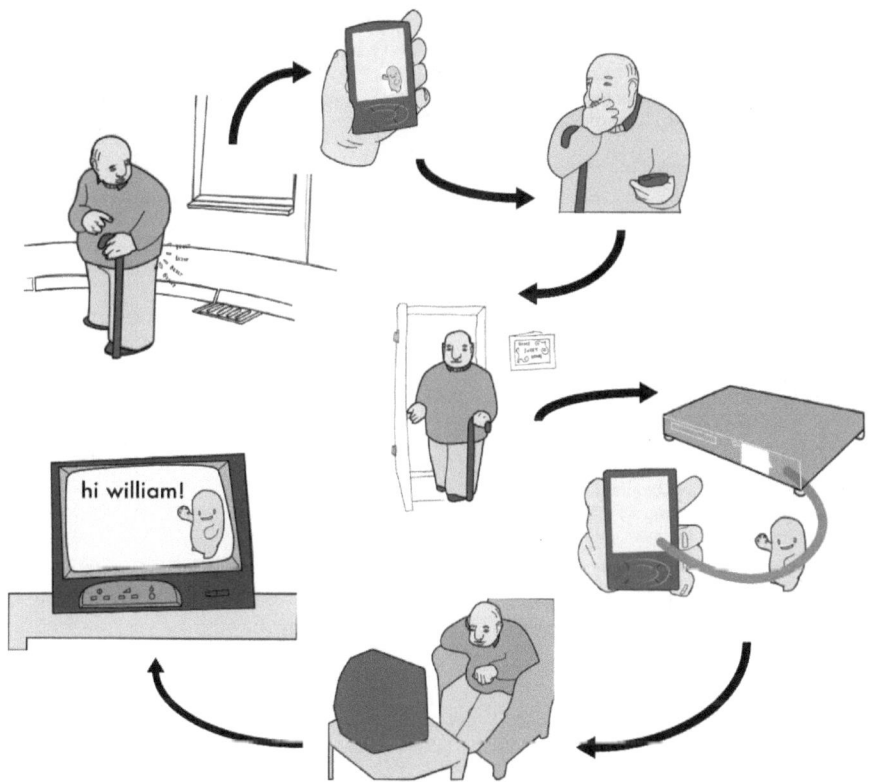

Fig. 3. The GoPal mobile companion scenario

3.3   Health and Fitness Companion

The notion of what would constitute a Health and Fitness companion (HFC), and more importantly what design considerations would differentiate it from the other companion technologies being explored was explored in a two day workshop between SICS, University of Tampere and Edinburgh Napier University. During and subsequent to this workshop, 3 personas were developed to explore the various needs of people with differing lifestyles, levels of fitness and exercise regimes.

One central theme of exploration was what motivational approaches are suitable to which scenarios and which personas? Thus the scenarios can outline differencing motivations, for example when someone trains well their companion subscription is reduced. Alternatively, should planned training not reach a required level the companion could prevent a recorded television program from being shown until training is completed.

1. We meet Sandy in a hospital room, he's being visited by his kids.

2. They are worried about his health, he does little exercised and since his wife left him his diet has become appalling.

3. They give him a HFC (what is this!?) which will combine with his current home system. They explain that it's intended to help raise his general level of fitness, monitor his health and set and maintain a healthy balanced diet.

4. They all leave the hospital and Sandy starts the configuration.

5. Being ex-army Sandy decides that a tough-love drill instructor personality would suit him best (he's on board with the fact that he needs to get healthy), so he selects Alf, a non-nonsense archetype companion character.

6. He opens his exercise regime to be accessible by his children, on their request, as he feels this will be an added incentive for him to exercise.

7. Configuration involves biometrics such as weight, height etc, allowing Alf to suggest appropriate training and diet.

8. It's aim is to understand whether the owner is in bad condition needing to get better, wanting to maintain current health or aim for high performance.

9. Alf reprimands bad behaviour (such as buying unhealthy food) nags when he doesn't exercise, but offers positive motivation when he does.

SANDY

- age 46

- drives a lot

- drinks and eats too much
- recently divorced

- children in early 20's

- had recent health scare
  (suspected heart attack which was actually angina)

- kids have bought him a HFC

Fig. 4. The Sandy persona for HFC scenario

These aggressively proactive stick or carrot approaches would of course not be suitable to all owners, however the HFC scenario is rather unique in its potential necessity to be, at times, disliked, as anyone who has worked with a personal trainer would concede. This issue is presented in the Sandy persona (Figure 4), whilst motivation is less of an issue for the Mari persona (Figure 5). The role of the HFC for Mari is more about training analysis and advice. Thus the HFC scenario is of particular interest when exploring the impact of human-companion relationship on task and functionality success.

1. She's set up a long term schedule with her HFC to enable her to run her first marathon in under 4 hours.

2. This includes target goals such as what times she should be running distances by which stage of the regime.

3. The HFC adapts to maintain the regime when Maris social circumstance impacts her ability to train.

4. If she runs too far or too fast the companion will advice that this may have a negative impact on her training and may result in potential injury.

5. Explicit instructions in real time run ("ok, now we're gonna push hard for 2 minutes….ok, well done, let's take it easy for the next 5….etc")

6. The HFC has access to her social schedule (through social companion?) and suggests going to a party the night before a long run may not be a great idea.

7. At the actual marathon her HFC becomes a motivating force and gives her real time advice (eg, "there's a hill coming up, pace yourself", it knows this from a run plug-in she bought for the HFC).

- age 23

MARI

- aerobics instructor

- training seriously for first marathon

- her usual training partner has moved away

- she leads a wild social life and tends to burn the candle at both ends

- she's got a targeted schedule

- companion is very proactive in pace making and motivation

Fig. 5. The Mari persona for HFC scenario

Other important areas involved in the HFC scenario are professional and social networking. For example, linking to a doctor to ensure the owner remains within healthy parameters, or linking to a social networking system (such as facebook or twitter) to engage in shared exercise activity, planning and experience.

3.4   Multimodal Interaction

The PhotoPal prototype discussed in section 3.1 stemmed from original explorations on what a Photo Companion would enable. Figure 6 illustrates a scenario in which someone has a large collection of photographs and wishes to search for a specific image to exemplify a recent trip. She applies both speech and touch during the interaction, the choice of which is task driven. For example, it is much quicker to specify specific search parameters through speech than by typing or clicking a series of check boxes (part 2 in the scenario). However, when it comes to flicking through the search generated group or applying certain other editorial functional tasks such as scaling and cropping, touch becomes the more natural interaction. This again is due to the context of the interaction. For example, it's quicker to drag a finger or stylus back and forth to resize an image in a serendipitous or haphazard fashion than it is to say, "Make that image a little bigger...bit bigger....bit bigger...no, that's too big...bit smaller...too small" and so on. However, for specific categorical edits speech may be best, for example "make this image 4 by 6 inches and print". The true power of the interaction experience comes from the considered use of both in conjunction.

A further consideration is environmental influence. For example, Figure 7 shows the potential for moving between displays. Small displays (eg digital photoframes) have a more limited touch capability than a larger display (in the case of Figure 7, an interactive coffee table).

In this scenario we considered many other options such as when the display that is too far from the user to be touched; a situation that reflects the current living room environment. In such a situation physical gesture becomes an appropriate option, either by using ones hands or by wielding an object, such as is used in the Nintendo Wii games console, or Microsoft's Kinnect. This allows for parameters such as speed, direction and shape of movement. An alternative of course is to use two displays, a for example a tablet device connected to the large living room screen. This would actually allow for a combination of speech, touch and gesture.

1. The user is moving from a standard view of their photos to a search mode. This is a voice driven function.

2. Here the user narrows down the field by establishing a search parameter again by voice. Note that the user could search for any metadata parameter or combination of parameters that the system has established. Indeed the system could proactively suggest additional ones.

3. Having used voice to establish the smaller field, the user now applies touch to quickly flick through the pictures. Additional touch functionality could include scaling, croping or editing.

4. Having found the photo they want to send , the user now combines speech with touch to indicate that the gesture of flicking to the left means email that specific image to the users uncle.

Fig. 6. An example of a multimodal interaction with a Photo Companion

Fig. 7. An example of a multimodal interaction moving between displays from a digital photoframe to a smart coffee table

3.5   Discussion

In these scenarios we can see how the many considerations of utility, form, emotion, personality and trust and social attitudes get woven together to create companion experiences. The contexts for the human-companion interactions are critical to providing a good companion experience. Probably the most well-known companion-type system, was the universally hated 'clippy' that formed a central part of Microsoft Word in the early 2000s before being gently removed from service. Clippy did not distinguish any individual characteristics of people, nor did it consider the context of the interaction. It had a very limited set of behaviours that soon became annoying, and there was no attempt at interacting in an emotional or sensitive manner. In short it failed on all the key design components that we have identified. This is not, however, the case any more and we are starting to see some good examples of companion technologies emerging.

4   Emerging Companion Technologies

The critical design consideration for companion technologies is to ensure a sensitivity in understanding their context of use and employing suitable, appropriate interaction modalities. For example, a cooking companion may be a perfect example of where touch based technologies, as are proving ever more popular in the consumer market, is not a suitable modality for interaction due to the context of use namely hands covered in ingredients. In such a scenario high level non-contact gestures such as swiping above a device to move between stages of a recipe would be far more useful. With the application of simple high level gestures and a voice driven interface and feedback the interaction becomes more companionable as the technology provides an assistive feedback in a natural modality to the context and environment, ie voice. A further advantage of this multimodal approach is the capacity for a "no-look" interface with the owner companion interaction governed by a very natural and companionable experience, a conversation. For example the owner may ask "when should I add the flour?". The companion can respond "add the flour once all the butter has melted".

The enabling factor for many of the current wave of companion technologies has been the emergence of the smartphone as the archetypal mobile electronic communication device. With Apple's launch of the original iPhone in January 2007 there was a paradigm shift in the consumer attitude to, and desire for, a computationally and graphically powerful, always connected device capable of replicating or exceeding a desktop web experience. With this shift has come a tidal wave of products, operating systems and associated development environments spearheaded by Apple's iOS mobile platform and App store as well as Google's Android OS and associated App marketplace. With the advent of the powerful mobile and tablet devices utilising these and other software platforms there is now far less of a case for a dedicated piece of hardware for many context specific tasks, from remote controls to barcode scanners.

Typically a modern smartphone or tablet has all the I/O hardware that is required for the majority of mobile computing tasks, namely GPS, cellular network and various other communication protocol radios; gyroscopes and magnetometers; speakers and microphones; high resolution screens and high resolution front and rear cameras. More critical to the case of iPhone or HTC Incredible or Blackberry as someone's companion is their sheer mobility and ever presence to a user/owner's location. Allied to this persistence is the Apple App store induced shift in software model from large, sophisticated, complex, multi-functional and expensive applications to small, simple, easy to use, uni-functional and cheap applications. With it has come a plethora of companion-type applications across the whole spectrum from useful to useless, from basic to advanced, from entertaining to functional.

Some applications have addressed the functional aspects of potential companion scenarios, for example the Nike+ iPhone application mirrors in many ways the Health and Fitness scenario discussed earlier including training regimes, monitoring and motivation. What it lacks is any anthropomorphism, there is no associated personality, ECA or personification to enhance emotional investment in the experience. The examples that have done this are almost exclusively at the other end of the functional spectrum, ie not really useful but entertaining.

Many clones of the original Tamagotchi experience are available as well as functionally similar applications replicating the experience of more sophisticated "care for me" companions such as NintenDogs. It will be interesting to see if there is a difference in the emotional engagement owners experience towards such applications when they are embedded within a multi-function device such as a smartphone as opposed to a dedicated piece of hardware designed purely for the facilitation of the relationship as was the case with the original Tamagotchi and Furby.

A notable example of mobile applications that have tried both to have functional purpose as well as some form of embodied personality is Siri. Siri is marketed as a personal assistant who resides on your mobile device and with whom you interact with in natural language. This naturalistic, conversationally based interface is a very powerful factor in the anthropomorphism of the experience even when no specific personality quirks are present other than politeness and there is no associated ECA. The interaction begins with the user/owner asking Siri something out loud, for example "I'd like a romantic place for Italian food near here". Siri will apply voice recognition and then respond through the paradigm of a text message conversation, for example whilst undertaking the search (derived from the application of server side natural language processing on the utterance) Siri will respond "Ok, let's see..." and once appropriate sources of information are determined they will be presented in a conversational manner, for example "Ok, I found these Italian Restaurants which reviews say are romantic and are close to you now". Important here is the use of the word "I" in the conversation, this semantic choice very subtly, but very powerfully, suggests self-awareness and sentience where of course none exist. The fact that Siri indicates knowledge of where you are without asking or without that information being proffered (through the simple use of the GPS radio on the mobile device) simply adds to this and increases a sense of presence, a sense of being *with* the person who is participating in the interaction.

It is through these subtle but powerful methods that designers can seek to attribute personification and potentially provoke emotional investment by those people that interact with these technologies, and in doing so shift those interactions into relationships. What is clear is that despite the ever increasing power, engineering sophistication and sensory capabilities of today's mobile computing devices, they still only serve as platforms for the delivery of companion experiences and those experiences still require the interaction design consideration that they always have. In short it not the technology that is important, it is what you do with it that counts.

5   Conclusions

In this chapter we have set out to explore the notion of a companion. One such manifestation, of course, is the Virtual Butler, but we think that companion is more general. The Virtual Butler is a particular type of companion, based on the butler metaphor. Thus, for example, one would not expect the butler to share social attitudes; the 'upstairs-downstairs' relationships of people and their butlers almost prohibit shared social attitudes by definition.

We see companion technologies as embracing a whole range of experiences that are designed to encourage people to develop relationships with technology. Naturally there are many moral and ethical issues arising from this that must be debated and understood. There are safety, security and privacy issues. But there are also many potential benefits. Companions might help to relieve loneliness for the elderly. They might help care for the infirm. They might make interacting with the Internet and navigating through the mass of information more effective and enjoyable. Indeed we expect them to do all these things.

Companions seek to establish a sense of social presence with the people who interact with them. It is this sense of presence that allows people to form and maintain relationships. Social presence is concerned with being-with, with feeling connected to and aware of other entities. This, much richer form of interaction, will lead to quite different forms of relationships between people, technologies and information.

References

1. Benyon, D.R., Leplatre, G., Mival, O., Cringean, S., Vaswani, G.: Artificial Companions for Older People. In: Proceedings of AISB 2004 Symposium on Expressive Characters, Leeds (April 2004)
2. Cringean, S., Benyon, D.R., Leplatre, G.: Explorations of Personality Rich Artificial Companions. In: Humaine workshop. HCI 2005 Conference The Bigger Picture, Edinburgh (September 2005)
3. Benyon, D.R., Mival, O.: From Human-Computer Interaction to Human-Companion Relationships. In: Proceedings of IITM Conference, Allahabad, India, December 28-30 (2010)
4. Benyon, D.R., Mival, O.: Landscaping Personification Technologies. In: Proceedings of CHI Human Factors in Computing Systems, Adjunct Proceedings (2008)
5. Mival, O., Cringean, S., Benyon, D.R.: Personification Technologies: Developing Artificial Companions for Older People. In: Proceedings Chi Fringe 2004. ACM Press (2004)
6. Wilks, Y.: Artificial Companions as a new kind of interface to the future internet. Oxford Internet Institute, Research Report 13 (October 2006)
7. http://www.lirec.org/
8. http://project-sera.eu/
9. http://www.semaine-project.eu/
10. Smith, C., Crook, N., Dobnik, S., Charlton, D., Boye, J., Pulman, S., Santos de la Camara, R., Turunen, M., Benyon, D.R., Bradley, J., Gambäck, B., Hansen, P., Mival, O., Webb, N., Cavazza, M.: Interaction Strategies for an Affective Conversational Agent Telepresence Journal (2011)
11. Pelachaud, C.: Brave new topics 2: affective multimodal human-computer interaction: Multimodal expressive embodied conversational agents. In: Proceedings of the 13th Annual ACM International Conference on Multimedia 2005, pp. 683–689 (2005)
12. Bickmore, T., Picard, R.: Establishing and maintaining long-term human-computer relationships. ACM Transactions on Computer-Human Interaction (TOCHI) 12(2) (2005)
13. Norman, D.: How Might People Interact with Agents? Communications of the ACM 37(7), 68–71 (1994)

14. Shneidermann, B., Maes, P.: Interface Design vs. Agents. Interactions Magazine 4(6) (1997)
15. http://en.wikipedia.org/wiki/AIBO
16. Mori, M.: The Uncanny Valley Energy 7(4), 33–35 (1970)
17. Norman, D.: Emotional Design: Why we love (or hate) everyday things. Basic Books, New York (2004)
18. Reeves, B., Nass, C.: The Media Equation. CSLI Publications, Stanford (1996)
19. Lester, J.C., Converse, S.A., Kahler, S.E., Barlow, S.T., Stone, B.A., Bhogal, R.S.: The persona effect: Affective impact of animated pedagogical agents. In: Proceedings of CHI 1997, pp. 359–366 (1997)
20. Fogg, B.J.: Persuasive Technologies. Morgan Kaufman (2003)
21. Benyon, D.R., Murray, D.M.: Special Issue on intelligent interface technology: editor's introduction. Interacting with Computers 12(4), 315–322 (2000)
22. Carroll, J.M.: Making Use. MIT Press (2000)

Care-O-bot® 3 – Vision of a Robot Butler

Ulrich Reiser[1], Theo Jacobs[1], Georg Arbeiter[1], Christopher Parlitz[2],
and Kerstin Dautenhahn[3]

[1] Fraunhofer IPA, Abteilung Robotersysteme, Nobelstr. 12,
70569 Stuttgart, Germany
[2] SCHUNK GmbH & Co. KG, Bahnhofstr. 106-134, Lauffen/Neckar, Germany
[3] University of Hertfordshire, Adaptive Systems Research Group,
School of Computer Science, College Lane, Hatfield Herts AL10 9AB, United Kingdom

Abstract. This chapter promotes the idea of a robot butler and investigates the advantages and disadvantages of embodiment for the proposed scenario „Tina and her butler". In order to make the discussion more tangible, Care-O-bot® 3 is introduced, which is the newest version of the Care-O-bot® series developed by the Fraunhofer Institute for Manufacturing Engineering and Automation IPA in Stuttgart, Germany. Remarkably, the prominent role of this robot was chosen to be a butler's. A brief overview is given of current human-robot interaction research, focusing on how users react to the idea of a robot companion. The results of different user studies provided inspiration during the design phase of Care-O-bot® 3, in particular with respect to the robot's appearance and the user interaction concept. The technological aspects are covered shortly before user interaction scenarios embedded in research projects related with Care-O-bot® 3 are presented. Results from real life trials conducted in an elderly care facility are given afterwards. Against the background of these scenarios, the benefits and drawbacks of embodiment for the virtual butler scenario are discussed using the example of Care-O-bot® 3.

1 Introduction

The scenario "Tina and her butler" presented in the preface of this book proposes a future vision of an artificial companion helping elderly people to better master their lives. In the scenario, the active elderly woman Tina is supported by a virtual butler, whose capabilities intensively rely on communication and information acquisition services. The butler is highly networked with home appliances, the internet and butlers of other persons, enabling it to e.g. quickly setup a communication channel to Tina's niece, to get the departure time of the next bus or to have the living room cleaned by autonomous vacuum cleaners.

Another important property of the butler is its ability to adapt to persons' individual preferences, learning about their special needs, their music taste and their social network. It is even able to be empathic about the current emotional state of the user, taking it into account for its planned actions.

Considering all these abilities, there seems to be no stringent need for an embodiment of the butler as a robot at first sight. However, the scenario is rather

R. Trappl (Ed.): Your Virtual Butler, LNAI 7407, pp. 97–116, 2013.

unspecific about how exactly the communication between user and butler takes place. How does the user address the butler? When does the butler know that it is addressed? How does the user know, when the butler is ready for communication? These are typical problems for which an embodiment could provide an easy solution. The benefits of a robot embodiment will be discussed in more detail in this article.

The chapter is organized in the following way: At first, current user studies concerning the expectations of users from an artificial assistant will be presented. How the results of these studies were considered in the design concepts of the newest development of the Care-O-bot® series, Care-O-bot® 3 [19], will be pointed out subsequently. In particular, the user interaction concept of Care-O-bot® 3 is introduced. Thereafter, scenarios guiding through the development process of the robot as well as scenarios from related research projects are presented. Finally, the potential contribution of Care-O-bot® 3 for the "Tina and her butler" scenario will be discussed, concluding with a short outlook to the next development goals of Care-O-bot® 3.

2   User Studies: The Role of an Artificial Butler from a User's Perspective

The research field of human-computer interaction (HCI) is well established and has existed for many decades, while human-robot interaction (HRI) is a fairly new research field that is related to, but also distinctly different from HCI and has gained a lot of attention recently. Concerning a mobile service robot, additional aspects with respect to the users' acceptance and their expectations have to be considered. So, what are people's views on the role of an intelligent service robot in their home?

Several studies have been conducted to investigate people's attitudes towards domestic robots. Syrdal [23] carried out a survey in order to examine adults' attitudes towards an intelligent service robot. Participants were 21-60 years old, while most of them were in the age of 21-30. Results show that most participants were positive towards the idea of an intelligent service robot and view it as a domestic machine or a smart intelligent equipment that can be 'controlled', but is intelligent enough to perform typical household tasks. Participants also prefer a robot to be neutral towards gender and age.

Scopelliti [24] investigated people's representation of domestic robots across three different generations and found that while young people tend to have positive feelings towards domestic robots, elderly people were more frightened of the prospect of a robot in the home.

Studies within the European research project COGNIRON assessed people's attitudes towards robots via questionnaires following live human-robot interaction trials [6]. Responses from 28 adults (the majority in the age range 26-45) indicated that a large proportion of participants were in favour of a robot companion, but would prefer it to have a role of an assistant (79%), machine/appliance (71%) or servant (46%). Few wanted a robot companion to be a 'friend'. The majority of the participants wanted the robot to be able to do household tasks. Also, participants preferred a robot that is predictable, controllable, considerate and polite. Human-like communication was desired for a robot companion, however, human-like behaviour and appearance were less important.

These three studies, conducted in different European countries, agreed with respect to the desired role of a service robot in the home: an assistant able to carry out useful tasks, and not necessarily a 'friend' with human-like appearance.

From the latter fact arises the following question: why do people possibly not want the artificial companion to be a friend? This question also impacts the virtual butler scenario in the sense that users might not want the butler to behave like a friend, knowing their personality, their interests, their preferences and even their current mood. These considerations led to the definition of a robot companion which must be a) able to perform a range of useful tasks or functions, and b) must carry out these tasks or functions in a manner that is socially acceptable and comfortable for people it shares the environment with and/or it interacts with [23].

This creates the following challenge for the development of such a robot: we have to bridge the gap between functionality, which goes along with hard technological properties of e.g. an industrial robot, and social acceptance, which goes along with the comfortable design of e.g. an electronic pet.

3   Care-O-bot® 3: Convergence of Design and Technology

Motivated by the user studies which brought the insight that artificial companions need not be necessarily humanoid to be well accepted, further considerations were made about the robot's appearance.

3.1   Considerations on Embodiment Appearance

Humans sometimes talk not only to persons, but also to inanimate objects like their cars, computers, alarm clocks or other devices, identify them by gender and give them sometimes even names [1], [10]. This phenomenon, that humans attribute human-like characteristics to inanimate objects is called anthropomorphism [10].

Anthropomorphism is a constant pattern in human cognition [2], [7], [14], [25], and the interaction of a human with a robot (or any kind of machine) cannot completely elude it. This becomes apparent also in the scenario, as Tina's neighbour, Dorry, gives her butler a name, 'Djinn', which does not perfectly fit to a human, but much less to a technical device.

According to Mori [11], the so-called uncanny valley would suggest to either stay in the domain of very non-human, toy-like robots, or to create a robot that appears to be almost perfectly human-like, because a robot that has many human-like features, but is still recognizable as non-human may elicit rather fearful responses. Unfortunately, at present the uncanny valley is not a good starting point for robot engineering and lacks a solid empirical foundation [12].

Furthermore, there is disagreement. The matching hypothesis [8] predicts the most successful human-robot interaction if the robot's appearance matches its role in the interaction. In highly interactive social or playful tasks participants in a study preferred the human-like robot. In serious, less emotional tasks, however, they did prefer the machine-like robot [8]. Similarly, a highly human-like robot may not be the best choice for a medical task that may involve people feeling embarrassed [28].

We must be aware of the fact that the appearance of the robot communicates its strengths, weaknesses and competences to the user, as well as psychological aspects such as perceived personality. User personality and the perceived personality of a robot impacts how people perceive robots and their behaviour [29]. It remains unclear of whether people would prefer their own personality and the robot's to match [30] or not [33] but, as discussed above, any such differences are also likely to be influenced by the task and context of the interaction as well as the robot's appearance and functions. A systematic study into people's perceptions of robot appearance and behaviour as well as robot and user personality attributions in a robot home companion scenario exemplified different factors [31]. It was shown that while the majority of people prefer robots with human-like appearance and attributes, introverted participants and those with lower scores for emotional stability tended to prefer the mechanoid (mechanically looking) appearance to a larger degree than other participants. From the perspective of robot designers who may wish to satisfy the preferences of as many potential users as possible, this suggests that less human-like robots may represent the 'best comprise' and find greater acceptance of a large target user group. It has been suggested that a variety of non-human cues may be used successfully in human-robot interaction [32] and indeed, this has been confirmed by a recent HRI study [34]. Note, finding a 'best compromise' is a design heuristic that can be important in situations where users may either not have the choice to choose from a variety of different designs, or if one system is being used by many users (e.g. in a care facility).

Human-like appearance is likely to trigger expectations that go beyond the capabilities of a machine. But being humanoid in appearance does hardly suffice to meet the expectancy of human-like reactions. To achieve this, the robot needs to interpret situations correctly to adapt its behaviour. This requires elaborate models of cognition and emotion. Even though research makes progress in these matters, e.g. within the COGNIRON [4] or LIREC [35] projects, the technology is not yet readily available. Instead findings suggest, that if a machine triggers high expectations concerning its capabilities, the user adapts accordingly and tends to overchallenge the machine [17] while getting frustrated himself.

Furthermore, the relation between human and robot gets even more complicated if we expand the focus from the capabilities of the robot to the characteristics of the interaction. Patterns of social behaviour become more important [15], [16] in this context. Thus, the robot designer also needs to be familiar with issues regarding social interaction aspects. At present, however, findings are still too preliminary to serve as design guidelines for a socially acceptable *humanoid* service robot.

3.2   Key Features of Care-O-bot® 3 Design

Based on these arguments, a non human-like appearance for Care-O-bot® 3 was decided and measures to avoid anthropomorphic attributions were investigated to support technomorphic perceptions. The most important of these measures include the avoidance of any parts that resemble a face or produce gender specific expressions or interpretations. Furthermore, the robot behaviour was modeled under considerations described above; the robot should never refer to itself by "I", or express its needs in a human way like "I am hungry" if the battery is low, for example.

The basic concept developed is based on a two sided design. One side is called the 'working side' and is located at the back of the robot, away from the user. This is where all technical devices like manipulators and sensors which can not be hidden and need direct access to the environment are mounted. The other side is called the 'serving side' and is intended to reduce the users' possible fears of mechanical parts by having smooth surfaces and a likable appearance. This is the side where all physical human-robot interaction takes place. One of the first design sketches can be seen in Fig. 1 (left).

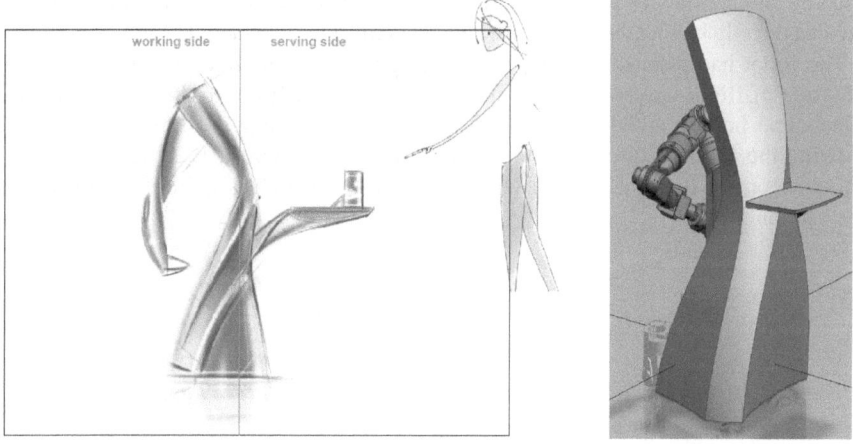

Fig. 1. Left: First design sketch, Right: first technical rendering

After several steps of design-technology convergence a simplified rendering was created (see Fig. 1, right hand side). Based on these images the underlying technology was integrated into this shape.

3.3   Technological Properties

Care-O-bot® 3 can be divided into the following components: mobile base, torso, manipulator, tray and sensor carrier with sensors.

The mobile base consists of four wheels, for each of which orientation and rotational speed can be set individually. This allows the robot an omnidirectional drive enabling advanced movements and simplifying complete kinematic chain (mobile base - manipulator - gripper) control. The wheeled drive was preferred to leg drive because of safety (no risk of falling) and stability during manipulation. The base also includes the battery pack for the robot, laser scanners and one PC for navigation tasks. The size of the base is mainly determined by the required battery space. Nevertheless, the maximal footprint of the robot is approx. 600 mm and the height of the base is approx. 340 mm.

The torso sits on the base and supports the sensor carrier, manipulator and tray. It contains most of the electronics and PCs necessary for robot control. The base and torso together have a height of 770 mm.

The manipulator is based on the SCHUNK LWA3, a 7-degrees-of-freedom (DOF) light-weight arm. It has been extended by 120 mm to increase the work area so that the gripper can reach the floor, but also a kitchen cupboard. It has a 6-DOF force-torque sensor and a slim quick-change system between the manipulator and the 7-DOF SCHUNK Dexterous-Hand SDH. The force-torque sensor is used for force controlled movements like opening draws and doors, but also for teaching the robot new tasks by physical interaction with the human.

The robot hand has tactile sensors in its fingers making advanced gripping possible. Special attention was paid to the mounting of the arm on the robot torso. The result is based on simulations for finding the ideal work space covering the robot's tray, the floor and area directly behind the robot following the 'two sides' concept developed.

The robot has a sensor carrier carrying high-resolution stereo-vision cameras and 3-D-time-of-flight-cameras, enabling the robot to identify, to locate and to track objects and people in 3-D. These sensors are mounted on a 5-DOF positioning unit allowing the robot to direct his sensors to any area of interest. It is very important in this concept not to create a face with these sensors which is quite difficult to avoid (see section 3.1).

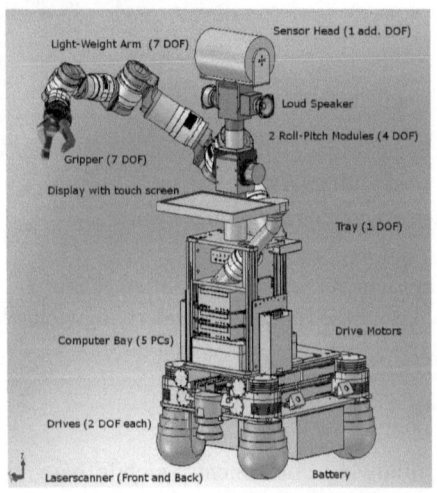 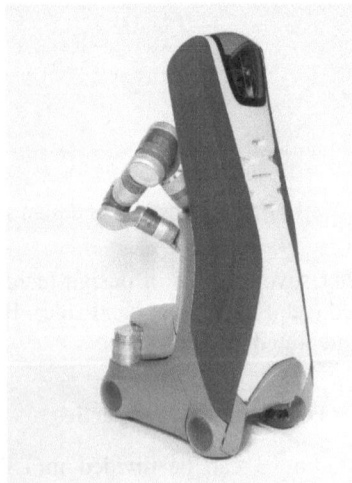

Fig. 2. Left: Hardware set-up of Care-O-bot® 3, Right: Care-O-bot® 3 with flexible casing

Fig. 2 shows the complete hardware set-up of the robot. The convergence of the original design idea and the underlying technology can be seen in on the right hand side, showing the robots final appearance.

4   User Interaction Scenarios

Development in robotics is mostly scenario driven. For Care-O-bot® 3, user interaction played an important role, such that a couple of user interaction scenarios were worked out during the development of the robot.

Variations of the "Tina and her butler" scenario get more and more the focus of research projects on national and European level. The research scenarios in contrast however mostly include handicapped or elderly people that suffer from mobility constraints, sensory and perceptual impairments or mental degeneration that complicate simple every day tasks and often prevents them from being able to stay in their homes, independently any more. But mobile robots cannot only assist people in their homes but also in elderly care-facilities. In the following, scenarios from current research projects with Care-O-bot® 3 as a project platform are presented. The section starts presenting guiding scenarios in the Care-O-bot® 3 development phase.

4.1   Guiding Scenarios during the Development of Care-O-bot® 3

The Care-O-bot® 3 project [3] particularly aims at the area of household helper robots and developed different user interaction scenarios, of which in the following those will be presented that are relevant to the "Tina and her butler" scenario. The fetch-and-carry service represents the robot's core functionality and is to some extent contained in all following scenarios. The scenario based design method [21] is applied to produce interface concepts. Each of the following scenarios is based on a single persona [18].

The personae developed in the Care-O-bot® design phase ranged from millionaires with the need for an electronic butler, retired engineers with the wish to have a technical companion to diabetic programmers with the need to have a dependable nurse.

Because of the diversity of the personae, different hardware solutions were considered, ranging from small form PDAs to full size Tablet PCs. As diverse as the hardware were the results for the actual user interfaces (UIs). The UI represents the traditional gateway to the Care-O-bot® 3 hardware. Its abilities can be accessed through all designed UI variants. As an example three personae will be described along with respective UI designs. A forth UI design is presented that was developed independent from a certain persona, as it simply comprises the core functionality of Care-O-bot® 3: the fetch-and-carry service.

The first UI version is based on a persona called 'Hartmut von Geiss'. He is a young manager of an IT business. He uses the robot at his home to support his daily housework. Casually his robot helps him in multitasking situations: Video phone call from his boss, during his diner while a parcel service is ringing. Fig. 3 (top left) shows the first design of an UI for this scenario. It is a very straightforward design using a small tablet PC with a decent segmentation of the available screen.

The second design is based on a PDA and uses the guidelines that are appropriate for stylus passed input devices. The story behind the design contains a persona called 'Fabian Krasse'. He is a diabetic programmer who wants a reliable nurse that fits his technophile life-style. The interface of this scenario (see Fig. 3, top right) is based on a PDA that fits Fabians way of life and working.

The last concept presented is based on a persona called 'Patricia van der Dellen' and represents the group of so called 'soccer moms' - meaning they have the technical equipment, but not necessarily the knowledge of the underlying technology, a characteristic which could also apply to elder persons that are not afraid of using technology. This is a more challenging group of users and leads to an interesting UI concept. The hardware consists of a tablet PC with finger touch capabilities. The interaction concept is based on various 'genies' that represent the different characteristics and services that Care-O-bot® 3 can offer (see Fig. 3, bottom).

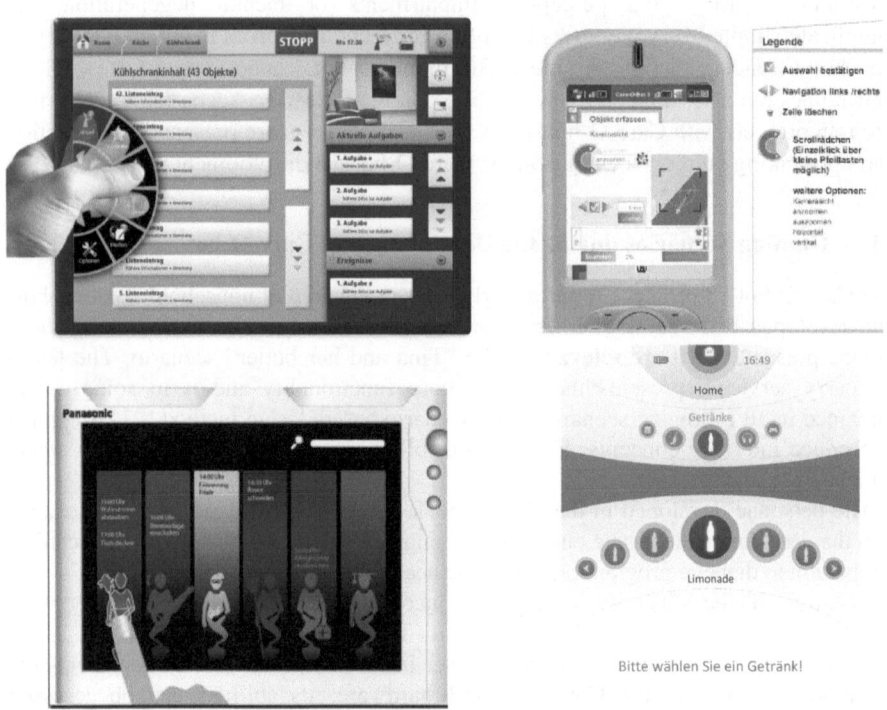

Fig. 3. User Interfaces for the different scenarios: Top left: User Interface for technical assistance at home (IT professional); Top right: User Interface for young technophiles; Bottom left: 'Soccer Mom' User Interface. Bottom right: Serving Drink User Interface [20]

The different genies cover the following areas: Household, entertainment, medical, education, cooking and personal secretary. Remarkably, the genie metaphor is also used in the „Tina and her butler" scenario – it seems to fit well for the high-tech butlers: the user does not know how the work is done, but can be absolutely sure that it is done.

The forth UI is more general and focuses on the classical fetch-and-carry service in form of a serving drink scenario. The UI is not designed for a dedicated persona and can be implemented on the touchscreen of Care-O-bot® 3. The user may choose from an assortment of drinks Care-O-bot® is able to deliver and order the desired drink through the UI. Furthermore, the UI reflects the current state and operation the robot is performing, e.g. navigating, moving the arm or using its cameras.

All described scenarios were developed during the development of Care-O-bot® 3 to target the applicability of Care-O-bot® 3 for different user groups. In the following, scenarios from current research projects are presented that focus on supporting especially elderly people in their daily lives.

4.2   Home Assistant Scenario

The main idea behind the recently started European research project SRS (Multi-Role Shadow Robot for Independent Living) [13] is to allow elderly persons to live longer in their own homes instead of moving into an elderly care facility and therefore enable a more independent life. The prominent aspect of the project is to use a tele-operated robot to assist elderly persons at fulfilling household tasks. The robot acts in a semi-autonomous manner which means that it tries to accomplish a task autonomously until something unexpected happens. If the robot is not able to solve this problem, a remote operator is asked for help. The robot is also able to learn new actions by observing the actions of the human operator.

To identify appropriate scenarios for a tele-operated home assistant, a survey among three potential user groups was conducted. The three user groups for the SRS system are

- elderly persons as local users and beneficiary,
- private caregivers, e.g. relatives of the elderly person as remote operators
- employees of 24-hour teleassistance centers as professional remote operators.

The scenarios obtained from this survey were ordered with respect to both the feasibility and the benefits of a potential realization with a tele-operated robot.
The two top-ranked scenarios are defined as follows:

1) Fetch-and-carry service
   The fetch-and-carry service constitutes the base scenario for SRS. The robot gets a request by the local user to an object to a certain location. For example, if the elderly person is sick and has to stay in bed, the request could be to bring a glass of water to the bed (see Fig. 4, lower left) or if the elderly person wants to read a book, the robot can be requested to retrieve this difficult to reach object (see Fig. 4, upper right). After receiving the request, the robot navigates to the location where the object should reside, detects it using its sensors, grasps the object and drives back to the location of the local user where it delivers the object. If, for example, the object is not located at its usual place and the robot cannot find it, it can request the remote operator for help. The remote operator then scans the room by moving the robot manually and

observing the camera image in order to find the missing object and tell the robot where to find it.

Preparing food is a slight variation of the fetch-and-carry scenario (see Fig. 4, upper left). Additionally, it includes opening and closing furniture objects like a fridge or a microwave.

2) Emergency assistance

The second SRS scenario is emergency assistance (see Fig. 4, lower right). If an elderly person falls at night, the robot might help by giving support at standing up or by starting a video call with the tele-operator. The remote operator can then use the robot to observe the elderly person and decide to set up an emergency call. This scenario is based on the assumption that the local user is equipped with a fall sensor as the robot is not able to detect this with its sensors at every place in the elderly person's home.

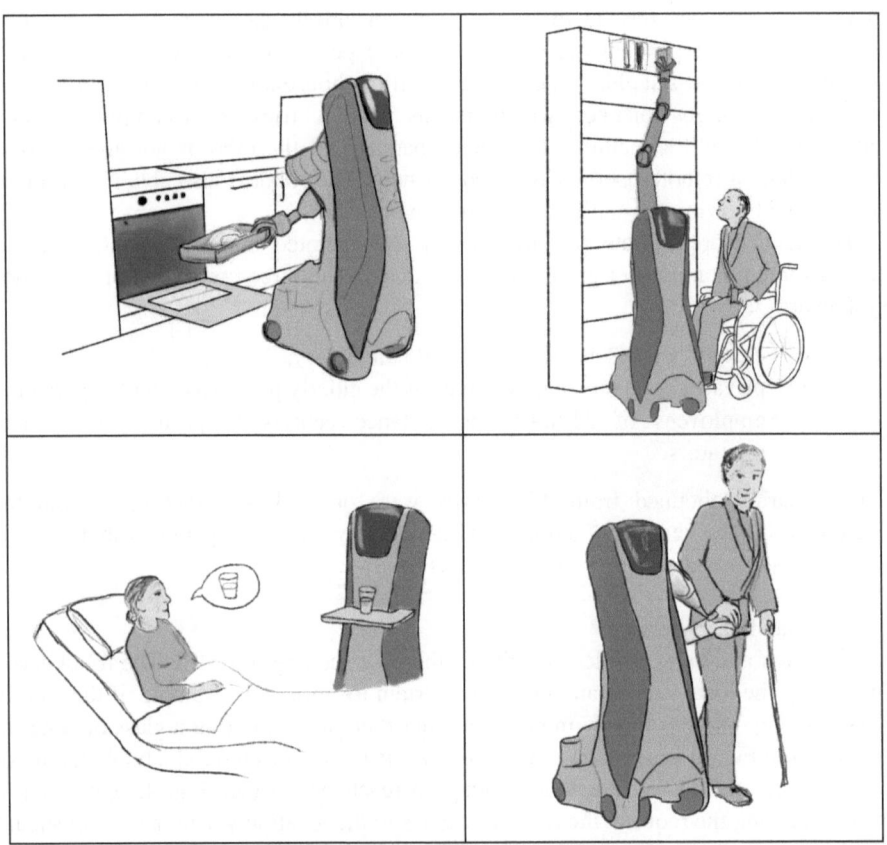

Fig. 4. Envisaged SRS Scenarios

4.3   Scenarios to Support Service Personal in Elderly Care Facilities

In contrast to the SRS project, the project WiMi-Care [26] is focused on the application of a robot butler in elderly care facilities. Here, tasks are mainly focused on supporting care workers in their daily work, taking over routine tasks such as transporting goods and journalizing their work to leave them more time for work in direct contact with the inhabitants. Regarding the background that a shortage of care workers is foreseeable in the future, taking over tedious, walk-intensive tasks can help to ensure adequate care for the increasing number of elderly people in the next decades. In the WiMi-Care project, two scenarios for Care-O-bot® 3 were identified following the method of scenario based design. To determine where support work in elderly care facilities is really needed and appreciated, a requirement analysis was conducted in an elderly care facility based on visits of the facility and interviews with care workers.

In the scenario "potation supply" (Fig. 5, left) Care-O-bot® 3 offers water which was drawn autonomously from a water cooler to the inhabitants. As elderly people generally tend to drink too little, the work of offering drinks to inhabitants is usually very time-consuming for care workers. In addition, journalizing the amount of consumed potation is usually error-prone as care workers often have to do several tasks at once and have to react to sudden alarms.

The potation supply scenario begins with Care-O-bot® 3 moving to the water cooler which is set up in a kitchen area on the ward. The cup of water is then placed on the robot's tray and is carried to a sitting area where Care-O-bot® 3 identifies the inhabitants sitting at the tables. The robot then chooses a person which according to the potation supply journal has not drunk enough water and offers the drink. Here special attention is paid to motivate the elderly people to drink, for example by addressing the people individually via speech output. If the drink is taken Care-O-bot® 3 thanks the inhabitant and moves back to the kitchen area where the next cycle can be started. Apart from the credible interaction with inhabitants, the development of Care-O-bot® 3 during the project aims on a safe and reliable task execution among people on corridors and in sitting areas.

The idea of the "entertainment" scenario (Fig. 5, right) is to offer individual entertainment functions and activities to inhabitants such as to read out texts, to play music or to play games like chess or memory. This allows the care facility to extend the program of activities for the inhabitants. Furthermore, memory training applications can complement occupational therapy. To start an entertainment function, a care worker selects an appropriate activity on the touchscreen of Care-O-bot® 3 or operates the robot with a smartphone. The robot then moves to the inhabitant and offers to start the selected entertainment program.

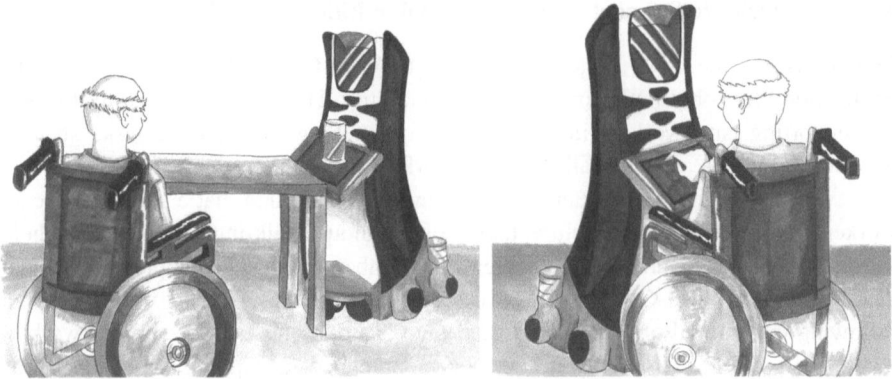

Fig. 5. Care-O-bot® 3 supporting care workers in an elderly care facility: Potation supply (left) and entertainment functions (right)

5   Experimental Results

In this section a short evaluation is given for the implementation of two scenarios presented in section 4: the fetch-and-carry service, which was shown at an international exhibition, and the "potation supply" scenario from the WiMi-Care project.

5.1   Implementation of the Fetch-and-Carry Service

Though many different scenarios guided the development process, the fourth and simplest of the scenarios described in section 4.1, the fetch-and-carry service, was implemented. This scenario contains the core functionality of Care-O-bot® 3, the fetch-and-carry service, in form of drink delivery. As described in section 4.1, the user may choose a drink from the user interface, which the robot then fetches autonomously and serves it to the user by putting it on the tray. Despite the low complexity of the scenario, the implementation was very challenging due to the high requirements on the robot's autonomy.

The serving drink scenario was exhibited on international fairs, e.g. Automatica 2008 or IREX 2009, where the robustness and reliability of the service could be demonstrated.

5.2   Evaluation of Care-O-bot® 3 in an Elderly Care Facility

In May 2010 the potation supply scenario which was developed in the WiMi-Care project was tested in an elderly care facility in Stuttgart in a first practical test of one week. One goal of this test was to prove the feasibility of the potation supply scenario and to evaluate the acceptance of a robot performing support tasks in an elderly care facility. Another goal was to identify the need for further development of Care-O-bot® 3 during the project in order to ensure a reliable performance of the robot in the

Fig. 6. Implementation of the serving drink scenario at the IREX fair in Tokyo, November 2009

second and final practical evaluation which will take place in June 2011. For the first practical test, it was decided to implement the potation supply scenario in a simple, but robust version, leaving out for example the detection and grasping of cups in the kitchen, as well as the journalizing of the served fluid. The full potation supply scenario as well as the entertainment scenario will be implemented and evaluated at the second test phase.

The task of Care-O-bot® 3 in the first practical evaluation consisted of three steps (Fig. 7). At first, the robot drove to a kitchen and drew water from a water cooler. The second step was to transport the cup on a long corridor which was frequented by inhabitants and staff members to the sitting area. Here great requirements with respect to collision avoidance and path planning had to be met, especially when the corridor was crowded by inhabitants with wheelchairs and walking aids or when the way was temporarily blocked by carts carrying laundry or food. In the third step, the robot offered the drink to people sitting at a table. Here the challenges were to carefully approach chairs so that the water could be reached and to persuade inhabitants to take and drink the water.

All three steps were performed successfully [27]. Water was offered and handed over to inhabitants more than 20 times in a regular supply service that was installed after setup and basic tests were completed. The acceptance of Care-O-bot® 3 was very high. The test phase had been prepared with several information evenings so that care workers and inhabitants understood the idea of a robot supporting the staff without replacing them and showed no fear to interact with the machine. However, in many cases the elderly people did not drink the water, but just placed it in front of them. A reason for this might be that the inhabitants during testing were already offered beverages by the care workers. The inhabitants also were aware that the robot was tested and might have taken the drink to support the work of the scientists which of cause also was a distraction from their daily routine. It will be closely monitored in the second test phase, if this behaviour changed and if the robot will be able to convince the inhabitants to drink.

Generally the expectations towards the robot seemed to match its abilities, which surely can be accounted to the functional design of Care-O-bot® 3. Nevertheless, some inhabitants tended to treat the robot like a life form and for example thanked Care-O-bot® 3 and even tried to caress it when it brought them a drink.

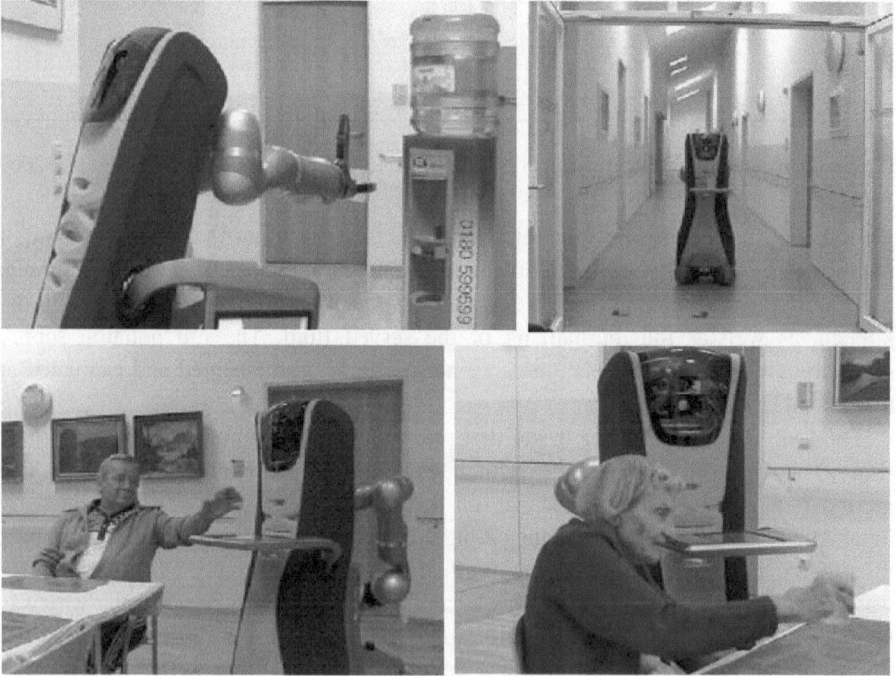

Fig. 7. Course of the potation supply scenario: Drawing water from a water cooler (upper left), transporting it to a sitting area (upper right) and offering it to the inhabitants (bottom)

6   Considerations on Physical Embodiment

In the last sections, it was pointed out that the guiding visions during the development process of Care-O-bot® 3 and the scenarios defined within the research projects had many ideas in common with the virtual butler scenario. The question is now, to what extent the embodied robot could serve this vision of supporting elderly people to live an independent and social active life, and in which regard it is maybe hindering.

On the one hand, an embodiment brings many additional challenges, from the mechanical and electrical engineering point of view, from the software and integration complexity point of view, and from the users' safety point of view. Besides engineers, many experts in other fields are necessary to create a robust, reliable and functional system, with an appealing design on top of that. We have seen in sections above that the robot design has to be chosen very carefully in order to not provoke overdrawn expectations by the users and disappointing them with respect to the actually available functionality. Furthermore, the embodied butler is less mobile than a virtual one and most probably bound to the home.

On the other hand, most capabilities of the virtual butler described in the "Tina and her butler" – if available – could be easily made available on the embodied butler, too. Most functions would probably be implemented in pure software, and even if some special hardware device should be required, it surely can be integrated into the hardware set-up. Care-O-bot® 3 offers already a touch display, for example. So the question is not "virtual or embodied butler?" but rather "What additional benefits do we gain from a robot butler?"

Embodiment bears much potential. User interaction can be designed much more natural, as humans are used to communicate with some kind of counterpart. Besides human-machine communication via some kind of input device or speech, also visual cues like gestures or mimics can be used more easily and more intuitively. Care-O-bot® 3 is also able to give feedback via simple gestures like nodding, shaking the „head" or bowing. It can thus signal the user that he has understood the assigned task, in fact in the manner of a discreet butler. There is also a technical aspect: to be able to communicate with the user independently of his location and focus of attention, there's a need for extensive installation of fix sensors. A mobile robot relieves this challenge a lot by carrying sensors on board. Most commonly, the user will be directed to the robot if he intends to give it any commands or requests.

Finally, and importantly, the embodied butler is able to support the user physically – by doing housework like clearing the dish washer, bringing objects or even helping handicapped people to get up and walk (see scenarios in section 4 and [8]).

Concerning the user's perception of the robot butler, several previous studies found differences in terms of how people react to a physical robot, as opposed to a virtual, animated, projected or even 'disembodied' robot. Lee et al. [43] have shown positive effects of physical embodiment on the quality of interaction between robots and people. Participants preferred interaction with physical robots, compared to virtual robots. More specifically, they found that the physical embodiment enhanced the agent's social presence [43]. Likewise, Bartneck [44] suggested that physical embodiment facilitated social interaction with an emotional robot (eMuu), whereby participants gained a higher score in a negotiation experiment with the robot than with a computer screen character.

Tapus and Mataric [46] identified differences in how patients with cognitive impairment reacted towards a physical robot or a computer animation playing recorded songs. The studies in [41, 45] further support the importance of physical embodiment on performance and people's perception of social interactions. Here, participants perceived a physical robot as more appealing, helpful, watchful and enjoyable than a non-embodied robot. Note, while some studies [42] did not find strong differences between a physical robot and a projected robot in terms of people's perception and experience of the interaction, significant evidence is supporting the existence of such differences. Pereira et al. [40] found in studies with children that physical embodiment, compared to a virtually embodied agent, had a positive effect on children's enjoyment of a game. Kose-Bagci et al. [39] carried out a systematic study where 66 children played a drumming game either with an embodied child-sized, humanoid robot, a 'hidden robot' (only the sound could be perceived), or a real-time projected image of the same robot. Statistical analysis of the results of questionnaires and behavioural performance showed that the presence of the physical, embodied robot led to more interaction, better drumming and turn-taking performance, as well as more enjoyment of the interaction. Thus, concerning the user's perspective, there is support in favour of a robotic home companion, rather than a virtual butler. However, we need to consider that the task and function, efficiency and utility of the system also influence the acceptance of new technology. One area that is often contrasted to the vision of an autonomous robot butler is ambient assisted living (AAL). Indeed, many functions for elderly care may be performed by a virtual butler or non-robotic physical systems used in the domain of AAL where we find specific solutions e.g. for fall detection using radio tags [36], health and human activity monitoring using biometric sensors [37], or other sensors that can be integrated in a smart home [38]. However, for scenarios where several functions need to be combined into a single system, where physical tasks need to be performed by the system, and where the physical presence of a single robot as a focus of attention and interaction will enhance the user's experience and acceptance of the services provided by the system – in such situations an embodied robot companion, as described in this chapter, seems to be a very promising solution with many advantages over alternative, non-robotic systems.

7   Conclusion and Outlook

In this chapter, the robot butler Care-O-bot® 3 was presented, including design, technology and user scenarios. An important insight was the fact, that the appearance of a device provokes users' expectations with respect to its functionality. Embodiment consequently bears the risk of unsatisfying anticipations, e.g. that the robot is able to manipulate if it is equipped arms. It was shown that the robot's appearance was therefore designed carefully to express not more and not less than the discreet service of a butler.

How far are we then from the realisation of the "Tina and her butler" scenario? There is probably still a long way to go to make a robot butler robust, reliable and functional enough in dynamic environments like households, especially in connection with elder users. There exist many examples of robots performing very well in complex, but well defined and specific scenarios. Often this performance degrades rapidly when the scenario changes – mostly the loss of performance is disproportionate to the degree of change. This means in the worst case that the robot fails completely if the scenario differs in any respect (e.g. type and position of objects, obstacles or persons in the environment, etc.).

In other words, major challenges in robotics are about handling unstructured and unknown environments, user safety and particularly human-robot interaction. Integration effort increases steadily with the increase in complexity of the single components of a robot, such that in the first place specialists like autonomous vacuum cleaners or lawn mowers will propagate on the market rather than the all-rounding generalist. A fully autonomous household assistant might even not be necessary: the robot's deficiencies and unreliability could e.g. be diminished by the support of remote operators as proposed in the research project SRS.

At the moment, artificial intelligence and robotics research are conducted rather concurrently with only few contact points in some research projects like COGNIRON [4], LIREC [35] or competitions like RoboCup [22]. One community would possibly end-up with a virtual butler, the other with a physical one. As indicated in the section above, however, both approaches could be combined quite easily in the long run. Almost all functions of an intelligent virtual butler can be implemented on a robot, while the benefits of the robot can help in scenarios with more physical interaction of butler and person.

References

1. Benfield, J.A., Szlemko, W.J., Bell, P.A.: Driver personality and anthropomorphic attributions of vehicle personality relate to reported aggressive driving tendencies. Personality and individual Differences 42, 247–258 (2007)
2. Caporael, L.R.: Anthropomorphism and mechanomorphism: two faces of the human machine. Computers in Human Behaviour 2, 215–234 (1986)
3. The Care-O-bot project, http://www.care-o-bot-research.org, http://www.care-o-bot.de
4. COGNIRON-The Cognitive Robot Companion, European project in the 6th framework (FP6-IST-002020), Duration: 2004-2007 (2008), http://www.cogniron.org
5. Dautenhahn, K.: Socially intelligent robots: dimensions of human-robot interaction. Philosophical Transactions for the Royal Society B: Biological Sciences 362(1480), 679–704 (2007)
6. Dautenhahn, K., Woods, S.N., Kaouri, C., Walters, M.L., Koay, K.L., Werry, I.: What is a robot companion – friend, assistant or butler. In: IEEE IRS/RSJ International Conference on Intelligent Robots and Systems, IROS 2005, Edmonton, Alberta, Canada, pp. 1488–1493 (2005)
7. Eddy, T.J., Gallup, G.G., Povinelli, D.J.: Attribution of cognitive states to animals: Anthropomorphism in comparative perspective. Journal of Social Sciences 49, 87–101 (1993)

8. Goetz, J., Kiesler, S., Powers, A.: Matching robot appearance and behaviour to task to improve human-robot cooperation. In: Proceedings of the 12th IEEE Workshop on Robot and Human Interactive Communication, vol. IXX (2003)

9. Hans, M., Graf, B.: Robotic home assistant Care-O-bot® II. In: Prassler, E., et al. (eds.) Advances in Human-Robot Interaction, pp. 371–384. Springer, Heidelberg (2004)

10. Luczak, H., Roetting, M., Schmidt, L.: Let's talk: anthropomorphism as means to cope with stress of interacting with technical devices. Ergonomics 46(13/14), 1361–1374 (2003)

11. Mori, M.: Bukimi no tani [the uncanny valley translated by K. F. MacDorman and T. Minato]. Energy 7, 33–35 (1970)

12. MacDorman, K.F.: Androids as an experimental apparatus. In: Proceedings of CogSci-2005 Workshop: Toward Social Mechanisms of Android Science, Stresa, Italy, pp. 106–118 (2005)

13. Multi-Role Shadow Robot for Independent Living (SRS), funded in the 7th European framework with Grant agreement no.: 247772, Duration (February 2010-January 2013), http://www.srs-project.eu

14. Nass, C., Steuer, J., Tauber, E., Reeder, H.: Anthropomorphism, agency, and ethopoeia: computers as social actors. In: CHI 1993: INTERACT 1993 and CHI 1993 Conference Companion on Human Factors in Computing Systems, pp. 111–112. ACM Press, New York (1993)

15. Nass, C.: Etiquette equality: exhibitions and expectations of computer politeness. Communications of the ACM 47(4), 35–37 (2004)

16. Parise, S., Kiesler, S., Sproull, L., Waters, K.: Cooperating with life-like interface agents. Computers in Human Behavior 15(2), 123–142 (1999)

17. Pearson, J., Hu, J., Branigan, H.P., Pickering, M.J., Nass, C.I.: Adaptive language behaviour in HCI: how expectations and beliefs about a system affect users' word choice. In: Proceedings of the SIGCHI Conference on Human Factors in Computing Systems, CHI 2006, pp. 1177–1180. ACM Press, New York (2006)

18. Pruitt, J., Grudin, J.: Personas: practice and theory. In: Proceedings of the 2003 Conference on Designing for user Experiences, DUX 2003, pp. 1–15. ACM Press, New York (2003)

19. Reiser, U., Connette, C., Fischer, J., Kubacki, J., Bubeck, A., Weisshardt, F., Jacobs, T., Parlitz, C., Hägele, M., Verl, A.: Care-O-bot® 3 – Creating a product vision for service robot applications by integrating design and technology. In: The 2009 IEEE/RSJ International Conference on Intelligent Robots and Systems (IROS), St. Louis, USA, pp. 1992–1997 (2009)

20. Reiser, U., Parlitz, C., Klein, P.: Care-O-bot® 3 – Vision of a robot butler. In: Beyond Gray Droids: Domestic Robot Design for the 21st Century: Workshop in Cambridge, UK on 1 September 2009 at HCI 2009, Cambridge, UK (2009)

21. Rosson, M.B., Carroll, J.M.: Usability engineering: scenario-based development of human-computer interaction. Morgan Kaufmann Publishers Inc., San Francisco (2002)

22. (2010), http://www.robocup.org

23. Syrdal, D.S., Dautenhahn, K., Woods, S.N., Walters, M.L., Koay, K.L.: Doing the Right Thing Wrong' - Personality and Tolerance to Uncomfortable Robot Approaches. In: The 15th IEEE International Symposium on Robot and Human Interactive Communication (RO-MAN 2006), pp. 183–188 (2006)

24. Scopelliti, M., Giuliani, M.V., D'Amico, A.M., Fornara, F.: If I had a robot at home. Peoples' representation of domestic robots. In: Keate, S., Clarkson, J., Langdon, P., Robinson, P. (eds.) Designing a More Inclusive World, pp. 257–266. Springer (2004)

25. Watt, S.N.K.: Seeing things as people. Ph.D. Thesis, Knowledge Media Institute and Department of Psychology, Open University Walton Hall Milton Keynes, UK (1997)

26. Supporting the Knowledge Transfer for a Participative Design of the Care Work Sector through Microelectronics (WiMi-Care), funded by the German Federal Ministry of Research and Technology (BMBF, support code: 01FC08024-27), Duration (November 2008-October 2011), http://www.wimi-care.de

27. Jacobs, T., Graf, B.: Working Brief 23: Pilotanwendungen: Ergebnisse für die Weiterentwicklung des Care-O-bot® 3 hinsichtlich benötigter Fähigkeiten und Akzeptanz (2010), http://www.wimi-care.de/outputs.html#Briefs

28. Bartneck, C., Bleeker, T., Bun, J., Fens, P., Riet, L.: The influence of robot anthropomorphism on the feelings of embarrassment when interacting with robots. Paladyn – Journal of Behavioral Robotics 1(2), 109–115 (2010)

29. Syrdal, D.S., Dautenhahn, K., Woods, S.N., Walters, M.L., Koay, K.L.: Looking good? Appearance preferences and robot personality inferences at zero acquaintance. In: Proc. AAAI - Spring Symposium 2007: Multidisciplinary Collaboration for Socially Assistive Robotics, March 26-28, pp. 86–92. Stanford University, AAAI Technical Report, AAAI Press, Palo Alto (2007)

30. Tapus, A., Tapus, C., Matarić, M.J.: User-Robot Personality Matching and Assistive Robot Behavior Adaptation for Post-Stroke Rehabilitation Therapy. Intelligent Service Robotics Journal, 169–183 (2008)

31. Walters, M.L., Syrdal, D.S., Dautenhahn, K., te Boekhorst, R., Koay, K.L.: Avoiding the uncanny valley: robot appearance, personality and consistency of behavior in an attention-seeking home scenario for a robot companion. Autonomous Robots 24(2), 159–178 (2008)

32. Bethel, C.L., Murphy, R.R.: Survey of Non-facial/Non-verbal Affective Expressions for Appearance-Constrained Robots. IEEE Transactions on Systems, Man, and Cybernetics - Part C: Applications and Reviews 38, 83–92 (2008)

33. Woods, S.N., Dautenhahn, K., Kaouri, C., te Boekhorst, R., Koay, K.L., Walters, M.L.: Are Robots Like People? - Relationships between Participant and Robot Personality Traits in Human-Robot Interaction Studies. Interaction Studies 8(2), 281–305 (2007)

34. Syrdal, D.S., Koay, K.L., Gácsi, M., Walters, M.L., Dautenhahn, K.: Video Prototyping of Dog-Inspired Non-verbal Affective Communication for an Appearance Constrained Robot. In: Proceedings IEEE RO-MAN 2010, 19th IEEE International Symposium in Robot and Human Interactive Communication, September 12-15, pp. 632–637. IEEE Press, Viareggio (2010)

35. LIREC: Living with Robots and Interaction Companions, FP7 Integrated Project (2008-2012), http://www.lirec.org/

36. Luštrek, M., Kaluša, B.: Fall detection and activity recognition with machine learning. Informatica 33, 205–212 (2009)

37. Jara, A.J., Zamora-Izquierdo, M.A., Gomez-Skarmeta, A.F.: An Ambient Assisted Living System for Telemedicine with Detection of Symptoms. In: Mira, J., Ferrández, J.M., Álvarez, J.R., de la Paz, F., Toledo, F.J. (eds.) IWINAC 2009, Part II. LNCS, vol. 5602, pp. 75–84. Springer, Heidelberg (2009)

38. De Silva, L.C., Petra, M.I., Punchihewa, G.A.: Ambient Intelligence in a Smart Home for Energy Efficiency and Eldercare. In: Kim, J.-H., Ge, S.S., Vadakkepat, P., Jesse, N., Al Manum, A., Puthusserypady K, S., Rückert, U., Sitte, J., Witkowski, U., Nakatsu, R., Braunl, T., Baltes, J., Anderson, J., Wong, C.-C., Verner, I., Ahlgren, D. (eds.) FIRA 2009. CCIS, vol. 44, pp. 187–194. Springer, Heidelberg (2009)

39. Kose-Bagci, H., Ferrari, E., Dautenhahn, K., Syrdal, D.S., Nehaniv, C.L.: Effects of Embodiment and Gestures on Social Interaction in Drumming Games with a Humanoid Robot. Advanced Robotics 23, 1951–1996 (2009)

40. Pereira, A., Martinho, C., Leite, I., Paiva, A.: iCat, the chess player: the influence of embodiment in the enjoyment of a game. In: Proc. 7th Int. Conf. on Autonomous Agents and Multiagent Systems, Estoril, pp. 1253–1256 (2008)
41. Wainer, J., Feil-Seifer, D.J., Shell, D.A., Matarić, M.J.: Embodiment and human–robot interaction: a taskbased perspective. In: Proc. Int. Conf. on Human–Robot Interaction, Jeju Island, pp. 872–877 (2007)
42. Powers, A., Kiesler, S., Fussell, S., Torrey, C.: Comparing a computer agent with a humanoid robot. In: Proc. ACM/IEEE Int. Conf. on Human–Robot Interaction, Washington, DC, pp. 145–152 (2007)
43. Lee, K.M., Jung, Y., Kim, J., Kim, S.R.: Are physically embodied social agents better than disembodied social agents?: the effects of physical embodiment, tactile interaction, and people's loneliness in human–robot interaction. Int. J. Hum.-Comput. Stud. 64, 962–973 (2006)
44. Bartneck, C.: eMuu — an embodied emotional character for the ambient intelligent home. PhD Thesis, Eindhoven (2002)
45. Wainer, J., Feil-Seifer, D.J., Shell, D.A., Matarić, M.J.: The role of physical embodiment in human–robot interaction. In: Proc. IEEE Int. Workshop on Robot and Human Interactive Communication, Hatfield, pp. 117–122 (2006)
46. Tapus, A., Matarić, M.J.: Socially assistive robotic music therapist for maintaining attention of older adults with cognitive impairments. In: Proc. AAAI Fall Symp. AI in Eldercare: New Solutions to Old Problem, Washington, DC, pp. 297–298 (2008)

Part III
Further Developments

Spoken Language Processing:
Where Do We Go from Here?

Roger K. Moore

Dept. Computer Science, University of Sheffield, Regent Court, 211 Portobello,
Sheffield, S1 4DP, UK
r.k.moore@dcs.shef.ac.uk

Abstract. Recent years have seen steady improvements in the quality and performance of speech-based human-machine interaction driven by a significant convergence in the methods and techniques employed. However, the quantity of training data required to improve state-of-the-art systems seems to be growing exponentially, and yet performance appears to be reaching an asymptote that is not only well short of human performance, but which may also be inadequate for many real-world applications. This situation suggests that there may be a fundamental flaw in the underlying architecture of contemporary speech-based systems, and the future direction for research into spoken language processing is currently uncertain. This chapter addresses these issues by stepping outside the familiar domains of speech science and technology, and instead draws inspiration from recent findings in fields of research that are concerned with the neurobiology of living systems in general. In particular, four areas are highlighted: the growing evidence for an intimate relationship between sensor and motor behaviour in living organisms, the power of negative feedback control to accommodate unpredictable disturbances in real-world environments, mechanisms for imitation and mental imagery for learning and modelling, and hierarchical models of temporal memory for predicting future behaviour and anticipating the outcome of events. The chapter shows how these results point towards a novel architecture for speech-based human-machine interaction that blurs the distinction between the core components of a traditional spoken language dialogue system; an architecture in which cooperative and communicative behaviour emerges as a by-product of a model of interaction where the system has in mind the needs and intentions of a user, and a user has in mind the needs and intentions of the system. It concludes with a roadmap of technical pre-requisites and desiderata that would seem to be necessary if voice-based interaction with an autonomous agent such as a virtual butler is to become a practical reality.

1   Introduction

One of the enduring features of almost all science fiction stories is the ubiquitous assumption that the primary means for future human-machine interaction will be vocal communication. It is often portrayed that the linguistic abilities of future technology will match those of a typical human being, and that conversational

R. Trappl (Ed.): Your Virtual Butler, LNAI 7407, pp. 119–133, 2013.
© Springer-Verlag Berlin Heidelberg 2013

interaction between humans and robots will be both possible and desirable. The same is true for the "virtual butler" concept addressed in this volume – how else are people to develop a long-term and productive relationship with such an autonomous agent if not by using everyday speech to express their needs and desires? Indeed, it is precisely with such futuristic scenarios in mind that scientists and engineers have spent the past 50 or so years developing the core spoken language technologies that would support such a facility – automatic speech recognition, text-to-speech synthesis and spoken language dialogue systems.

2   Spoken Language Technology

2.1   Speech Recognition

Automatic speech recognition (ASR) is the term given to the technology that is intended to take a human speech signal from a microphone input and convert it into digital information in some form of text-like representation by recognising the words that are being spoken. Such a technology has long been of interest in the commercial marketplace because it offers people the possibility of using their voice to control a piece of equipment by speaking a relevant command or to enter text or data by voice dictation. The attractiveness of ASR is that all of these actions could be performed 'hands-free', thereby avoiding the need to use a physical input device such as a keyboard or mouse. This could provide a real advantage in applications that involve a person performing multiple simultaneous tasks - piloting an aircraft, for example.

Research into automatic speech recognition goes back several decades. One of the first scientific papers to be published on ASR appeared in the early 1950s [8], and since that time a considerable amount of effort (in both person-power and funding) has been devoted to the development of a technology that can recognise (and even understand) spoken input. The very earliest ASR devices could only accommodate small vocabularies of the order of tens of words (e.g. the digits *"zero"* to *"nine"*), and each word had to be spoken in isolation with a distinct pause preceding and following each utterance. Also, such early systems were 'speaker-dependent' and could only be used by people who had 'trained' them (i.e. by individuals who had provided examples of each word in advance). In contrast, since the late 1990s, modern ASR technology has been able to handle vocabularies consisting of tens of thousands of words; it is able to operate in a 'speaker-independent' mode for a wide range of individuals without any system training; and it can recognise continuous speech with no unnatural pauses between the words. The key scientific breakthroughs occurred in the 1970s and 80s when researchers started to investigate the use of dynamic programming (DP) for performing the recognition search process [42], context-sensitive sub-word structures to facilitate the recognition of words not observed in the training data [44], and hidden Markov modelling (HMM) for handling the immense variability observed in speech signals within a formal mathematical and statistical (Bayesian) framework [20].

For a contemporary review of current techniques for automatic speech recognition, see [13].

2.2   Speech Synthesis

Text-to-speech synthesis (TTS) is the opposite side of the coin to ASR. Digital data, usually in some form of text-like representation, is converted into speech and read out automatically to a human listener. TTS is of commercial interest because it allows people to receive information 'eyes-free', thereby avoiding the need to look at a dedicated screen or display. Again, this technology offers a real benefit in applications involving simultaneous tasks - listening to navigation instructions whilst driving, for example.

Like ASR, the earliest speaking machines also appeared in the 1950s, with the first end-to-end TTS system published in 1964 [18]. Based on electrical analogues of the structure and functioning of the human vocal tract, such speech synthesisers sounded rather unnatural, but the 1990s saw a significant jump in quality when researchers abandoned the modelling approach in favour of one based on the cut-and-past of segments taken from recordings of actual speech [10, 22, 47]. Such concatenative/unit-selection-based TTS systems sounded very much like a real person (since they were essentially recordings), although there was a tendency for occasional disturbing discontinuities to arise where the speech had not been put back together too well (usually in relatively unpredictable material). These problems could only be overcome by using larger and larger quantities of recorded material, which was not only challenging for the speaker that had to provide the data, but it also meant that the best systems required many gigabytes of storage [21].

In the last ten years, these practical limitations have started to be overcome by the appearance of a new type of TTS system - HMM-based speech synthesis systems (HTS). Like ASR, HTS exploits the benefits of stochastic modelling to achieve a more compact and economical representation of the speech data [54].

2.3   Dialogue Systems

Given even primitive technologies for ASR and TTS it is natural to consider combining the two together in order to create a two-way conversation or dialogue. A spoken language dialogue system (SLDS) does just this, and it typically connects ASR and TTS with an application 'back end' through a dialogue manager component that is responsible for organising the turn-taking between user and system. SLD systems are of commercial interest because they offer the possibility of automating transactions that are normally conducted face-to-face with a human agent - buying train tickets over the telephone, for example.

Some of the earliest research into spoken language dialogue took place during the 1980s [46], and much of this work employed finite-state automata to represent the intended course of an interaction [14, 25, 27]. More recently, emphasis has switched away from prescribed interactions to more flexible arrangements, again exploiting the stochastic modelling approach to handling variability and uncertainty using 'Partially observable Markov decision processes' (POMDPs) [50, 48, 53].

2.4   The Current State-of-the-Art

The current situation in contemporary spoken language processing is that each area of technology has enjoyed steady year-on-year progress since the 1980s; ASR accuracy, TTS quality and SLD usability have been improving constantly (as evidenced by the large number of scientific and technical articles that are published each year). These improvements have arisen from main four areas:

- the increasing use of data-driven statistical modelling approaches (such as HMMs, HTS and POMDP) based on very large corpora of spoken language to estimate the parameters of the underlying statistical models;
- the relentless increase in available computer power that has facilitated ever more powerful search techniques (such as DP);
- the sustained existence of formal public benchmark testing that has encouraged quantitative comparisons between different research laboratories; and
- the emergence of published standards (such as VoiceXML) that permit fast application deployment.

This is a remarkable success story and all three technologies have matured sufficiently to support moderately large and lucrative markets. For example, the majority of mobile telephones support 'voice dialling', a feature through which a user can create a voice tag for each entry in their phone book and then call the appropriate contact by speaking the appropriate name. Likewise, software for 'large vocabulary continuous speech recognition' (LVCSR) for dictating documents has been available for PCs since 1997. Indeed, with the release of the Windows Vista operating system in 2007, LVCSR has become available as a standard feature on a PC, and in 2010 the same software could be downloaded as a free application on Apple's iPhone. Also, interactive voice response (IVR) systems have become increasingly commonplace since the mid-2000s, and many members of the general public have now experienced attempting to book a train or cinema ticket by talking to an automated spoken language dialogue system.

From the earliest applications to those extant today, most are marketed under the banner of speech being the most natural mode of human-machine interaction. Indeed, one supplier promoted the advertising catchphrase *"You have been learning since birth the only skill needed to use our technology"*.

On the surface this appears to be a very satisfactory situation – spoken language technology has matured steadily over a significant period of time, and a genuine market for speech-based applications has emerged. However, despite the successes in terms of applications, and the great steps forward that have been made in our understanding of how to model and process spoken language, there remain a number of what turn out to be rather significant challenges – especially for conversational interaction with an autonomous agent such as a virtual butler.

2.5   Performance Shortfalls

As anyone who has encountered a voice-enabled application will testify, spoken language processing turns out to be actually rather fragile in real everyday conditions.

Often users approach such a new technology with enthusiasm, only to find that success is blighted by recognition errors, unintelligible responses and hard to navigate dialogues. After one or two failed attempts to use a voice-enabled application, the typical user simply reverts to more familiar and reliable methods. Whilst it is true that most people do indeed own a mobile phone with a voice dialling feature, it turns out that only a small proportion have actually tried to use it, and very few of those individuals actually continue to use it on a regular basis. A similar story applies to document dictation on a PC – many people try it out, but then soon discover that two-fingered typing is actually faster [31]! Likewise, the unreliability of IVR systems is sufficiently infamous that they often feature in the stage routines of stand-up comics, and the popularity of the website http://gethuman.com/ is a testament to people's frustration with automated voice-based services.

Overall it seems that, from a user's perspective, unless they are obliged to use the technology (for example being unable or unwilling to type, or being faced with an automated system with no obvious means for reaching a human operator), spoken language processing does not seem to be quite ready for everyday use. In fact, it also turns out that it is definitely not natural to talk to a machine – at least, not using current spoken language technology. This situation was expertly parodied in a sketch broadcast on the US Saturday Night Live show that depicted a strange and stilted conversation between two people on a blind date, one of whom - Julie - does *"the voice recordings for companies such United Airlines, Blue Cross and Amtrak"* and, as a consequence, talks just like a typical IVR system. Whilst the sketch is hilarious – *"I think you said you are nine Gary ... did I get that right?"* - it also reveals an important truth; current spoken language technology gives rise to rather unnatural and difficult to navigate vocal interactions.

Of course performance in the research laboratory is significantly in advance of that encountered by users in the commercial marketplace. Nevertheless, even the best ASR systems still make 20-50% errors on spontaneous speech (i.e. at best, one word in every five is wrong!), and this places fundamental restrictions on the ability to construct conversational interaction with an autonomous agent such as a virtual butler. For example, the capabilities of even the most advanced prototype conversational system [49] is severely restricted by the limitations of the spoken language processing components and their interfaces with the rest of the system.

The question is thus whether these frustrations and difficulties simply reflect the fact that there are still shortfalls in the performance of the spoken language components, and that continued steady progress will iron out the problems, or are they indicative of a more fundamental limitation intrinsic to the current approaches? Unfortunately it appears to be the case that the latter is true. For example, not only is current performance well short of that which a human being is able to achieve using spoken language [24], but there is also evidence that performance appears to be reaching an asymptote despite training systems on orders of magnitude more data than is needed by a small child to learn language [30]!

2.6   Research Challenges

There is no shortage of opinion on the main obstacles that need to be overcome [1, 6, 9, 28, 38, 55]. Most recently, a pair of linked review articles identified *"six ambitious, achievable, and testable grand challenge tasks"* [2, 3]: everyday audio, rapid portability to emerging languages, self-adaptive language capabilities, detection of rare key events, cognition-driven speech and language systems, and spoken language comprehension. This list is accompanied by the usual request for collecting and annotating even greater quantities of spoken language data.

Of course what is needed are solutions not challenges, and for many years it was thought that these problems could be overcome by "bridging the gap" between the speech technology research community and those involved in studying the form and structure of speech, such phoneticians and linguists [29, 43]. The assumption was that solutions to the challenges identified above lay in bringing together knowledge about spoken language with the relevant computational processes for manipulating it. However, despite numerous attempts over many years it has proved singularly difficult to extend performance beyond that achieved using state-of-the-art engineering approaches.

So if, as it seems, performance improvements are going to become harder and harder to come by, and even then we are still heading for capabilities that are well short of those that the markets and applications demand, and the speech sciences are not providing the necessary insights, where can we turn for inspiration? Clearly human beings provide an existence proof that robust spoken language processing is possible, so what critical piece (or pieces) of the jigsaw are we missing? Where do we go from here?

3   Where Do We Go from Here?

One of the features of spoken language which is so often overlooked (especially by engineers) is the simple, yet in the author's view, critical fact that speech is a sophisticated interactive, affective and communicative behaviour that is grounded in both an individual's cognition and the external world in which they exist. Spoken language expresses relationships between the minds of individuals and between objects and events taking place in the past, present and future (imagined and real). It is an activity that is founded on more general behaviours exhibited by human beings and, although somewhat special to human beings, it also shares characteristics with those possessed by other living systems. This broader perspective is almost completely ignored in the spoken language processing field; for example, one of the six challenges identified by Baker et al. [2, 3] is "cognition-driven speech", but the topic is only treated very lightly and it is not referred to again in their follow-up article.

It is thus the author's view that non-incremental progress will only come from stepping outside the usual domains of speech science and technology, and instead drawing inspiration from recent findings in the neurobiology of living systems. In particular, the author has recently identified four areas that could have significant implications for the future of spoken language processing [32]: the growing evidence for an intimate relationship between sensor and motor behaviour in living organisms [40, 41], the power of negative feedback control to accommodate unpredictable disturbances in real-world environments [39, 23], mechanisms for imitation and mental imagery for learning and modelling [19, 51], and hierarchical models of temporal memory for predicting future behaviour and anticipating the outcome of events [16].

The implications of these findings for future spoken language processing have been discussed in more detail elsewhere [32, 33], and a novel architecture for speech-based human-machine interaction has been proposed: *"PREdictive SENsorimotor Control and Emulation"* (PRESENCE). The PRESENCE architecture blurs the distinction between the traditional components of an SLP system; communicative behaviour is modelled as a loosely-coupled heterogeneous network of feedback-control systems that exhibit continuous but synchronised coactive behaviours. The implications are that systematic behaviour resulting from speaker-listener interaction should no longer need to be modelled as random variation, and thus the relevant models could be calibrated with significantly less training data. In particular, PRESENCE suggests a new model of speech generation that selects its characteristics appropriate to the needs of the listener, monitors the effect of its own output and modifies its behaviour according to its internal model of the listener; a new model of speech recognition that uses a forward/generative model based on an internal emulation of the intentions of the speaker and which adapts its model to the voice of the speaker based on knowledge of its own voice; and a new model of dialogue that is driven by the need to satisfy a users' needs and which uses emotion to appraise its success.

Research into PRESENCE is ongoing and ranges from detailed studies of the energetics of speech production using the world's first anatomically-correct animatronic tongue [17] through to the use of emotion as a controlling variable in open-ended conversational dialogue between a user and an 'embodied conversational agent' (ECA) [7, 52]. So, what are the implications of this new perspective for a voice-enabled virtual butler?

3.1   Towards a Voice-Enabled Virtual Butler

The PRESENCE architecture places its main emphasis not on the traditional components for spoken language processing, but on the needs and intentions of both the users and the system. These are aspects of interactive behaviour that are almost completely ignored in contemporary operational systems, and yet it is clear that the behaviour of many living organisms (especially human beings) is fully conditioned on such hidden variables. It is hardly surprising that people have a hard time interacting with current spoken language technology when such systems have no concept of satisfying a user's needs or understanding a user's intentions. Without such 'drives' (and the necessary feedback to determine the ongoing success on any interaction) a system can only follow a set of prescribed behaviours almost independently of the user's actions – clearly a recipe for disaster.

By its very nature, a virtual butler should be configured to serve the needs of its users, and this means that it has to be given the means to determine those needs. However, recognising the needs and intentions of human beings is clearly an almost impossible task given the complexity and sophistication of human behaviour and our primitive understanding of how to configure a cognitive architecture (such as PRESENCE) to accommodate such an advanced requirement. In the short term, the theory underpinning PRESENCE leaves only one possible line of approach – to manage users' expectations such that their behaviours fall automatically within the capabilities of the autonomous agent.

In practice, this suggests that a virtual butler should exhibit visual, vocal and interactional 'affordances' [15] that make it apparent to a user just what it can and, more importantly, cannot do. Clearly, a humanoid robot (or photo-realistic ECA) with a human-sounding voice is going to encourage a user to behave much differently to one that looks and sounds like a robot [34]. Likewise, any disparity between the affordances exhibited visually, vocally and behaviourally is highly likely to confuse a user [36]. What is needed is a unified approach to designing a virtual butler in which the look, feel and sound of the robot is 'appropriate' to the limited complexity of its internal cognitive structures. In just the same way that human beings and cooperative animals such as dogs achieve joint tasks very successfully using a mixture of gestural and vocal interactive behaviours, so a virtual butler needs to occupy a behavioural niche that is intuitively understandable to a human user. Any mismatches in behaviour lead inexorably to the user falling into an interactional chasm, not unlike the famous 'uncanny valley' [35] in which near-human representations are significantly more disturbing than those that are clearly not human.

Several of these ideas have been expressed already [4, 36] but, as yet, there are few practical solutions to the problem. What is needed is an approach that focuses on the coherent design of a cognitively-limited virtual butler service agent that is motivated by clearly defined needs, and whose externally-visible behaviours all contribute to support the rapid communication and assimilation of its operational affordances. Its vocal behaviour needs to be embedded in a wider interactional framework, and its vocal characteristics can be used to confirm its limited communicative affordances.

3.2   A Technical Roadmap

Taking such an approach leads to a suggested roadmap of technical pre-requisites and desiderata that would allow a virtual butler to engage in effective vocal interactivity:

- All of the agent's behaviours should be driven by a defined set of internal needs and intentions that specify the purpose and function of the agent in the context of the shared environment with user(s) with whom it is expected to interact (in order to satisfy those needs and intentions). This can only be achieved by the agent's designers taking an ethnomethodological perspective on the application scenario and environment.
- The agent should attempt to recognise and understand the needs and intentions of the user(s) by referencing its' own needs and intentions. This will allow it to empathise with the user(s), and to optimise its' behaviour in the face of uncertainty

in a complex environment. For a service robot such as a virtual butler this will almost certainly require the establishment of analogous relationships between the internal and external morphology of humans and the robot (the virtual butler doesn't need to drink wine in order to recognise and understand that a human has asked for some wine, but it does need to know that wine is a sustaining substance for human beings in the same way that electricity is a sustaining substance for robots).

- The virtual butler needs to exhibit its intentionality by making it clear to the user what the agent's role is and what its capabilities are. This information is manifest passively by virtue of the robot's general appearance (visual, vocally and behaviourally) and actively by its attempts to engage the attention of users by physical approach, gestural behaviour (e.g. pointing at a full wine glass) and/or vocal enquiry (e.g. by making an announcement).

- The agent needs to know when and how to engage with user(s). This means that the virtual butler must be capable of recognising user(s) in space and time, and selecting the appropriate location and moment to interact. This implies, for example, that ongoing human-to-human conversations should not be interrupted (unless there is an overriding necessity to do so). In general, the establishment of shared attention would require that the realisation of the robot's needs and intentions should be modulated by its knowledge of appropriate norms of human social behaviour. Even a seemingly simple vocal norm such as not talking at the same time as the user(s) could appear as an emergent behaviour resulting from the management of a purposeful interaction, rather than as a result of slavishly following potentially faulty rules of turn taking. Such behaviour would be a natural extension of recent work on 'incremental dialogue' [45] in which there is a tight coupling between interlocutors who are modelled as jointly engaged on a common task rather than simply passing information back and forth.

- The agent will have a range of hidden variables that affect its behaviour, such as its responsiveness, its 'willingness' to interrupt human activity and its style of speaking (e.g. formal vs. informal, rapid vs. slow, degree of helpfulness etc.). Any particular collection of settings in such variables constitutes the 'individuality', and hence 'personality, of the agent. Clearly the personality of a virtual butler needs to be set to be appropriate to the social setting – configurations that are appropriate for an autonomous virtual trainer (who's intentions may be to coerce the user) are likely to be quite inappropriate for a virtual butler (who's intentions are to serve the user). It is also crucial to set a personality that reflects the actual abilities of the robot, and which ties together the visual, vocal and behavioural affordances discussed earlier. This may entail a specific robotic appearance coupled with a robotic voice appropriate to the size and range of behaviours available to the physical agent.

- A crucial part of an agent's intention to service the needs of the user(s) is its ability to determine whether those needs are being met. A key feedback mechanism is thus the monitoring of user behaviour, especially with regard to affective states and emotions, and this can be achieved through a variety of established analyses, including an assessment of the user's voice. Action selection in the agent could then be conditioned on such information, and would guide it towards satisfying the user needs through behaviours that optimised the user's affective state (e.g. by making them 'satisfied' or even 'happy'). Such an approach to managing human behaviour has been shown to be viable in the setting of a robot companion [52].

- The corollary of the immediately preceding point is that the agent also needs to exhibit emotion, so that it is able to indicate whether its own needs and intentions are being met (which, you will remember, also subsumes the users needs and intentions). Hence a virtual butler that is unable to fulfil a given request could manifest its own disappointment through its general demeanour and, of course, its linguistic behaviour and vocal characteristics – i.e. not mimicking sadness, but in some limited sense being genuinely sad.

- In general, an autonomous agent such as a virtual butler needs to monitor the effect of its own behaviour, and adapt accordingly. This means that learning is a critical function that allows an agent to keep track of a constantly changing environment. Most contemporary learning schemes (especially in processing patterns such as speech) are overly reliant on substantial quantities of carefully annotated material. In the case of the virtual butler, learning mechanisms need to be based on episodic/case-based (rather than statistical) [11, 26] events in order to facilitate one-shot learning. Such an approach would naturally lead to the possibility of the immediate re-use (imitation) of user's behaviours by the robot [5, 12, 37] in just the same way that people mirror each other/align in body posture and conversation.

- Likewise, the virtual butler's lexicon should arise, not only from training data obtained in a simulation environment, but from the conceptual framework/ontology that is grounded in the given domain of cognitive behaviour. Of course, this needs to be coupled with more general-purpose linguistic functionality that is within the constraints of what is available from state-of the-art language understanding and generation, and that is appropriate to the cognitive and interactional skills of the robot.

The purpose of this list of desiderata is not simply to identify the technical pre-requisites for vocal interaction with an agent such as a virtual butler, but also to underline the argument that such behaviours cannot be easily divorced from all of the other behaviours manifest by such an agent. The argument being presented here is that where we go with spoken language processing depends on a more integrated view of its relation with other components, and its intimate link with wider aspects of cognition and action. These seemingly high-level cognitive constraints need to be brought to bear on the low-level vocal components in order to create an ability to engage in conversational interactions and to recognise and understand what people are saying, all within the context of a given social interaction.

3.3   What It Might Be Like When We Get There

An illustrative example of just such a robot is provided by the famous talking 'toaster' in the UK TV science fiction comedy drama "Red Dwarf". The dialogue between Lister (one of the human characters) and the toaster progresses as follows (Lister is sitting on his bunk trying to read a book):

TOASTER:	*"Would you like some toast?"*
LISTER:	"Hmm-mm"
TOASTER:	*"… some nice hot crisp brown buttered toast?"*
LISTER:	"Hmm-mmmm!"
TOASTER:	*"You don't want any toast then?"*
LISTER:	"No"
TOASTER:	*"What about a muffin?"*
LISTER:	"Nothing"
TOASTER:	*"You know the last time you had toast – 18 days ago, 11:36 Tuesday the 3rd – two rounds"*
LISTER:	"Shh"
TOASTER:	*"I mean, what's the point of buying a toaster with artificial intelligence if you don't like toast?"*
LISTER:	"I do like toast!"
TOASTER:	*"I mean, this is my job – this is cruel"*
LISTER:	"Look – I'm busy"
TOASTER:	*"Oh, you're not busy eating toast are you!?"*
LISTER:	"I don't want any!!"
TOASTER:	*"I mean, the whole purpose of my existence is to serve you with hot buttered scrummy toast – if you don't want any, then my existence is meaningless."*
LISTER:	"good!"
TOASTER:	*"I toast, therefore I am."*
LISTER:	"Will you shut up!"

In this short sketch, the robotic toaster is represented as a one-dimensional bread-obsessed electrical appliance. Its entire perception of the world is conditioned on its core function, and the conversational interaction revolves entirely around the service that it provides. It exhibits drives and motivations for its actions, and emotional responses when its objectives are repressed. It also engages in interaction using a voice that is clearly robotic yet fully expressive, and its vocal characteristics convey the robot's increasing frustration as the dialogue progresses.

Of course this is an example taken from science fiction, which is not usually cited as the most reliable guide for future technological progress. However, this particular exchange does nicely illustrate some of the main implications of the roadmap presented in this chapter. In the short-term, the likelihood of us being able to create a highly focussed and self-centred device such as the toaster is much higher than that the possibility of constructing a more general-purpose robot. The arguments presented here do indeed suggest that such a device is not only very likely to exhibit the characteristics depicted by the Red Dwarf toaster, but that it is essential that it should do so if it is to truly engage in meaningful interaction with human users.

4   Conclusion

This chapter has addressed the issue of conversational interaction with an autonomous agent such as a virtual butler. It has been argued that, despite impressive technological progress over many years, the state-of-the-art in spoken language processing falls short of what would be required in order to fulfil such an ambitious requirement. A suggested way forward involves embedding vocal interactivity within a wider cognitive framework that links drives and motivations with communicative behaviour. It has also been argued that in order for an agent such as a virtual butler to be effective, its look, sound and behaviour should actively reflect its interactional affordances – not to do so risks confusion and rejection on the part of the human user. A roadmap of technical pre-requisites and desiderata has been outlined which provide a coherent approach to embedding the spoken language abilities of a virtual butler within a wider cognitive and affective context.

Acknowledgements. I'd like to thank my colleagues Dr. Peter Wallis and Dr. Simon Worgan, both of whom have been willing to engage in vocal interaction with me on many of the ideas expounded in this chapter. Also, during the period in which I was preparing this chapter, I have received partial support by the European Commission under grant agreement number ISTFP7-231868 SERA - *"Social Engagement with Robots"* - and ISTFP6-034434 COMPANIONS - *"Intelligent, Persistent, Personalised Multimodal Interfaces to the Internet"* - both of which have been concerned with integrating spoken language processing into autonomous agents/robots.

References

1. Atal, B.: Speech technology in 2001: New research directions. Proc. Natl. Acad. Sci. USA 92, 10046–10051 (1995)
2. Baker, J.M., Deng, L., Glass, J., Khudanpur, S., Lee, C.-H., Morgan, N., O'Shaughnessy, D.: Research developments and directions in speech recognition and understanding, part 1. IEEE Signal Processing Magazine, 75–80 (2009)
3. Baker, J.M., Deng, L., Khudanpur, S., Lee, C.-H., Glass, J.R., Morgan, N., O'Shaughnessy, D.: Updated MINDS report on speech recognition and understanding, part 2. IEEE Signal Processing Magazine, 78–85 (2009)
4. Balentine, B.: It's Better to Be a Good Machine Than a Bad Person: Speech Recognition and Other Exotic User Interfaces at the Twilight of the Jetsonian Age. ICMI Press, Annapolis (2007)
5. Billard, A.: Imitation: a means to enhance learning of a synthetic proto-language in an autonomous robot. In: Dautenhahn, K., Nehaniv, C.L. (eds.) Imitation in Animals and Artifacts, pp. 281–311. MIT Press (2002)
6. Cole, R., Hirschman, L., Atlas, L., Beckman, M., Biermann, A., Bush, M., Clements, M., Cohen, J., Garcia, O., Hanson, B., Hermansky, H., Levinson, S., McKeown, K., Morgan, N., Novick, D., Ostendorf, M., Oviatt, S., Price, P., Silverman, H., Spitz, J., Waibel, A., Weinstein, C., Zahorian, S., Zue, V.: The challenge of spoken language systems: research directions for the nineties. IEEE Trans Speech and Audio Processing 3, 1–21 (1995)

7. Crook, N., Smith, C., Cavazza, M., Pulman, S., Moore, R.K., Boye, J.: Handling user interruptions in an embodied conversational agent. Paper presented at the AAMAS 2010: 9th International Conference on Autonomous Agents and Multiagent Systems, Toronto (2010)

8. Davis, K.H., Biddulph, R., Balashek, S.: Automatic recognition of spoken digits. Journal of the Acoustical Society of America 24, 637–642 (1952)

9. Deng, L., Huang, X.: Challenges in adopting speech recognition. Communications of the ACM 47(1), 69–75 (2004)

10. Dutoit, T.: An Introduction to Text-to-speech Synthesis. Kluwer Academic Publishers (1997)

11. Eliasson, K.: A case-based approach to dialogue systems. Journal of Experimental & Theoretical Artificial Intelligence 22(1), 23–51 (2010)

12. Erlhagen, W., Mukovskiy, A., Bicho, E., Panin, G., Kiss, C., Knoll, A., van Schie, H., Bekkering, H.: Goal-directed imitation for robots: a bio-inspired approach to action understanding and skill learning. Robotics and Autonomous Systems 54, 353–360 (2006)

13. Gales, M., Young, S.: The application of hidden Markov models in speech recognition. Foundations and Trends in Signal Processing 1(3), 195–304 (2007)

14. Gibbon, D., Moore, R.K., Mertins, I. (eds.): Handbook of Multimodal and Spoken Dialogue Systems: Resources, Terminology and Product Evaluation. Springer (2000)

15. Gibson, J.J.: The theory of affordances. In: Shaw, R., Bransford, J. (eds.) Perceiving, Acting, and Knowing: Toward an Ecological Psychology, pp. 67–82. Lawrence Erlbaum, Hillsdale (1977)

16. Hawkins, J.: On Intelligence. Times Books (2004)

17. Hofe, R., Moore, R.K.: Towards an investigation of speech energetics using 'AnTon': an animatronic model of a human tongue and vocal tract. Connection Science 20(4), 319–336 (2008)

18. Holmes, J.N., Mattingly, I.G., Shearme, J.N.: Speech synthesis by rule. Language and Speech 7, 127–143 (1964)

19. Iacoboni, M.: Understanding others: imitation, language, empathy. In: Hurley, S., Chater, N. (eds.) Perspectives on Imitation: From Mirror Neurons to Memes, vol. 1, pp. 255–282. MIT Press (2005)

20. Jelinek, F.: Continuous speech recognition by statistical methods. Proc. IEEE 64, 532–555 (1976)

21. Keller, E.: Towards greater naturalness: Future directions of research in speech synthesis. In: Keller, E., Bailly, G., Monaghan, A., Terken, J., Huckvale, M. (eds.) Improvements in Speech Synthesis. Wiley & Sons, Chichester (2001)

22. Keller, E., Bailly, G., Monaghan, A., Terken, J., Huckvale, M. (eds.): Improvements in Speech Synthesis. Wiley & Sons, Chichester (2001)

23. Lindblom, B.: Explaining phonetic variation: a sketch of the H&H theory. In: Hardcastle, W.J., Marchal, A. (eds.) Speech Production and Speech Modelling, pp. 403–439. Kluwer Academic Publishers (1990)

24. Lippmann, R.P.: Speech recognition by machines and humans. Speech Communication 22, 1–16 (1997)

25. Lopez Cozar Delgado, R., Araki, M.: Spoken, Multilingual and Multimodal Dialogue Systems: Development and Assessment. Wiley (2005)

26. Maier, V., Moore, R.K.: The case for case-based automatic speech recognition. Paper Presented at the INTERSPEECH, Brighton, UK (2009)

27. McTear, M.F.: Spoken Dialogue Technology: Towards the Conversational User Interface. Springer (2004)

28. Minker, W., Pittermann, J., Pittermann, A., Strauß, P.-M., Bühler, D.: Challenges in speech-based human–computer interfaces. International Journal of Speech Technology 10(2-3), 109–119 (2007)
29. Moore, R.K.: Whither a theory of speech pattern processing? Paper Presented at the EUROSPEECH 1993, Berlin, September 21-23 (1993)
30. Moore, R.K.: A comparison of the data requirements of automatic speech recognition systems and human listeners. Paper Presented at the EUROSPEECH 2003, Geneva, September 1-4 (2003)
31. Moore, R.K.: Modelling data entry rates for ASR and alternative input methods. Paper Presented at the INTERSPEECH 2004 ICSLP, Jeju, Korea, October 4-8 (2004)
32. Moore, R.K.: Spoken language processing: piecing together the puzzle. Speech Communication 49, 418–435 (2007)
33. Moore, R.K.: PRESENCE: A human-inspired architecture for speech-based human-machine interaction. IEEE Trans. Computers 56(9), 1176–1188 (2007)
34. Moore, R.K., Morris, A.: Experiences collecting genuine spoken enquiries using WOZ techniques. Paper Presented at the 5th DARPA workshop on Speech and Natural Language, New York (February 1992)
35. Mori, M.: Bukimi no tani (the uncanny valley). Energy 7, 33–35 (1970)
36. Nass, C., Brave, S.: Wired for Speech: How Voice Activates and Advances the Human-computer Relationship. MIT Press, Cambridge (2005)
37. Nehaniv, C.L., Dautenhahn, K. (eds.): Imitation and Social Learning in Robots, Humans and Animals. Cambridge University Press (2007)
38. O'Shaughnessy, D.: Automatic speech recognition: History, methods and challenges. Pattern Recognition 41(10), 2965–2979 (2008)
39. Powers, W.T.: Behavior: The Control of Perception. Aldine, Hawthorne (1973)
40. Pulvermüller, F.: Brain mechanisms linking language and action. Nature Reviews Neuroscience 6, 576–582 (2005)
41. Rizzolatti, G., Arbib, M.A.: Language within our grasp. Trends in Neuroscience 21(5), 188–194 (1998)
42. Sakoe, H., Chiba, S.: Dynamic programming algorithm optimisation for spoken word recognition. IEEE Trans. Acoustics, Speech and Signal Processing 26, 43–49 (1978)
43. Scharenborg, O.: Reaching over the gap: A review of efforts to link human and automatic speech recognition research. Speech Communication 49(5), 336–347 (2007)
44. Schwartz, R., Chow, Y., Roucos, S., Krasner, M., Makhoul, J.: Improved hidden Markov modelling of phonemes for continuous speech recognition. Paper Presented at the IEEE Conf. on Acoustics, Speech and Signal Processing (1985)
45. Skantze, G., Schlangen, D.: Incremental dialogue processing in a micro-domain. Paper Presented at the 12th Conference of the European Chapter of the Association for Computational Linguistics (EACL 2009), Athens, Greece (2009)
46. Taylor, M.M., Neel, F., Bouwhuis, D. (eds.): The Structure of Multimodal Dialogue. North Holland, Amsterdam (1988)
47. Taylor, P.: Text-to-Speech Synthesis. Cambridge University Press, Cambridge (2009)
48. Thomson, B., Young, S.: Bayesian update of dialogue state: A POMDP framework for spoken dialogue systems. Computer Speech & Language 24(4), 562–588 (2010)
49. Wilks, Y., Worgan, S., Dingli, A., Catizone, R., Moore, R.K., Field, D., Cheng, W.: A prototype for a conversational companion for reminiscing about images. Computer, Speech and Language 25(2), 140–157 (2011)
50. Williams, J.D., Young, S.J.: Partially observable Markov decision processes for spoken dialog systems. Computer Speech and Language 21(2), 231–422 (2007)

51. Wilson, M., Knoblich, G.: The case for motor involvement in perceiving conspecifics. Psychological Bulletin 131(3), 460–473 (2005)
52. Worgan, S., Moore, R.K.: Enabling reinforcement learning for open dialogue systems through speech stress detection. Paper Presented at the Fourth International Workshop on Human-Computer Conversation, Bellagio, Italy, October 6-7 (2008)
53. Young, S., Gašić, M., Keizer, S., Mairesse, F., Schatzmann, J., Thomson, B., Yu, K.: The hidden information state model: A practical framework for POMDP-based spoken dialogue management. Computer Speech & Language 24(2), 150–174 (2010)
54. Zen, H., Nose, T., Yamagishi, J., Sako, S., Masuko, T., Black, A.W., Tokuda, K.: The HMM-based speech synthesis system (HTS) version 2.0. Paper Presented at the 6th ISCA Workshop on Speech Synthesis, Bonn, Germany (2007)
55. Zue, V.: Conversational interfaces: advances and challenges. Paper Presented at the EUROSPEECH (1997)

Virtual Butlers and Real People: Styles and Practices in Long-Term Use of a Companion

Sabine Payr

Austrian Research Institute for Artificial Intelligence (OFAI)
Freyung 6/6/7, 1010 Vienna, Austria
sabine.payr@ofai.at

Abstract. In this chapter, we argue that it is already possible, with existing technologies, to go beyond fictional scenarios of virtual butlers or assistive robot companions, and that realistic, long-term studies of their use contribute much needed knowledge about user styles and hence design requirements. Such a study, undertaken by the EU project SERA (Social Engagement with Robots and Agents) is reported, and the data collected are presented, compared, and discussed. The striking difference between idealized personae (such as "Tina") and real users motivated a detailed case study about the frequently observed issue of initiative and floor management. The case study shows the considerable degree to which users shape human-robot interaction with their individual styles. In conclusion, a few such user styles, together with design consequences, are outlined on the basis of the data analysis, with the aim of enriching future scenario descriptions with more realistic personae.

1 Who Is Tina?

Semi-fictional stories like that of "Tina and her Butler" ([1] this volume) are a familiar way to describe use scenarios for technology design. "Tina" is a persona here [2], a single archetypical user as distilled from real user observations and studies and laid down in a narrative to guide design. The fact that the technology described is in some respects futuristic is consistent with the character of the story as an inspiration and orientation for research and development. The problem I have in accepting the story therefore does not reside in the virtual butler, but in the "Tina" persona: she is curiously colour- and featureless, more an empty outline of a person than an archetypical character.

The reason for this lies in the lack of users of any really future technology: if the technology does not exist yet, how can one study what users would do with it? The use of "personae" stems from classic software design tasks, where existing organizations, workflows, and people can be observed doing without the software what the software would then do for them. The archetypical user could be based on the study of a number of real users-to-be, and one could avoid inventing the unreal, idealized user who, like Tina, appears in the narrative as the always happy, perfectly satisfied, and smoothly interacting counterpart to the technology. While the archetypical user can be of considerable help for the designers, the idealized user is

R. Trappl (Ed.): Your Virtual Butler, LNAI 7407, pp. 134–178, 2013.

their enemy: he (or she) could lead them to believe that users are a docile, well-functioning, and homogeneous race at the receiving end of their inventions.

Even if designers are well aware of this trap - how can it be avoided if there are no real users around, if they are developing technologies that do not only satisfy single well-defined needs but have the potential to change lifestyles and cultures, as do the socially assistive robots and (virtual or embodied) companions this book is concerned with? How and where can one observe real users in real life when there is, as yet, nothing for them to use?

Assistive robots (like Car-O-Bot: [3]) have not left the laboratory yet and are neither safe nor functional enough to be tested in uncontrolled real-life situations in their potential users' homes. On the other hand, there are toy robots already on the market (e.g. Paro: [4]; [41]), a few non-mobile robotic interfaces with a handful of functions (like Mindscape's Karotz, formerly Nabaztag, in rabbit form, or Kysoh's Tux Droid in penguin form), plus single-function mobile robotic appliances such as vacuum cleaners and lawn mowers. There is also research being undertaken about people's lives with them (e.g. about the vacuum cleaner Roomba: [6]).

So, in a way, there are already some robots "in the wild", and even if their capabilities fall far short of the full-fledged socially assistive robot or the virtual butler of our story, they could serve as at least a start for studying their users. In this chapter, I will not be concerned primarily with the technical side of the story, i.e. the virtual butler and its functionality, but with the human side. The aim is to give the "Tina" persona more life-likeness and colour, based on knowledge about real users of robotic companions.

Section 2 gives an overview of a field study where data from long-term home use of a robotic companion were collected. Section 3 contains a description and comparison of the data using a range of qualitative criteria. Section 4 discusses, in more detail, the phenomenon of alternating and mixed initiative which turned out, in the analysis, as being an important criterion to distinguish what will be presented, in section 5, as different "styles of usage".

2   The SERA Field Study

2.1   Set-Up[1]

The intention of this field study, undertaken in the framework of the EU-funded FP7 research project SERA (Social Engagement with Robots and Agents, no. 231868, 2009-2010, see http://showcase.project-sera.eu/) was to contribute to filling some gaps in our knowledge about the users of robot companions. We collected audio-visual data on participants' involvement with the robot in their daily lives throughout a period of ten days. This duration allowed enough time for the novelty to wear off and for routine to build.

The project used a portable set-up with a robotic interface. The robot is always on and so can interact at any point in time, thus constituting a continual social presence in the participant's home. As opposed to a computer interface which has to be turned on to be active and remains a passive responder to user action, the embodied interface

---

[1] For a more detailed discussion of the set-up see [7].

is able to actively initiate interactions. The set-up therefore has similarities to the "Tina" scenario which also assumes an "always-on" attending virtual butler which takes the initiative in certain situations.

The scenario chosen for the SERA field study was that of a robot companion in the role of a health and fitness coach, with a view to possible practical uses of assistive robots for example in rehabilitation. The application was built as consistently as possible around this role so that e.g. questions and initiatives of the robot were motivated by its concerns and thus understandable for the participant.

The SERA application was developed to assist older users in adopting and maintaining an exercise routine over time. It was based on the Transtheoretical Model of Behaviour Change [8] in which the change of any kind of behaviour is represented as a process in five stages: pre-contemplation, contemplation, preparation, action, and maintenance. Initially, the application assumed users in the preparation and action phases of a change toward having more physical exercise. It turned out in the data collection, in particular in the interviews, that practically the behaviour of all participants was better described as being in the maintenance stage. The users provided the researchers with a self-devised activity plan before the study. It contained details of what exercise (sports, walking, gardening etc.) they had planned for the 10 day trial period. This plan served as the knowledge base for the robot's interactions.

This application is, in many aspects, similar to the FitTrack screen-based system [9, 10] or the AUTOM robot [5]. FitTrack was a purely screen-based application that users started when they wanted rather than a social presence. The SERA field study hypothesised that the robotic set-up would emphasise the persuasive and monitoring effect. A central goal of the study was to explore the novel phenomenon of always-on, socially aware, and pro-active companions in the home of older persons.

The system used in the field study consisted of a Nabaztag (the predecessor of the Karotz, see http://www.karotz.com) as a robotic frontend. The Nabaztag comes in the form of a rabbit with movable ears and flashing coloured lights on its front. It was mounted, together with a PC and periphery, in a piece of transportable furniture (see Fig. 1). The periphery consisted of a webcam for data collection and an array microphone which was intended for speech recognition (not implemented). The background for the study was the idea of having robotic companions also function as a conversational frontend to a "smart home", equipped with sensors to monitor the user's whereabouts and well-being. We simulated such a scenario with a few sensors: a PIR motion sensor and a switch in a key hook. The intention was that participants should store their house keys on this hook for the trial period, so that the system could monitor when the subject left the house and came back, in acccordance with the activity-related application. The robot communicated with a synthesised voice.

For user input, we used yes/no-buttons in the first iteration of the study and, for the second and third iteration, the built-in RFID-reader of the Nabaztag. Participants received a set of flashcards each equipped with an RFID-tag. The cards bore words, numbers and symbols suitable for the different topics and questions that could occur in the system's dialogs: multi-purpose smileys (looking friendly, neutral, unfriendly) for yes/don't know/no, good/neutral/bad etc.; numbers for rating (1 to 5), numbers for minutes of activity (10 to 60), and some additional commands and possible topics (message, weather, system, repeat, add-to-log, and, in iteration 3, an "aargh!"/reset/stop card).

Collection of video data was only done when the user consented to it by pressing a button. This button did not start the recording per se (which was instead triggered by the sensors) but did affect whether the video data were permanently stored on the local harddisk. In this way it was possible to record also the beginnings of interaction before the video button was pressed.

The dialog manager was a state-based system written in Java. The dialog state networks were developed to be self-contained and closed in that there had to be a path for every possible input, including no input. The aim was to develop coherent dialog that imitated the intuitive strategies employed in human-human conversations and that continued the interaction whatever the user input.

Fig. 1. SERA Field Study setup in a participant's home

2.2   Participants

Recruitment of the participants was done via a local older persons' advisory group Sheffield 50+[2]. Potential participants were contacted using a flyer with details of the project via email and post. The initial recruitment criteria were that the participants were over 50 years of age and healthy with no known pre-existing condition which placed restrictions on doing exercise. They had to be willing to be video-recorded and to have the system in their homes for a 10 day period. The participants recruited for the project are shown in table 1 along with their demographic details and in which iterations they were involved.

Table 1. Participant information: participant number, sex, age, whether they live on their own or with others and in which iterations they were involved

Participant	Sex	Age	Live alone?	Iterations
P1	F	65	Y	1, 2, 3
P2	F	50+	N (1 other)	1, 2, 3
P3	F	60	Y	1, 2, 3
P4	F	50+	N (1 other)	2, 3
P5	M	76	N (1 other)	2, 3
P6	M	71	N (1 other)	3

The participants were visited by one of the researchers who explained the project in more detail and collected their consent to participate when appropriate. Before the trial began, the participants provided the researcher with a self-devised activity plan for the trial period which was then input into the system. The plan detailed their planned activities for the period including any other diary events which they were happy to provide and which could form the basis of an interaction with the robot.

The robot was installed in the users' homes in a position where the participant was happy and that maximised privacy for them, the other people who lived in the house and any visitors. The initial site suggested was in the participant's hallway to allow reasonable function of the set-up as storage for the participants' house keys, and as the least intrusive position, ensuring frequent passage but less sustained presence. The priority in positioning the system was placed on the participant's preference. On installation of the robot, the system was explained to the participant in terms of the interaction method and what types of interactions the system would have with them. The participants were given a booklet of instructions in case they needed some clarification of how the system worked along with all the contact details for the researchers. The participants were contacted after three days to ensure that they were happy to continue with the trial and also to make sure that the technology was functioning as expected.

---

[2] http://www.sheffield50plus.co.uk

From that point until the end of the trial, the participants were not contacted by the researchers unless they initiated contact with questions, problems or organisational issues. There was no remote access to the rabbit, except for sending messages to the robot, and therefore no real time viewing or interference in the function of the system. In addition to having videoed data for analysis the participants were left with a notebook if they wished to make notes on what they liked or disliked about the robot or the trial itself. The notes were then used to help prompt questions during the follow-up interview which took place after the trial had finished.

2.3   Method of Analysis

Whenever the participants chose to record an interaction, the images from the video camera were stored. At the same time, logfiles of the interactions were written and stored in iterations 2 and 3. Additonally, open interviews were made with all participants after each iteration, audio-recorded and transcribed.

Several research teams analysed the data or part of them during the project's lifetime using different methods, e.g. content analysis of the interviews [11, 12] and coding for non-verbal signals [13]. Interaction analysis of individual video sequences from iteration 1 and 2 allowed to bring up issues like routine building [14], closings [15] and topic management [16], and also led to methodological considerations about the transfer of experience to design [17, 18, 19]. A wealth of observations and characterizations of interactions and users became obvious in project-internal discussions of the data, but none of the methods used seemed to be able to capture and describe this abundance, and in particular the strong inter-individual differences between subjects that were observed. This deficit has motivated the study presented here: what could and should be coded to characterize interactional behaviour both over a stretch of time and on the level of the individual interaction, without losing the relationship between the two? Which codes were reliable without losing the richness of observable behaviour? How to make visible and verifiable the informal impressions of individual user styles?

The primary codes used in this study were the "hard facts" that could be found both in the video sequences and the logfiles: date and time of the interaction, mode of communication, the dialog scripts that were activated, the people present at the time of the interaction, and the overall initiative (who started the interaction?). The following table lists these categories with their dimensions:

Case studies such as the ones in [16] and below in section 4 show that overall initiative is much too coarse a category to capture the problem of floor management. Therefore the category "Topic management" was introduced, mainly in order to be able to answer the question of how frequent topic changes and topic negotiations were in the data, and hence how relevant an issue they are for dialog management in conversational companions.

Table 2. Coding categories

Category	Dimensions	Note
Day and Time	day of trial (usually 1 to 10), 1-hour time slots	multiple videos of one extended interaction were observed and counted as one interaction
Persons present	User only, partner, other persons, researcher, unknown	only 1 choice for the whole sequence
Interaction mode	Button (for iter.1), RFID card (iter. 2 and 3), Talk, None	combinations of button + talk or RFID + talk are possible (and frequent)
Dialog scripts	mainly, the dialog types as discussed in section 3, with some more distinctions	multiple scripts can be activated during an interaction.
Initiative	User, robot	codes the overall initiative - who started the interaction?
Topic management	proposed, accepted, refused (each for user and robot)	multiple topic changes can occur throughout an interaction; topic changes made by the robot "normally" as part of a complex dialog (e.g. in the GoodMorning dialog) were not coded.

The database tool used for this study also allows to add and retrieve any kind of textual information. It was therefore possible to add unlimited free notes and keywords which was done regularly during the repeated viewings of the video sequences. Some of the keywords developed into categories, e.g. the ways of closing as used in [15], while other keywords served directly for finding, filtering and comparing (or contrasting) records. To date, there are still some keywords and keyword groups that could lead to further specific analyses e.g. with regard to conversational repair activities and their success or failure, both by robot and human. Only some of these notes and keywords have been followed up in enough detail to enter into the present study.

Although a total of over 300 video sequences, of which 174 in iteration 3, could be considered a sufficient basis for statistical analyses of the data, this would make no sense because they only stem from six subjects. We did some counting and numerical comparison for a number of the coded categories, but we intentionally refrain from any statistical generalizations about user behaviour.

3   Description of the Data

3.1   Number of Interactions in Iteration 3

The present study focuses on the data collected in iteration 3 of the field study. Data from other iterations were used for comparison where this seemed useful. In iteration

3, there were six participants. P1, P2 and P3 had participated in both previous iterations, P4 and P5 in iteration 2, while P6 was new. P5 and P6 are male. P1, P3, and P4 are living alone, whereas the others live with their partners (see table 1 above). In [7], only the video recordings are listed as data, while in our analysis, the logfiles of the interactions were also taken into account, especially in order to include P3 in the analysis who, although she had given prior consent, never switched on the camera so that there are no video data from her interaction. The study of the logfile however shows that she had a considerable number of interactions, too. The logfiles show unrecorded episodes for other participants as well. In some cases, the robot starts a dialog but the participants do not respond and therefore do not record such an episode.

Table 3. Overview of interactions in iteration 3

	video	no video	total
P1	7	0	7
P2	26	7	33
P3	0	28	28
P4	14	4	18
P5	31	0	31
P6	51	6	57
all participants	129	45	174

Table 4. Recordings per iteration and participant (from [7])

Iteration	Participant	N videos (participant only)	N videos (with researchers)	Total
1	1	35	4	39
1	2	10	3	13
1	3	7	7	14
total	3 participants	52	14	66
2	1	28	0	28
2	2	14	1	15
2	3	5	3	8
2	4	25	4	29
2	5	36	3	39
total	5 participants	108	11	119
3	1	6	1	7
3	2	25	1	26
3	3	0	2	2
3	4	12	2	14
3	5	30	1	31
3	6	39	12	51
total	6 participants	112	19	131

The number of episodes for P1 is small because of technical troubles that made it necessary to break off the data collection. In the first two iterations, P1 had been very active with 35 and 28 recordings, respectively. The following table gives an overview of videos recordings in all iterations.

3.2   Persons Present

As mentioned above, only a minority of participants live alone. Beside the co-habitants, there are also other persons who are present at some time or other during the interactions with the robot: the researchers, guests, or other members of the family.

The following chart (Fig. 2) shows the distribution of these events. For episodes where no video recording is present, the status is obviously "unknown".

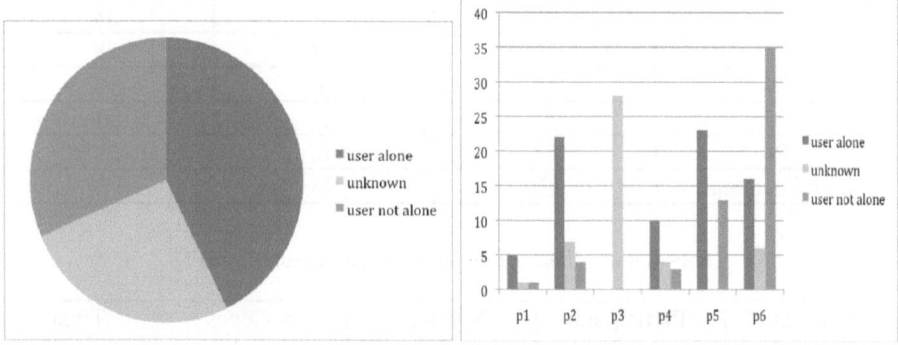

Fig. 2. Persons present during interactions: overall (left) and by participant (right)

As there are no video recordings of P3, we do not know whether there were other persons present at any time. P6 is much more often in company than alone when he[3] interacts with the robot, the others are more often alone than not.

The proportion of episodes where the test subject is not alone is higher than we had expected. The scenario of the field study was oriented toward the single participant. Neither the dialogs nor the perceptive capabilities of the robot prepared it for the presence of third parties in the experiment.

Although it was clear who in each household was the participant in the study, the co-habitants also participated to some degree. Sometimes they were present, watching and also commenting on the interaction. Sometimes they were in a different room, and the participants had two interactions - one with the robot and one with the partner - going on at the same time, often talking about the robot or commenting their own interaction with it. In one case (in iteration 1) the participant (P2) complained afterwards that her husband regularly rose earlier and thus became the addressee of the robot's "Good Morning!" greeting and dialog.

---

[3] Male and female personal pronouns are used according to the gender of the participant.

When guests or other family members (e.g. grandchildren) were present, they were "shown off" the rabbit and assisted as an audience, talking with the participant about it. On such occasions, participants tended to initiate a variety of dialogs and to let themselves be drawn into vivid social interaction (e.g. talking, showing strong facial expressions) so that these interactions make the impression of set-up "performances" for the benefit of the third person, cf. [14].

Most scenarios for assistive robots are based on the owner or user living alone, and assume therefore a dyadic relationship. Our small sample (see Table 3 above) with 4 out of 6 persons, of which both males, co-habiting with another person, does not contradict demographic facts, e.g. those of Austria:

Table 5. Living arrangements of older persons in Austria, by gender, 2010, in percent of the gender and age group (Source: Statistik Austria)

in %	Age 70-79	Age 80+
Men, in partnership	79,4	63,1
Men, living alone	16,4	27,5
Women, in partnership	46,2	18,1
Women, living alone	40,7	58,4

Note: the numbers do not add up to 100 % because other living arrangements are not reproduced here.

The table shows that the typical scenario of a robot in a single-person household captures only a minority of cases, except for women in their eighties. Even considering that, in absolute numbers, there are many more women in this age group than men (578 900 vs. 392 200 in Austria, 2010), it remains true that a large majority of the older population share their homes with a partner.

While these proportions will probably change over the next few decades when the younger generations who now live in single-person households more often than the older ones grow old in their turn, taking their living arrangements into the third and fourth age, new trends to reverse that development may not be ignored either: already there are emerging initiatives of private house-sharing among older persons or between older and younger persons (see http://www.alternative living.org/aboutus.html for just one out of many examples).

A consequence of these demographic facts and trends is that the design of assistive robots has to take into account the variety of living arrangements of the aging population. The robot is not necessarily one person's companion, but more often than not a household companion. Even if its user in the narrow sense may be a single person, other persons are likely to be around at times, to be ignored and/or acknowledged by the robot.

The capability of distinguishing different people - visually, but also by voice - is therefore a priority in the design of domestic companions. Furthermore, the behaviour of a companion robot has to adapt to the different social situations: some topics and services are private and should not be brought up when other persons are present. On the contrary, other topics (e.g. hints to events) are particularly appropriate to initiate conversations with more than one user.

3.3   Time of Day

In the search for patterns in the participants' interactions with the robot, we also analysed the times of day at which the interactions took place. The following diagram accumulates these data for all datasets from iteration 3.

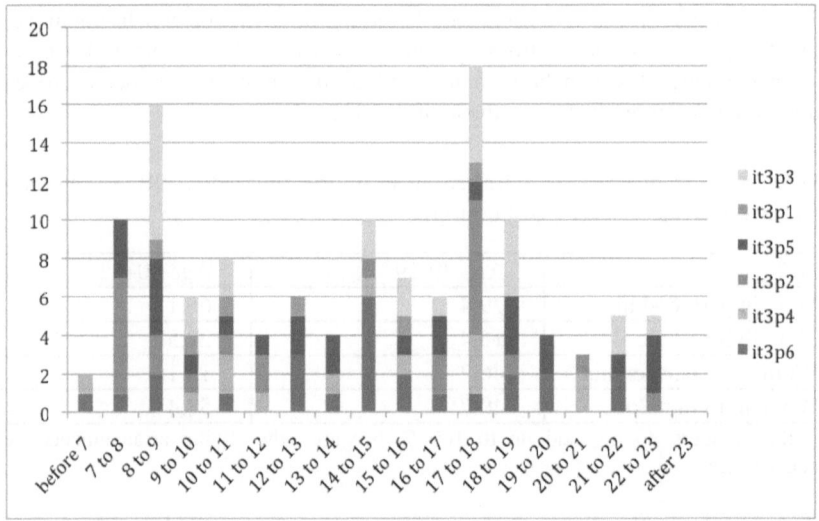

Fig. 3. Distribution of interactions over the day, all participants, iter. 3

The peaks in the morning and early evening are partly due to those participants who are still professionally active outside the home. The other reason for the higher number of interactions in the morning and in late afternoon is however the rabbit itself, because it was designed to initiate dialogs at these times of the days, notably the GoodMorning and the Summary dialog (see below, Dialog Types).

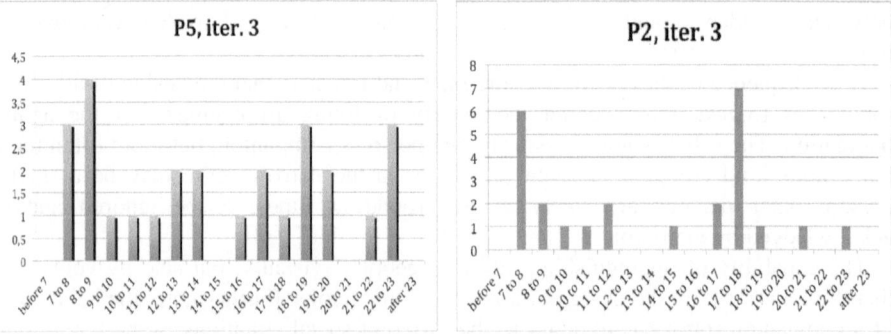

Fig. 4. Distribution of interactions over the day, P5 and P2, iteration 3

The charts in Fig. 4 show the daily interaction patterns for two participants in iteration 3. Both participants have a higher frequency of interactions in the morning, when the rabbit typically initiates the GoodMorning dialog. The rest of P5's interactions are then distributed more evenly throughout the day when compared to P2. P2 has another high interaction slot in the late afternoon.

3.4   Dialog Types

There were 8 types of dialog which are described below. An example for each dialog is reprinted from the logfiles, i.e. reproducing the RFID input, but not participants' verbal utterances.

GoodMorning: this dialog is launched by a signal from the PIR motion sensor at the first appearance of a person in the morning.

GoodMorning dialog: it3_P2_FOct5_0748s45.mov

```
<e k8055:PIR                                          <no state>
                                             Oct5_0748:45:156/>
<e mc: Good morning, how are you?            Oct5_0748:45:156/>
<e usr:"smile"
                                             Oct5_0748:58:359/>
<e mc: If it's okay to record you now,
please could you press the video button?     Oct5_0748:59:500/>
Would you like to hear what the weather
forecast is today?
<e k8055:PIR                                      AskWeatherRFID
                                             Oct5_0748:59:906/>

<e k8055:PIR                                      AskWeatherRFID
                                             Oct5_0749:5:156/>

<e k8055:VIDEO                                    AskWeatherRFID
                                             Oct5_0749:5:156/>
<e mc: Video recording on.                   Oct5_0749:5:156/>

<e usr:"smile"                               Oct5_0749:7:906/>

<e mc: The weather today is Mostly dry
with increasing amounts of sunshine.         Oct5_0749:13:375/>
<e mc: Some people find it useful to weigh   Oct5_0749:19:375/>
themselves daily as part of their exercise
routine. I hope you don't mind me asking
but will you be weighing yourself today?


<e usr:"frown"                               Oct5_0749:29:171/>
<e k8055:PIR                                   RemindWeighingRFID
                                             Oct5_0749:30:156/>

<e mc: You haven't got any exercise
planned for today in your diary. If you do   Oct5_0749:30:875/>
some exercise then let me know and I can
add it to your activity log.
<e mc: Unless you'd like to talk about
anything else, I'll talk to you later. Bye   Oct5_0749:41:875/>

<e k8055:PIR                                     EndMorningRFID
                                             Oct5_0749:43:718/>
```

The dialog has a variant for days on which there is an entry in the activity plan. The example shows that not only the GoodMorning dialog as a whole is initiated by the rabbit, but also the different topics of which it consists: weather, weighing oneself, and activity for the day. In the later analysis of dialog types and topics covered this multitude of topics in the GoodMorning dialog is ignored. As will be seen in the other dialog types, the request to switch on the camera is part of every dialog. We will therefore, in the following sections, also ignore it as a topic.

GoingOut: this dialog type is triggered by the switch in the key hook, and initiated when the keys are taken off the hook. It has two varieties, depending on whether an activity for this day and (approximate) time has been found in the activity plan of the participant, as in the following example:

GoingOut (known activity): it3_P4_HOct2_1327s48.mov

```
<e k8055:KEYS-off                              GoodMorningRFID
                                          Oct2_1327:48:656/>

mc: Hello. If you're okay to be
videoed, please could you just put        Oct2_1327:48:656/>
the video button on as you go
past?
mc: From your plan it looks like          Oct2_1327:48:656/>
you're going to gardening. See you
soon.
<e k8055:PIR                                   OutKnownRFID
                                          Oct2_1327:53:359/>
<e k8055:VIDEO                                 GoodMorningRFID
                                          Oct2_1327:56:921/>
<e mc: Video recording on.                Oct2_1327:56:921/>
```

The general version of this dialog was more frequent, however:

GoingOut (unknown activity): it3 P3, rec.no. 330[4]

```
<e k8055:PIR                                        <no state>
                                          Oct18_2240:34:375/>
<e k8055:KEYS-off                                   <no state>
                                          Oct18_2240:34:437/>
<e mc: Hello. If you feel okay to be      Oct18_2240:34:437/>
videoed, could you please press the video
button on your way past?
<e mc: Are you going out?                  Oct18_2240:34:437/>
<e k8055:PIR                                   OutUnknownRFID
                                          Oct18_2240:52:265/>
<e usr:"neutral"                          Oct18_2240:56:250/>
<e mc: Okay, have a good time. Bye.       Oct18_2240:57:484/>
<e k8055:PIR                              ConfirmGoingOutRFID
                                          Oct18_2241:7:515/>
```

---

[4] As mentioned earlier, P3 did not turn on the video throughout the trial period. The record number in the database serves as reference in her case instead of the video file name generated at storage.

There were several pecularities with the GoingOut dialog in the field test:

- One participant did not want to leave her keys in a new unusual place. She used a placeholder to hang on the key hook, but she hardly ever thought of taking it off when leaving the house.
- When participants were really going out and took the key off the hook for that purpose, they often did not stop to interact with the rabbit or to turn on the video recording.

However, the most frequent type of use of the keys and the key hook seemed to be to trigger an interaction, to "wake" the rabbit, or the like (see discussion of this practice below). The keys were put back immediately after having been taken off, followed by the introduction of a different topic. As motivation for this action, we can assume, in some cases (especially P4), confusion about how to initiate an interaction (e.g. after unsuccessful attempts), in other cases the wish to show off the functions of the rabbit for the benefit of third persons (e.g. P2 in iteration 1, P6 in iteration 3).

ComingHome: this dialog corresponded to the GoingOut dialog; it also had variants for both "coming home from a planned activity" and "coming home from an unknown activity":

ComingHome (known activity): it3_P4_HSeP24_2054s38.mov

```
<e k8055:KEYS-on                    OutKnownRFID SeP24_2057:36:671/>
<e mc:  Hello.  Welcome  home.  If             SeP24_2057:36:671/>
you're okay to be videoed, please
press the video button.
<e mc: Did you have a good time?               SeP24_2057:36:671/>
walking the dog?
<e k8055:PIR                                    DiscussActivityRFID
                                                SeP24_2057:46:125/>
```

ComingHome (unknown activity): it3_P6_FNov5_1852s22.mov

```
<e k8055:PIR                       <no state> Nov5_1852:22:850/>
<e k8055:KEYS-on                   <no state> Nov5_1852:31:162/>
<e mc: Hello. Welcome home. If you're         Nov5_1852:31:162/>
okay to be videoed, please press the
video button.
<e mc: Did you have a good time?              Nov5_1852:31:162/>
<e k8055:PIR                       DiscussNullActivityRFID
                                              Nov5_1852:32:100/>
<e k8055:VIDEO                     DiscussNullActivityRFID
                                              Nov5_1852:38:287/>
<e mc: Video recording on.                    Nov5_1852:38:287/>
<e k8055:PIR                       DiscussNullActivityRFID
                                              Nov5_1852:40:537/>
<e usr:"neutral"                              Nov5_1852:44:990/>
<e mc:  Would  you  like  me  to  add         Nov5_1852:46:365/>
something to your exercise log?
<e k8055:PIR                                  InAddToLogRFID
                                              Nov5_1852:53:725/>
<e usr:"neutral"                              Nov5_1852:54:319/>
<e mc: How many minutes of exercise           Nov5_1852:55:365/>
would you like to add to your log?
<e k8055:PIR                                  AddToLogRFID
                                              Nov5_1853:6:287/>
```

The ComingHome dialog leads on to the AddtoLog, on the assumption that an outdoor activity of the user often corresponds to some physical exercise.

Although both GoingOut and ComingHome dialogs are triggered by an action of the user (taking off and putting back the keys), they are considered as initiated by the robot in our analysis. The reason is that manipulating the keys is not a communicative action per se. It is the rabbit that "uses" this event to start a dialog, while the user under normal circumstances does not intend to interact.

As noted above, however, some of our field study participants "re-invented" the manipulation of their keys as a communicative action. They took off and put back the keys without leaving the house in-between, one action almost immediately following the other. It is clear that they used the keys to initiate an interaction. One user (P1) inversed this practice to avoid the GoingOut/ComingHome dialog when she intended to leave the house only for a short time, e.g. to empty the trashbin: she had ready and used a second set of keys on these occasions.

The field study setup had not foreseen this use of the key switch: the users came up with a new, creative practice in interacting with their companion robot for their own purposes. By using the key switch to trigger certain dialogs, the key was transformed into a semiotic artifact [20] that acquired specific sign-like qualities and meanings in the action of entering and leaving the house. The ability of humans to create semiotic structure in their environment, including whatever representations and material objects there are, is a field in which, at the time being, intelligent artifacts are simply helpless.

AddtoLog: More often than in conjunction with ComingHome, the AddtoLog dialog was initiated by the users. The rabbit "understood" both the dedicated RFID-card ("Add to log") and any of the 10 to 60 number cards as an intention of the user to add a certain amount of minutes to the exercise log for that day.

AddtoLog: it3 P3, rec.no. 330

```
<e usr:"addtolog"                                    Oct18_2241:18:390/>
<e k8055:PIR                         <no state> Oct18_2241:29:140/>
<e usr:"smile"                                       Oct18_2241:29:453/>
<e mc: Hello?                                        Oct18_2241:29:453/>
<e usr:"addtolog"                                    Oct18_2241:33:953/>
<e   mc: If you're okay to be                    Oct18_2241:35:31/>
videoed, please could you just
press the video button?. Would
you like me to add something to
your exercise log?
<e k8055:PIR                                    AskAddToLogRFID
                                             Oct18_2241:40:781/>
<e usr:"smile"                                    Oct18_2241:48:0/>
<e   mc: How  many  minutes  of                  Oct18_2241:49:31/>
exercise would you like to add to
your log?
<e k8055:PIR                         AddToLogRFID Oct18_2241:52:593/>
<e usr:"60"                                          Oct18_2241:55:718/>
<e mc: 60 minutes of activity?                       Oct18_2241:57:31/>
<e usr:"addtolog"                                    Oct18_2242:2:656/>
<e k8055:PIR                         StateAmountExerciseRFID
                                             Oct18_2242:3:656/>
<e mc: I'll put that in your log                 Oct18_2242:4:31/>
now.
```

```
<e k8055:PIR                                              PutInLogRFID
                                                   Oct18_2242:8:906/>
<e usr:"smile"                                     Oct18_2242:10:859/>
<e mc: That makes a total of 60                    Oct18_2242:12:31/>
minutes of exercise so far today.
<e k8055:PIR                                          TotalAfterAddRFID
                                                   Oct18_2242:15:468/>
<e usr:"addtolog"                                  Oct18_2242:16:500/>
<e mc: Would you like me to add                    Oct18_2242:18:31/>
something to your exercise log?
<e k8055:PIR                                           AskAddToLogRFID
                                                   Oct18_2242:20:718/>
<e usr:"smile"

                              AskAddToLogRFID Oct18_2242:27:906/>
<e  mc:  How  many  minutes  of                    Oct18_2242:29:31/>
exercise would you like to add to
your log?
<e usr:"60"                                        Oct18_2242:31:31/>
<e mc: 60 minutes of activity?                     Oct18_2242:34:31/>
<e mc: I'll put that in your log                   Oct18_2242:37:531/>
now.
<e mc: That makes a total of 120                   Oct18_2242:41:31/>
minutes of exercise so far today.
<e mc: Unless you'd like to talk                   Oct18_2242:47:531/>
about anything else, I'll talk to
you later.
<e k8055:PIR                                            EndAddToLogRFID
                                                   Oct18_2242:49:656/>
```

This example shows one of the cases where participants repeated the add-to-log sequence which became necessary whenever they wanted to add more than the 60 minutes which was the maximum possible to input with a single RFID-card.

Summary dialog: This dialog can be either user- or robot-initiated. At a certain time of day, the robot actively starts a dialog, gives feedback about the amount of exercise accumulated throughout the day, and asks users to rate hwo they feel. The user can request this dialog at any time during the day.

Summary: it3_P2_FOct3_2011s41.mov

```
<e k8055:PIR                                              <no state>
                                                   Oct3_2011:41:703/>
<e mc: Hello. Have you got a couple of
minutes for a chat?  Oct3_2011:41:703/>
<e usr:"smile"

                                                   Oct3_2011:48:640/>
<e mc: If you're okay to be recorded,              Oct3_2011:49:812/>
please could you press the video button?
My record shows that today has been a day
off exercise. How are you feeling?
<e k8055:PIR                                       NoExerciseTotalRFID
                                                   Oct3_2011:52:343/>
<e k8055:VIDEO                                      NoExerciseTotalRFID
                                                   Oct3_2011:53:281/>
<e mc: Video recording on.                         Oct3_2011:53:281/>
```

```
<e mc: If you had to give the way you are          Oct3_2012:2:812/>
feeling a number between 1 and 5, where 1
is really awful and 5 is really great,
then where would you place yourself
today?
<e usr:"neutral"
                                                   Oct3_2012:3:15/>
<e k8055:PIR                                        ExplainAskRateRFID
                                                   Oct3_2012:6:906/>
<e mc: Oh..  I was expecting a rating              Oct3_2012:13:812/>
between 1 and 5. Please could you use the
rating cards to rate how you're feeling?
<e k8055:PIR                                             GetRatingRFID
                                                   Oct3_2012:20:31/>
<e usr:"2"                                          Oct3_2012:20:734/>
<e mc: 2. Oh. Perhaps things will go               Oct3_2012:23:812/>
better tomorrow..  I'll put that rating
in your log.
<e mc: Thanks then. Unless there's                 Oct3_2012:32:812/>
anything you'd like to talk about, I'll
see you later.
<e k8055:PIR                                             FinishEvalRFID
                                                   Oct3_2012:33:656/>
```

The example shows a case where the dialog is initiated by the rabbit. P2 answers the first - open - question "How are you feeling?" for which one of the Smiley cards (good - bad - neutral) is indeed expected as an answer. However, the dialog is designed in such a way that it does not insist on user input where this is not absolutely necessary, and so the rabbit has gone on to the rating question in the meantime, which requests a number card as input.

Weather: The current weather report is part of the GoodMorning dialog, but the user can also initiate this report with an RFID card at any time.

Weather: it3_P6_FNov5_1427s20.mov

```
<e k8055:PIR                      <no state> Nov5_1427:30:834/>
<e k8055:PIR                      <no state> Nov5_1427:42:834/>
<e usr:"smile"                               Nov5_1427:43:240/>
<e mc: Hello?                                Nov5_1427:43:240/>
<e usr:"smile"                               Nov5_1427:53:990/>
<e mc: If you're okay to be videoed          Nov5_1427:55:115/>
now, please could you press the video
button?.  How are you?
<e k8055:PIR                                      ChatRabbitRFID
                                             Nov5_1427:57:22/>
<e k8055:VIDEO                                    ChatRabbitRFID
                                             Nov5_1427:59:209/>
<e mc: Video recording on.                   Nov5_1427:59:209/>
<e k8055:PIR                                      ChatRabbitRFID
                                             Nov5_1428:7:84/>
<e usr:"smile"                               Nov5_1428:8:225/>
<e k8055:PIR                                      ChatRabbitRFID
                                             Nov5_1428:14:897/>
```

```
<e mc: If you want to, we could talk          Nov5_1428:15:615/>
about the weather, or I could check
for a new message or read out the
latest old message. I could give you
some information about the system, or
I could add more minutes to your log
or give you a summary of what's in
there already. If you'd like to know
about any of that then just show me
the corresponding card.

<e usr:"weather"                              Nov5_1428:17:506/>

<e k8055:PIR                                    RemindTopicsRFID
                                              Nov5_1428:22:959/>
<e usr:"weather"                              Nov5_1428:36:959/>

<e mc: The up to date weather forecast        Nov5_1428:39:631/>
from the Met Office is Feeling cooler
than yesterday, and after a breezy
start the wind will gradually ease.
There will be sunny intervals and
scattered showers, with the showers
perhaps turning heavy at times.
Maximum temperature 12 &deg;C.
<e k8055:PIR                                     GetWeatherRFID
                                              Nov5_1428:46:22/>
```

This sequence starts with a general user initiative: when the user starts an interaction by showing any card other than one that directly introduces a topic, the rabbit goes into an equally general opening sequence that lays out the possibilities of topics to choose from. P6 here chooses the weather topic.

Recommendation (Message): this dialog can also be user- or robot-initiated. When a new message is present on the server, the robot initiates a dialog whenever the user's presence is detected. When the user initiates the dialog with the RFID card, the robot either delivers a new message if there is one, or asks whether the last (heard) message should be repeated. The messages themselves are "handcrafted" by the research team and tailored to the interests of the individual user where they are known. In the first two iterations, the authorship of the message and the nature of the robot as transmitter were made explicit. In the third iteration, the messages were authored as the rabbit's own recommendations and from the rabbit's own perspective, e.g. by adding comments from a rabbit's point of view. The following sequence is robot-initiated.

Recommendation: it3, P3 (no video), rec.no. 327

```
<o k8055:PIR                        <no state> Nov5_1608:58:84/>

<e mc: I've just found something that          Nov5_1608:58:84/>
you might like here.
<e mc: Would you like to hear it?              Nov5_1608:58:84/>

<e k8055:PIR                                     HearNewRecRFID
                                              Nov5_1609:6:178/>
<e mc: Would you like to hear the new         Nov5_1609:11:178/>
recommendation I've found for you?

<e usr:"smile"                                Nov5_1609:18:975/>
```

```
<e mc: If you don't want to go to the        Nov5_1609:20:178/>
Three Merry Lads tonight, there's an
alternative  family  bonfire  tomorrow
afternoon at Our Cow Molly's ice cream
farm in Dungworth with fire engine rides
from 2 o'clock and the bonfire is lit at
5 o'clock.. Do you think you might be
interested in that?
<e k8055:PIR                  SayRecRFID Nov5_1609:28:865/>

<e k8055:PIR                                 SayRecRFID
                                    Nov5_1609:43:365/>
<e mc: If you're wondering how to     Nov5_1609:44:678/>
respond then perhaps you could use the
smile or frown face for yes or no or use
the 1 to 5 cards to show how interested
you are.
<e k8055:PIR                                 SayRecRFID
                                    Nov5_1609:53:53/>
<e usr:"smile"                        Nov5_1609:56:475/>

<e mc: okay, thanks.  I'll try and find     Nov5_1609:57:678/>
something else that I can tell you about
tomorrow.
<e mc: Unless you'd like to talk about     Nov5_1610:5:678/>
anything else, I'll say bye for now.

<e k8055:PIR                                 EndRecRFID
                                    Nov5_1610:11:428/>
```

System: this dialog can only be user-initiated by an RFID card. It was already present in the first iteration, where it was initiated by pressing the in-built button of the Nabaztag. The idea of this dialog in the first iteration was to give users the opportunity to take the initiative and "make" the rabbit perform - e.g., for visitors. At the same time, this dialog is a quick help to operating the rabbit.

it3_P6_FNov5_1427s20.mov

```
<e usr:"system"                       Nov5_1430:20:459/>

<e mc: At any time you can get my     Nov5_1430:21:631/>
attention by letting me see the
cards with the faces on. After
that then I can give you your
messages, a weather forecast, add
minutes into your exercise log or
give you a summary of how much
exercise is in there for today,
yesterday or in total.



<e k8055:PIR                    FurtherSystemInfoRFID
                                    Nov5_1430:23:522/>

<e k8055:PIR              <no state> Nov5_1430:57:84/>
```

The sequence shown here is part of the long interaction from which we also took the "weather" sequence above.

3.5   Distribution and Frequency of Dialog Types

We wanted to know how many different dialogs individual participants had with the robot. "Dialog" here is used in a technical sense to refer to the robot's different script units, and not in the sense of conversations. More than one dialog could be activated during an interaction, which is why the total number (in Fig. 7) exceeds the number of interactions.

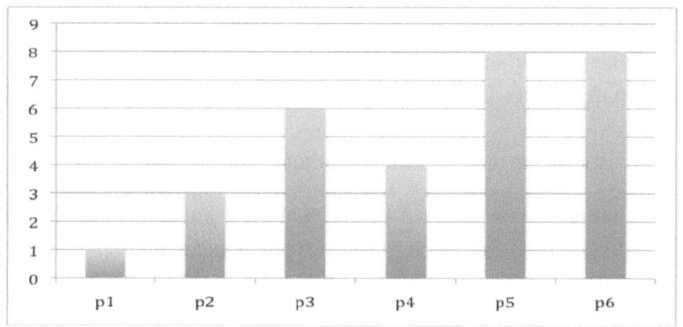

Fig. 5. Number of different dialog types per participant, iter. 3

In order to better reflect the habitual usage of the robot, the diagram shows only the number of dialog types that users had more than once. Participants were very different in this respect: while P5 and P6 had all types of dialogs at one time or the other, and more than once, P1 - the other extreme - only had a single type (but note the interrupted data collection for P1 in iteration 3). P2 and P4 also had only a limited range of different interactions with the robot, with P3 taking a middle position.

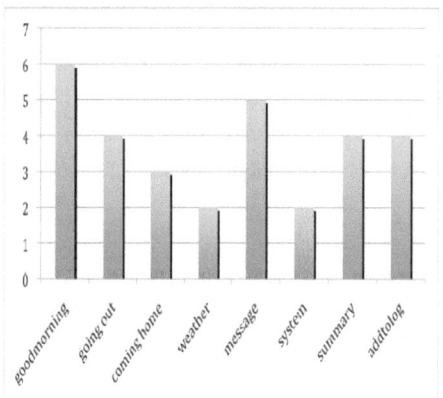

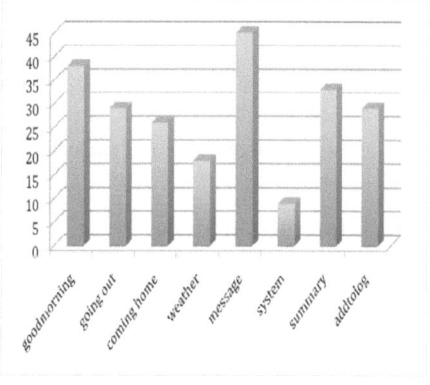

Fig. 6. How many participants had a dialog of type X?

Fig. 7. How many dialogs of type X were recorded in iteration 3?

Figures 6 and 7 show the distribution of dialog types by number of participants (left column) and the overall frequency of the different dialog types (right column). P2 and P3 are again quite similar in their behaviour: the three most frequent dialog types they had were GoodMorning, Message, and Summary.

The right column shows that for all participants taken together, the Message dialog was the most frequent in absolute numbers. It is also high in the distribution among participants. We can say, after this analysis, that

- all participants (n = 6) had at least one GoodMorning dialog,
- all but one participants (n = 5) had the Message dialog more than once,
- 3 to 4 participants had Summary, GoingOut, ComingHome, and AddtoLog dialogs,
- only 2 participants also had the Weather and System dialogs.

In fig. 8, we compare again the two participants, P2 and P5, here for the variety of dialogs they had. The predominance of three types is clear for P2. We will come back to discuss this distribution, comparing the same participants, in the section on initiative.

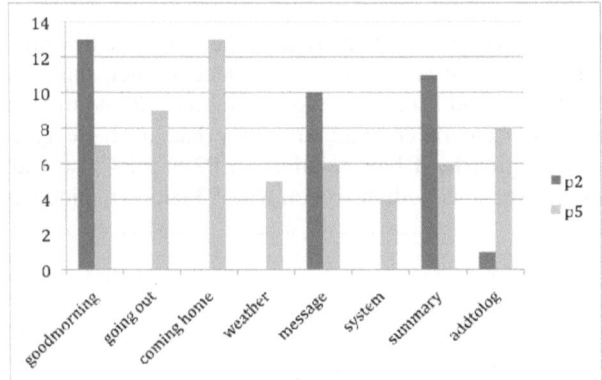

Fig. 8. Number and frequency of dialog types for P2 and P5, iteration 3

3.6   Interaction Mode

In iteration 1, participants had only yes/no buttons to interact with the Nabaztag. In iteration 2 and 3, they had cards with symbols and words, each with an RFID tag attached which could be read by the Nabaztag's in-built RFID reader. Participants also talked with the robot although it could not recognize or understand speech. Talk quantity ranged from single-word utterances, e.g. "Bye", to whole arguments.

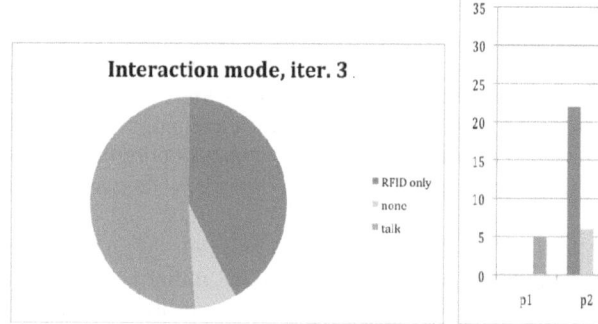

Fig. 9. Mode of interaction in iteration 3, without P3; "talk" here is with or without simultaneous use of RFID cards in an interaction.

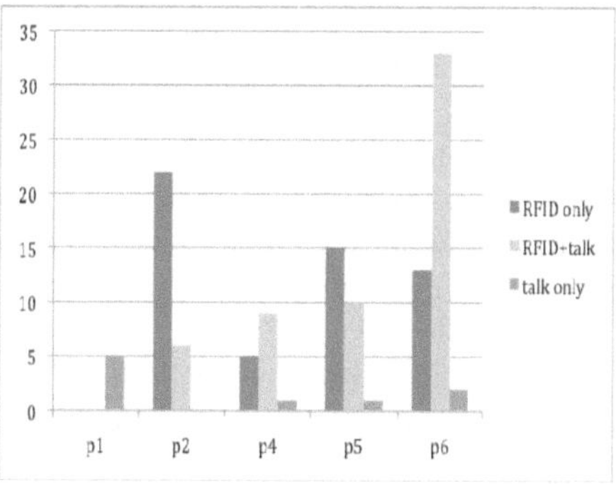

Fig. 10. Mode of interaction per participant, iteration 3, without P3.

The left diagram shows that in roughly half of the interactions, participants talked to the Nabaztag to some extent. These interactions include a few where participants only talked without using the RFID cards. In particular, P1, although briefed and trained like the others, hardly ever used the RFID cards throughout iterations 2 and 3, while she had used the yes/no button of iteration 1 frequently. She continued to record her "talks" with the robot nevertheless. The right chart shows the individual participants' interaction modes. P2 had the highest proportion of silent interactions, while P6 very often also talked when interacting.

At the start of the field study, we had no expectations about the mode of interaction. The fact that participants talked at all to the primitive robotic interface was therefore remarkable. It allowed us to treat the interactions as conversations in the analysis, and to apply the methods of conversation analysis accordingly.

The fact that participants also, and quite frequently, talked to the rabbit, does not by itself testify to the social skills of the experimental setup. The reason for this caveat is that we could observe quite the reverse: misunderstandings and breakdowns in the dialog "made" participants resort to verbal interaction as easily as a successful display of sociability. The utterances provoked by such failures and ensuing frustration tended to be longer and more numerous during one interaction (see below: topic management), while smooth interactions rather led to short confirmative or social utterances (such as greetings). "Talking" to the companion per se is therefore not a sign either of good or of bad quality of the interaction.

4   Initiative and Floor Management

4.1   Levels of Floor Management

Floor management in conversation is a concept that captures the mechanisms that participants use to organize the interaction on different levels. We will have to situate the concept first among several others that pertain to the organization of conversations: turn-taking, initiative, and topic leadership.

The basic problem that converstionalists, whether in dyadic or group talks, have to solve at any time is turn-taking, i.e. managing the change of speaker and hearer roles. It involves knowing when it is acceptable or obligatory to take a turn in conversation is essential to the cooperative development of discourse. This knowledge involves such factors as knowing how to recognize appropriate turn-exchange points and knowing how long the pauses between turns should be. It is also important to know how (and if) one may talk while someone else is talking--that is, if conversational overlap is allowed.

Initiative in talk has come into the focus of research mainly via the ambition of creating mixed initiative human-machine interaction. Mixed initiative has been defined as "a flexible interaction strategy, where each agent can contribute to the task what it does best." [21, 22] Obviously, this definition refers to task-oriented conversations, where system initiative ("Please enter your name first") and user initiative ("I want to fly to London next Tuesday") are easily and clearly distinguished. Rich data have been gathered and analysed both on human-human and human-machine task-oriented dialogs, mostly in experimental settings [23, 24, 25, 26, 27, 28, 29, 30]. The underlying assumption about mixed initiative is a relationship between the human and the machine where the machine *ideally* takes the role of an assistent which does not only give correct and helpful answers, but also takes the initiative where this appears to be necessary and fruitful for the advancement of the task. This ideal does not even apply to all human-human-conversations, as is shown in [31] where cases of collaborative task-oriented dialogs were analysed. It turned out that initiative can be distributed on "non-rational" grounds, i.e. it is not necessarily the contribution to the task that regulates who takes more of the initiative in such a dialog. There are many other possible factors that influence it: personality, mood, social relationship between the conversationalists, and so on.

Taking of initiative can involve a change of topic, but it need not. Initiative can be passed from one participant to the other while one and the same topic is being dealt with. Initiative, then, is the broader concept. It includes change of topic, but is not limited to it. In other words: who changes the topic necessarily also takes the initiative, while the inverse does not apply. The commonsense understanding is that the topic is what the conversation is about. Conversation analysts turned their attention more to the structural aspects of topic change [32, 33], a perspective that highlighted topic changes as "a solution to the problem of producing continuous talk" ([32], p. 265). The motivation for this perspective lies in the difficulty to determine, from the conversationalists' standpoint, what the content of a sequence is:

> *Disparate topics can occur coherently within the framework of a single, expanded sequence and achieve coherence by being framed by it. An utterance apparently coherent topically with preceding talk can appear incoherent nonetheless if it is structurally anomalous within the sequence it is part of. [34]*

The conversation that is the basis for Schegloff's statement shows an intricate intertwining of things that are "talked about" which, nevertheless, are made coherent by the particpants. His paper reminds us that "the topic" of a conversations is whatever the participants jointly construe as the topic, including and excluding things in the process. Although we will stick with the simpler notion of "topic" as the content of the dialog in the following analysis (on the side of the robot, it is technically determined by the currently active dialog script), this observation still has some influence: a topic can be brought up by one participant (human or robot), but it becomes "the" topic of conversation only by an agreement which is achieved with a range of different techniques, from tiny non-verbal signals (listening behaviour) to explicit negotiation (meta-discourse).

In order to distinguish the overall initiative to interact ("who starts an interaction and when?") from the concept of initiative as it is more often used (as in "mixed initiative", see below), namely as initiative during an ongoing interaction, we prefer to call it "interaction management". We have, in this section, distinguished three "levels" of floor management in a talk so far: turn-taking, initiative, and topic leadership. The level of interaction management has to be added as a fourth level, although it is, strictly speaking, outside the interaction proper, but nevertheless important for always-on companions. The following table resumes the organization levels of conversation.

Table 6. Levels of floor management

Level	Questions
Turn-taking	Who talks? Who talks next? How is the change of speakers organized?
Initiative	Who controls the conversation? Who shapes the other's input?
Topic management	Who brings up successfully what is going to be talked about?
Interaction management	Who starts a conversation? Who decides what is being talked about at what time?

In Conversation Analysis (CA), the level of interaction management is almost by definition ignored, the unit of study being the single conversation. However, it becomes an important design issue once we envision robots or virtual butlers which are always on and always present in the human working or living environment. Here it has to suffice to say that both knowledge and technology are lamentably deficient when it comes to detecting and appraising the situational and relational cues that lead to the decision when a moment is "right" to initiate and interaction, and which kind of interaction and conversational mechanisms are called for in a given situation.

4.2   Interaction Management in the SERA Data

The SERA field study is no exception to this: socially intelligent interaction management was not in its scope. Initially, the rabbit was designed so as to take the initiative in starting interactions. The motivation behind this pro-active approach was the goal of data collection. We could not rely on the robot's design, functions, and capacities to evoke enough interest in the participants so that they would start enough interactions themselves. The secondary motivation was related to the potential applications of such assistive robots: as the current vision goes, they would also have functions that require their pro-activity, e.g. to remind users of tasks and activities, to alert them to possibly dangerous situations in the house, to collect information for health monitoring, or to transfer messages and support social contacts - just as the virtual butler in the "Tina" story, which takes the initiative to start interactions at certain moments. The story makes it seem effortless for the virtual butler to come up with a reminder at just the right time:

> *"In the meantime, you could water the flowers for Dorothy, madam"*
> *James reminds her. "You promised to take care of the flowers until she*
> *gets back from her educational leave." [1]*

What is more, the user - Tina - obediently accepts this suggestion, although she is uncomfortable with the task. Taking the initiative to talk plus taking the authority to propose the other's course of actions is a socially sensitive undertaking. In human-human conversations, we find a whole range of strategies to mitigate the forcefulness of such actions. For example, preliminary enquiries whether the other is ready to start a conversation ("could I just say something?" or the like), appeal to external forces and obligations to justify one's intrusion, etc. - sometimes explicit, sometimes implicit, or even as reduced as an initial "a-hem" that signals that some talk is to follow. One of our research questions then was how real users would accept and react to sensitive questions and suggestions, and to learn more about when and how a companion robot is socially allowed to take the initiative and to raise such issues.

As laid out above in the discussion of the dialog types, some dialogs were started by the rabbit on the presence of a signal from the motion sensor at certain times of the day. Other dialogs were triggered by the key hook, or by the presence of a new message on the server. The number of dialogs that could only or also be initiated by the participants increased in later iterations (namely, Summary, Weather, and AddtoLog), made possible by the somewhat greater variety of input options through the RFID cards, and motivated also by user feedback in iteration 1.

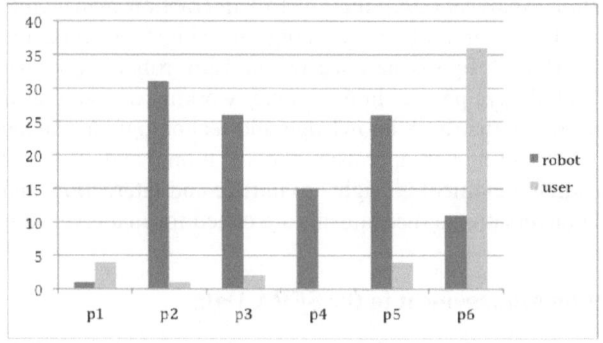

Fig. 11. Distribution of user- and robot-initiated interactions, iteration 3

Nonetheless, even in iteration 3 most interactions were initiated by the robot, just as we had expected. P6 is the striking exception here, with many more user- than robot-initiated interactions. However, a close inspection of all the video sequences revealed that the issue of initiative is much more complicated and that this simple analysis does not represent them correctly:

Commonsense prompts that taking the key off the hook or putting it back is an action (manipulation of an object) and not the initiation of an interaction. Only the utterance of the rabbit that the signal activated was considered (and coded as) such an initiative. As we have discussed above in the description of the GoingOut/ComingHome dialogs (see section 3.4), it turned out that several participants transformed the key into an element of interaction and used it only or primarily to start an interaction. This is then clearly a user-initiated interaction, but was not counted as such.

The motion sensor signal, captured in one of the periods where a dialog initiation by the rabbit was "due", led the robot to initiate such a dialog, e.g. in the morning. It also happened of course when the participant approached the rabbit at such times in order to initiate him/herself a dialog. This happened frequently, especially to P4, and led to a number of difficult or "broken" interactions. One reason for this conflict of initiative was the location of the Nabaztag in the participant's home: it was designed for a hallway, a place near the entrance, or similar locations of transition - in general for places where participants pass through on their way out of the house and back into it. P4 seemed to have placed the Nabaztag in a location where she did not usually pass by, but went intentionally to interact with the rabbit. An example of the often conflictuous interactions that resulted from this is discussed below in the case study (section 4.3). For this section, it is sufficient to say that these interactions were coded as robot-initiated, again under the (dubious, as it turned out) assumption that "being near" the robot, i.e. detected by the motion sensor, was not a sign that the user wanted to initiate a dialog.

4.3   A Case Study on Topic Management

4.3.1   Introducing the Case
Participant P4 entered the field study in iteration 2. From the briefing and the interview we know that she was actually interested in the fitness monitoring role of the rabbit. So she had certain personal expectations:

> "... I was really quite excited about it ... and it was an opportunity for me to kind of really focus on my physical activities... you know I decided that I wanted some use out of it." (it2_P4_part1)

This distinguished her from most of the other participants, especially P1 and P2 who repeatedly stressed that they were active anyway and didn't need support or encouragement in that respect, and that they participated for the "general good" of helping research to help others in their generation, who would need such a function more than they.

P4's expectations however translated into the clear intention to use the rabbit for logging, adding, and summarizing daily exercise. The rabbit, on the other hand, had its pre-defined agenda of events and dialogs that it was designed to go through (see section 3.4 above). By design, user-initiated interactions should only happen at the end of these sequences, or at times of the rabbit's inactivity. This is how P4 resumed this conflict:

"... But whenever I got to the rabbit it was always kind of another story. Either it didn't read the card, or it wanted me to do something else." - "I was giving it a job, because it's my rabbit, my tool, and it was giving me tasks." (it2_P4_part1)

The interaction we use here as a case study shows very well how this conflict of interests is managed in the conversation. Here is the beginning of the dialog:

(it2P4, May8, extract 1)

Row	User actions (not available Nabaztag)	User input to (available to Nabaztag)	Nabaztag output (available to user)	Nabaztag internal state (not available to user)
1				PIR sensor signal, GOODMORNING dialog
2			Good morning, how are you?	
3		card "addtolog"	(blue light)	
4			before we start talking about that, can I just give you the weather and let you know how much exercise you've got planned today first? Afterwards, please remind me that you wanted to add something to your log.	
5	okay		If it's okay to record you now, please could you press the video button? Would you like to hear what the weather forecast is today?	

The example interaction it2P4May8-09:58 is typical for P4's approach: from the start, she wants to take the initiative and to carry out her plan, i.e. to add an amount of exercise time to the log. Whereas the rabbit is programmed to initiate the "good morning" dialog when it gets a signal from the motion sensor for the first time in the day (row 1), she immediately presents to it the card "addtolog".

What has happened here? The rabbit's dialog is built on the adjacency pair of greeting - greeting, question-answer, as in:

```
(ex1)
A: "Good morning, how are you?"
B: "Fine, and you?" or "Good morning, fine!" or some other variant
```

With neither answer does B go beyond the opening of the conversation, but sticks to what is usually dealt with in this phase of the conversation. The opening only prepares the ground for the participants to a) introduce a topic and b) negotiate who introduces the first topic.

If B, in our example, does not return the greeting and completely skips the opening by starting topical talk (ex1 a and b), A would seek for reasons to account for such behaviour: B could be in a hurry, or the topic could be urgent (ex1a); or B is being rude and ignores conventions (ex1b); or B is usually not up to socially adequate conversations in the morning.

(ex1a)	(ex1b)
A: Good morning, how are you?	A: Good morning, how are you?
B: Where's the newspaper?	B: Where's the newspaper?
A: on the kitchen table; what's so urgent?	A: on the kitchen table; can't you say good morning first?

It is not difficult to think of a dozen more variants. One of them could be that A never addresses B's behaviour explicitly, either waiting that a good reason comes up by itself, or else taking (silent) offense because of B's rudeness. But whether rudeness, urgency or something else, A will interpret B's behaviour as having a "reason".

P4, in the sample dialog, is not in a hurry, as far as we can see. Is she, then, being "rude"? We have to ask whether the category of (im)politeness can be applied to this conversation at all. It rather looks as if P4, at the start, does not intend to interact socially with the rabbit. She wants to use it - as her "tool", see the quote from the interview above - for keeping the log of her activities. Her stance is one of machine user who wants to push a button to set the device in action.

The rabbit, on the other hand, is set up as a conversational agent, and starts talking. In row 4, the rabbit has reacted socially to P4's operation of row 3. The verbal "okay", then acknowledges this switch. P4 thus agrees to interact conversationally with the rabbit. She starts talking extensively after that and throughout the interaction. In row 30, the persistent troubles in the dialog lead her to reflect upon this with the question: "Why am I talking to you?" Subjects know of course that the rabiit cannot understand speech, but only the RFID-cards, buttons, and the key-hook switch. Most of them talk to the rabbit nevertheless at times, some quite often and at length (see Figs. 9 and 10).

Other participants in our study did not feel similarly disposed to talk to the rabbit. At this point, we can only conclude that humans deal with being socially addressed in different ways. Some do not seem to have a problem with asymmetric interaction: they are being talked to, but respond using the RFID-cards without speaking. For the companion to fulfill its function, it does not make any difference whether it is talked to or not, as long as there is some alternative way of operating it. Hutchby [35] called the apparently automatic transfer of conversational mechanisms to human-machine interaction the "persistence of conversation". He states that "the affordances of interactional competence may lead humans to bring into play normative expectations that the system turns out to be unable to manage." (p. 171). On these grounds, the interaction that we analyse here can be called a "conversation" although no speech understanding by the robot is involved. Within its narrow limits, the robot's dialog is built on the assumption of a conversational (socially interacting) stance of the user and tries to create an illusion of conversation. We observe that where users accept this offer, they apply the norms of conversational behaviour to both the robot and to themselves - at least as long as the robot is able to maintain the illusion.

4.3.2   "Before We Start Talking about That ... " - Successful Topic Change

In extract 1 above, the Nabaztag registers and recognises the unexpected input (row 4). It rejects the topic proposed by P4 and suggests to postpone it. Instead it announces its own topics. This takes the form of a question, but no answer is expected here.

Contrary to the designers' intentions of creating a rather "shy" and "friendly" persona, the rabbit here imposes its own course of conversation - clearly dominant behaviour. Such contradictions between intended character and actual behaviour are frequent in dialog systems Technical limitations don't allow for the conversation to evolve freely and to follow whichever path is suggested by the user. The rabbit shares this limitation with current task-oriented dialog systems. "Politeness" understood as the use of formulae cannot undo the underlying face-threatening act of taking the floor and introducing a topic. Indeed, they risk to be understood as quite the contrary by the hearer, namely sarcasm. In chatbots and dialog systems, this mismatch between the action and the formulation is one of the reasons why users become frustrated and angry, sometimes to the point of abusing the system verbally. [36, 37]

The rabbit does better in this regard. It mitigates this usurpation of initiative by promising to give it up later and to be then ready to accept the other's topic (row 4). The explicit mention of P4's topic is a clever move in the talk at this point, because the rabbit thus acknowledges that it has understood and accepted P4's topic, only just not at this time.

P4's "okay" in row 5, is a complex answer to this move [38]:

- First of all, P4 here changes the mode of usage from "machine use" to "conversation". The interaction shifts from tool operation to social (see section 2).
- By design, the rabbit's question is purely rhetoric: no user input is expected at this point. But this fact is not relevant here: by providing the preferred second-pair part, P4 orients toward it as a first part of a question-answer adjacency pair. We cannot know to what degree she is aware of this conversational illusion at this point. As mentioned above, participants know about the rudimentary input the rabbit can actually deal with, but talk to it nevertheless (see section 3.2)
- P4 also accepts the rabbit's proposal of dealing with its topics first, and that the rabbit takes the initiative from there on. P4's "okay" transforms the rabbit's announcement into the offer of a treaty and works as the conclusion of a negotiation of topic. She "reminds" the rabbit that a treaty has two sides to it, giving and taking: she gives up initiative for now, but announces that she will re-claim it later on (see section 3.3)

4.3.3   "The Weather or the Log?" - Conversational Illusions

The rabbit does not expect any input or confirmation of the proposal of topic and goes on immediately. In fact, there is a short pause between rows 4 and 5, enough for the "okay" to come in-between the rabbit's utterances. This pause is purely the technically motivated latency. However, by the subject, it can be understood as an intentional puse in which the rabbit waits for confirmation. The rabbit goes on "as if" it had understood and registered the subject's consent. This is pure coincidence on the dialog manager's part, but it creates the impression of a smooth conversation. There is an even nicer example of such a coincidence shortly afterwards.

After row 5, the rabbit expects two inputs: from the video button, to turn on recording (in fact, to store recorded data to disk), and a yes/no answer through a "smiley" card. P4 provides the first input (row 6). P4 also intends to provide the second input by showing a card, but the rabbit does not recognise it. We do not know which card the subject intended to show here.

Row	User actions (not available to Nabaztag)	User input (available to Nabaztag)	Nabaztag output (available to user)	Nabaztag internal state (not available to user)
6		presses video button		
7				ASKWEATHER dialog Video on
8			Video recording on.	
9	I would like to hear what the weather forecast said today ... and I await your response.			
10	(shows a card to N)			
11	(sits down in front of N)		Sorry, I struggle sometimes to read the cards, could you hold it up a bit closer to my nose?	
12	(gets up, shows other card) which card is that then? the weather or the log?			
13			Sorry, it's my fault, they're not easy to use. If you're having trouble and want to hear the weather try using the weather topic card instead	

14		card "weather"	(blue light)	
15	okay, you've got my weather card now. I saw the blue flashlight.			

In row 11, the rabbit starts the repair sequence for the case a card input was expected but not read. Note that the rabbit does not know at all whether the subject in fact had tried to show a card. The dialog proceeds only on the assumption that this was indeed the case. The assumption is right this time, and P4 complies by standing up and showing a card. It is visible from the video that she tries a different card from the first time (row 12). We can assume that one of the cards she is holding and showing (in rows 10 and 12) is still her topic card "addtolog". Unsure now, she asks which of the two cards she should show. The input fails again, and the rabbit takes another attempt at a repair. This one is built on the assumption that the user has tried and failed to show a yes/no card. So the rabbit, continuing with the "weather" topic, suggests to use the "weather topic card" instead. Again, this message coincides perfectly with P4's question "which card, the weather or the log?" by co-referring to one of them.

In this section, we tried to make clear the extent to which the human's contribution is necessary to make a "conversation". To say that at least two parties are needed to make a dialog is trivial, but in the case of human-machine dialogs, it tends to be ignored. Whether it "works" or not, i.e. whether the dialog is fluent and provides for sequentially relevant interpretations, or whether it breaks down, is all too often attributed to the machine alone. One has to remain wary of dialog transcripts in this respect. If the dialog above were reprinted here in the usual turn-by-turn manner, it would look like a perfect conversation. Only by incorporating the internal state of the machine we can make clear that there is no understanding or recognised input of any kind on the machine's part involved.

In this case, the good match between the user's and the machine's utterances is indeed pure coincidence. We have in our data other cases where the user has learned how the rabbit's dialog will go on, and provides suitable input or utterances just-in-time. The analysis of the data of P1 from iteration 1 [14] shows such a learning process. The occurrences of P1 talking to the rabbit decreased with the duration of the experiment. At the same time, the intervals between the rabbit's utterances and the pressing of the buttons in response became shorter. In between P1's approaches to press the input buttons, she now moves around the room to pursue other activities. She seems to know the sequence and length of the robot's utterances, and has adapted her movements and rhythm so that interacting with the robot is woven fluently into her everyday activities in the house.

4.3.4   "Now Let Me Add ... " Topic Change as Negotiation
In row 11, P4 has made explicit her consent with the first topic on the rabbit's agenda: "I would like to hear what the weather forecast said today ... and I await your response. " In row 17, P4 shows again that she has gone along with the topic introduced by the rabbit, by repeating part of the last utterance and "okay". Both are ways to close a topic [39].

Row	User actions (not available to Nabaztag)	User input (available to Nabaztag)	Nabaztag output (available to user)	Nabaztag internal state (not available to user)
16			the weather today is rain at first, soon brightening up.	
17	okay, yes, it is brightening up. And now add to log. You said t-			REMINDINGWEIGHING dialog
18			Some people find it useful to weigh themselves daily as part of their exercise routine.	
19	no, I will never do that.		I hope you don't mind me asking but will you be weighing yourself today?	
20	no, I won't ever be doing that ... But I want to... (shows card)			

After this unilateral topic-closing, she immediately comes back again to her topic. If we take the first "okay" (in row 5) as her initial consent to the rabbit's topic leadership and topic, and the explicit consent in row 9, she seems to withdraws this consent now, or has never intended to extend it beyond the "weather" topic. Maybe she simply has not listened to the rabbit's enumeration of intended topics (weather + exercise). P4 makes the second attempt to change to her topic, and tries to reinforce her claim by referring to the rabbit's utterance in row 4: "you said t-" - probably "... to remind you". it becomes clear here that P4 actually has taken the rabbit's utterance as a promise whose fulfillment she now claims, and that her consent had been given under the condition that her topic would be accepted later.

Instead, the rabbit goes on with its next topic - weighing oneself. P4 rejects this move strongly on several grounds, one of them being that her topic is again rejected. As there is more involved in this rejection than a negative answer, we dedicate a separate section to this issue (section 4).

In row 20, she shows again a card (most probably the "addtolog" card"), and, finally, the rabbit goes on to the topic "exercise" with a general statement. The rabbit has not recognised the input, but the topic following now in the normal "Good Morning" dialog is related to P4's intention, and so is taken by her as an acceptance of her topic. When the rabbit gives the amount of planned activity for that day, this is her cue for another "addtolog" request.

The card input is successful. Internally a new unrelated dialog is initiated. To P4 however, it is not evident that a new unrelated dialog has been started, but this makes no difference here. It does so in the dialog of May 12, where the card is not read immediately and the rabbit goes on to close the conversation - which, understandably, irritates her. Her frustration is not spontaneous, however, but has built up over the previous topic, "weighing oneself", which she wants to reject as a whole (see section 4.3.5).

In the May 8 dialog, however, things turn out well:

Row	User actions (not available Nabaztag)	User input to (available to Nabaztag)	Nabaztag output (available to user)	Nabaztag internal state (not available to user)
21			The NHS recommends doing at least 30 minutes of activity 5 times a week.	
22	I'm aware (?) ... mhmmm		From your plan it looks like you've got a total of 240 minutes of planned activity today.	
23	240 ... let me add	card "addtolog"	(blue light)	ASKADDTOLOG dialog
24			Would you like me to add something to your exercise log?	
25	YES, YES	card "60"	(blue light)	
26			60 minutes of activity? I'll put that into your log if that's right?	
27	Fantastic! And I've got two raised beds to dig erm, to line and to fill and to plant.		I'll put that in your log now.	

She greets the rabbit's question concerning the exercise log with an enthusiastic "YES, YES" and the confirmation of the added amount (60 minutes) with "Fantastic". The overall success of the interaction is confirmed by her closing statement "Okay, we're done" (row 51).

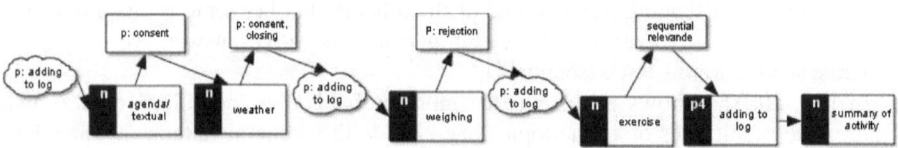

Fig. 12. The topic structure of the example dialog

Fig. 12 shows the overall topical structure of the dialog it2P4-May8-10:40. It shows that the user has made three failed attempts at changing the topic before she succeeds, while the Nabaztag has covered four topics in succession until that point. The design of the experimental companion was indeed to initiate and lead dialogs at certain times of the day, while it was passive and receptive for user input at others. In the sample dialog, it seemed to manage the user's initiative of introducing her topic quite well, but was not consistent. The negotiation of order and priority of respective topics is only superficial and not translated into conversational behaviour. Conversationalists faced with the problem of both having something they want to talk about have two options each: either "first me, then you" or "first you, then me". This can be negotiated explicitly. A motivation, excuse, or justification is often found in conversations for taking the floor first, showing that having the first topic is a socially sensitive issue. For both, however, the "then ..." part is important: it is understood that topics are only re-ordered, some of them postponed, but not ignored. The speaker who cedes the floor can expect that the other knows and acknowledges this, and that regaining the floor will re-establish the balance. Companions that have to cover different topics both self- and user-initiated, need to have the capacity to keep in evidence the topics to be covered by one and the other.

4.3.5   "I Don't Want That Reminder" - Beyond Topic Change

In this section, we will come back to the segment of the conversation about the topic "weighing oneself".

Row	User actions (not available to Nabaztag)	User input (available to Nabaztag)	Nabaztag output (available to user)
18			Some people find it useful to weigh themselves daily as part of their exercise routine.
19	no, I will never do that.		I hope you don't mind me asking but will you be weighing yourself today?
20	no, I won't ever be doing that ... But I want to... (shows card)		

In row 18 and 19, the rabbit changes the topic again, unilaterally and unlinked (ref.), which is considered the "strongest" kind of topic change. Moreover, this is a topic that has not been announced in the rabbit's key statement on topic management (row 3) which we have characterized as the offer of a "treaty". In this perspective, the rabbit is "cheating".

P4 answers with a series of negations (rows 19 and 20). If we list what she is negating at this point, it becomes clear that they are not just repeated for emphasis. There is a "target" or first pair part for each of the four negations (no - never - no - not ever):

1   the introduction of the topic (row 18) with the general recommendation
2   the question "do you mind me asking ...?"
3   the embedded question "will you be weighing yourself today?"
4   the topic as a whole: this becomes clear in row 20, when she tries to substitute her own topic in "but I want to ..."

P4, she makes clear, does not intend to weigh herself that day, but she does not even want the topic of weighing being brought up. In the second dialog we consider here (May 12), she makes her rejection of the topic as a whole explicit (row 11, overlapping with speech output):

it2P4-May12, 10:40:

Row	User actions (not available to Nabaztag)	User input (available to Nabaztag)	Nabaztag output (available to user)
	[I know. I don't want that reminder.]		Some people find it useful to weigh themselves daily [as part of their exercise routine]
			I hope you don't mind me asking but will you be weighing yourself today?
	How?		
	[How do I tell you no? Will I weigh myself today? How do I say no?]		The [NHS recommends doing at least 30 minutes of activity 5 times a week.]
	[Is it not very nice face?]		[From your plan it looks like you've got a total of 140 minutes of planned activity today.]
		card "frown"	
	[I'm not going to weigh myself today.] Okay, yeah, I know.	card "frown"	

Interestingly, though, she then starts talking about how to say "no", now referring to the embedded question "Will I weigh myself today?" (row 14). The problem she has to deal with again is the nested structure of the Nabaztag's treatment of this topic:

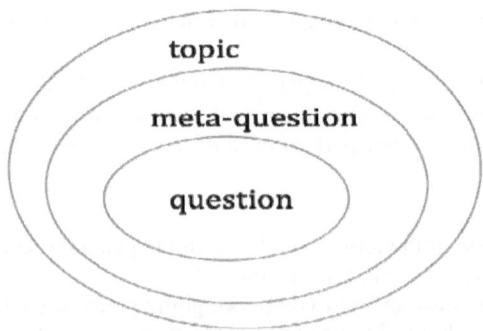

Fig. 13. Nested question structure: question = "Will you be weighing yourself?", meta-question = "Do you mind me asking, if ...?", topic = "weighing oneself"

The complexity of the segmental structure is not reflected by the options that the interaction offers. P4 has only one level and a small choice of possible answers. In contrast to the dialog on May 8, where she responds with an attempt to introduce her topic, here she tries to answer the "inner" direct question with "no". We have to assume that this does not mean that she has accepted the new topic, but that she simply does not see any other way out of it. (In fact, the dialogs were scripted in a way that ensured maximal fluidity, i.e. they did not break down even on unsuitable or missing input but went on "somehow").

The "weighing" topic had been introduced already in the dialogs of the first phase. Although weight control is not a necessary ingredient of the activity-related rehabilitation program the setup was inspired by, it was thought to be a sufficiently related topic to be consistent with it. The motivation for introducing this topic was the research question: how do users deal with active advices and reminders of companions that may not be entirely welcome? In iteration 1, it was formulated simply as: "Have you weighed yourself yet today?" Only few of the participants complied with the indirect recommendation, e.g. P1:

```
N: "Please press the no or yes button to get your answer. Have you
weighed yourself yet today?"
P1: "Yes" - presses button simultaneously
N: "Okay. Thanks"
P1 smiles
P1: "anything else. I even know I weighed 82.7 kilos or in english 12
10 and a half pounds - well stones and pounds."
(it1_P1_PSeP26_0948)
```

P2 always went through the topic quickly by pressing "No" (iter. 1) or having the "frown" card ready at hand (iteration 2). In the interviews and in feedback to the researchers after iteration 1, most participants expressed their dislike of the question. On these grounds, it was re-formulated for iteration 2 as reproduced here. The intention was to have the Nabaztag invoke external authorities both to give more weight to the issue and to pass responsibility for breaching the subject. This added little to make the question more palatable, as we found out. While P2 had found a routine way to go quickly through the topic, P4 showed stronger reactions, as for example in the interactions reprinted here. She would have liked to delete the whole topic from the dialogs.

The failure of the rabbit to adapt the plan of topics to cover to the user's needs and current intentions is one of the causes for this dialog (May 12) to finally fail: while she reflects on how to "say no", she misses the slot where she could introduce her topic, namely adding to the log, and the rabbit goes on to the closing of the dialog, thereby, for the user, clearly breaking the "promise" of coming back to the user's topic. P4's frustration is now building up quickly, to the point where she waves the cards in front of the rabbit instead of holding them still to be read. This, of course, still adds to her frustration, and she closes this interaction resuming:

```
P4: I'm leaving. I've had enough. You've not recorded, you've given me a
weather report I didn't want. You have asked me to remind you about
several things and then given me no way of doing it. I'm out of here.
(it2P4-May12_1040)
```

4.4   Topic Management in the Dataset

Topic management emerged as an important issue through interactions such as the one discussed in the previous sections. In order to determine whether problems with topic management were exceptional cases or phenomena that occurred regularly, data of iteration 3 were coded for topic changes. First we determined how often we could observe attempts or proposals to change the topic, and whether they were made by the robot or the user. Although the GoodMorning dialog script contains a sequence of different topics (about the weather, weighing, and exercise), we did not count the progress from one of these topics to the next by the robot as a topic change.

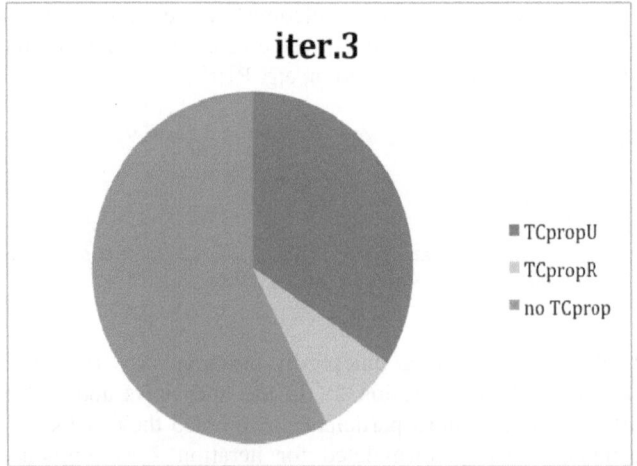

Fig. 14. Proportion of interactions where topic changes were attempted

The chart (Fig. 14) is based on a total of 158 interactions which were coded for topic management. We did not include, in the counting, the "GoodMorning" dialog (see section 3.4) which is already designed so as to propose and cover several topics. The proportion of interactions where a topic change was proposed by either the user (PCpropU) or the robot (TCpropR) is astonishingly high. Users tried to introduce new topics in 54 interactions, and the robot in 13 cases. Users did this more often in interactions they had initiated themselves.

Fig. 15 shows that roughly two out of three attempted topic changes were successful, and this independently of who made the attempt. Fig. 16 shows how the topic change attempts are distributed across participants (TCpropU) as well as the success rate of each participant. P5 and P6 made most attempts, and P3 had the highest relative success rate. Only P4 experienced more failures at introducing topics than successes. This result is consistent with her practice illustrated in the previous case study.

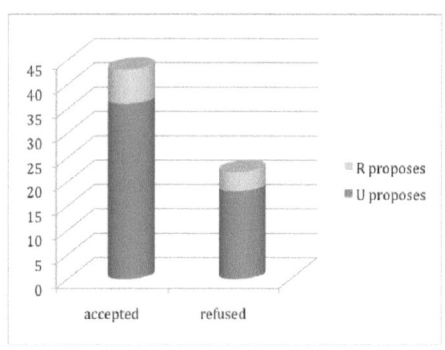 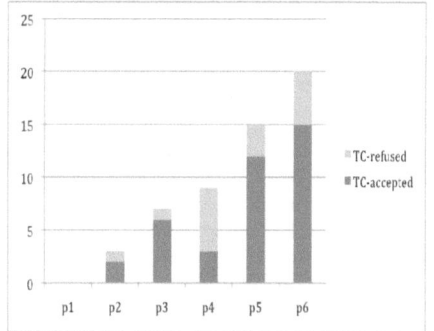

Fig. 15. Rate of acceptance/refusal of proposed topic changes

Fig. 16. Rate of acceptance/refusal of user-proposed topic changes by participant

The data of iteration 3 show that topic change can indeed be observed frequently in our field study. It may be noted, as an aside, that the interactions where it occurs have a higher degree of complexity, and are often longer, than exchanges about single topics. The data also show that, on average, topic changes went better than the detailed case study of P2 in iteration 2 leads to assume.

To close this section, we will present an example of P6 that is, in many respects, similar to the video from P4 in iteration 2 that was discussed above: the robot initiates the GoodMorning dialog.

it3_P6_FNov6_0834s33.mov

```
            <e k8055:PIR                                          <no state>
                                                        Nov6_0834:33:709/>
            <e mc: Good morning, how are you?            Nov6_0834:33:709/>
            <e k8055:PIR                                     GoodMorningRFID
                                                        Nov6_0834:43:37/>
            <e usr:"neutral                              Nov6_0834:43:819/>
            <e mc: If it's okay to record you            Nov6_0834:45:147/>
            now, please could you press the video
            button? Would you like to hear what
            the weather forecast is today?
            <e k8055:PIR                                      AskWeatherRFID
                                                        Nov6_0834:50:475/>
            <e k8055:VIDEO                                    AskWeatherRFID
                                                        Nov6_0834:51:350/>
            <e mc: Video recording on.                   Nov6_0834:51:350/>
            <e mc: Sorry, I struggle sometimes to        Nov6_0835:1:147/>
            read the cards, could you hold it up
            a bit closer to my nose?
            <e mc: Sorry, it's my fault, they're         Nov6_0835:13:147/>
            not easy to use. If you're having
            trouble and want to hear the weather
            try using the weather topic card
            instead
A ->        <e usr:"addtolog"                            Nov6_0835:14:287/>
            <e k8055:PIR                                      AskWeatherRFID
                                                        Nov6_0835:22:912/>
```

```
<e mc: Before we talk about that, can      Nov6_0835:26:397/>
I just give you the weather and let
you know how much exercise you've got
planned for the day? Please can you
remind me that you wanted to add
something to your log afterwards?.
The weather today is Chilly, with
sunny intervals and scattered
showers.
<e k8055:PIR                                    SayWeatherRFID
                                           Nov6_0835:27:225/>
<e usr:"neutral"                           Nov6_0835:35:178/>
<e mc: Some people find it useful to       Nov6_0835:44:897/>
weigh themselves daily as part of
their exercise routine. I hope you
don't mind me asking but will you be
weighing yourself today?
<e usr:"neutral"                           Nov6_0835:55:459/>
<e k8055:PIR                               RemindWeighingRFID
                                           Nov6_0835:56:600/>
<e mc: You haven't got any exercise        Nov6_0835:56:897/>
planned for today in your diary. If
you do some exercise then let me know
and I can add it to your activity
log.
<e mc: Unless you'd like to talk           Nov6_0836:7:897/>
about anything else, I'll talk to you
later. Bye
<e k8055:PIR                                   EndMorningRFID
                                           Nov6_0836:8:662/>
B ->  <e usr:"addtolog"                     Nov6_0836:10:865/>
      <e usr:"addtolog"                     Nov6_0836:12:475/>
      <e mc: Would you like me to add       Nov6_0836:14:397/>
something to your exercise log?
      <e k8055:PIR                            AskAddToLogRFID
                                           Nov6_0836:16:850/>
```

At point A P6 uses an "unexpected" topic card - "addtolog", as does P4 in the example above - to introduce a new topic. The robot refuses, as with P4, and goes on with the dialog script. P6 follows a different strategy: he accepts the robot's topic leadership and reacts with appropriate input (the "neutral" card). In this way, he follows the dialog to the end. Only then, after the rabbit's pre-closing, he introduces the topic again successfully (point B).

The two dialogs, of P4 and P6, are similar when one looks at the logs of the interaction, but they leave the participants with obviously very different impressions. Where P4 is frustrated, P6 closes the interaction with a friendly greeting, adding "it was nice talking to you". While the social skills designed into a robot companion are a necessary prerequisite for acceptance by and relationship with the user, the users' attitudes and practices are essential in fostering or hindering their deployment.

5   Styles of Usage

In this concluding section, we will therefore resume observations and comparisons of the data in the field study into the characterization of "user styles". A user style is understood here as a collection of typical attitudes and practices that appear repeatedly in the interactive behaviour of one or more persons. Given the few subjects in our study, user styles may strongly coincide with the characterization of a single user (like a "persona", in requirements engineering terms), but this is not necessary nor indeed intended. The claim is that elements of user styles will be found again and again in further real-life experiments with robot companions, of course together with new and other styles yet to be found.

The description of user styles is based on the analyses and comparisons presented in the previous sections, on qualitative observations annotated in open coding, and on the open interviews made with all participants after the data collection. To each user style, we add considerations about the companion design which would accommodate it best.

5.1   User Style "Minimalism"

This style is typically represented by P2 throughout all the iterations, but more widely shared than the others by the participants at certain times. P2 complied with the study requirements in that she kept up the (low) level of interactions. She did not initiate herself interactions and remained mostly passive. She made an effort to reduce time and effort for the interactions. Once she had learned when and what the rabbit would communicate, she kept the few RFID cards she needed ready and used them easily and without delay, so that the interactions went smooth and fast. The interaction became a daily routine. On the other hand, when the card input could not be read promptly by the rabbit, she quickly became impatient. The few verbal utterances she made were either angry outbursts caused by such delays, or short greetings. She had the fewest different types of dialog with the rabbit, and called it "mainly boring" in the interview, but did not make an attempt to explore its functionalities to make it, perhaps, less boring.

Companion Design: minimalist users are a challenge to design. On the one hand, they are open to a pro-active interaction style and even need it because they do not take the initiative themselves. On the other hand, they prefer interactions that are reduced to the essentials and do not take too much of their time and effort, and get easily frustrated by repetitions and "non-functional" (social) interaction. They react positively or negatively to the companion's initiatives based on the content, but do not seek out positive experiences by themselves. The companion has to be pro-active for them and to draw the minimalist user's attention to the functions that they do not explore by themselves. On the other hand, it has to adapt to the "minimalist" style by leaving out or shortening dispreferred topics and social utterances. Episodic memory and adaptation are most important for this user style.

5.2   User Style "Conflict"

This style is based on the data from P4 mainly, complemented with some elements in P2's behaviour. The "conflict user" has strong expectations about the companion's utility and the way of interacting. When these expectations are not immediately met, she gets frustrated easily and forms a negative image of the robot's capabilities.

> *"... I was really quite excited about it ... and it was an opportunity for me to kind of really focus on my physical activities... you know I decided that I wanted some use out of it." (it2_P4_part1)*

> *"... But whenever I got to the rabbit it was always kind of another story. Either it didn't read the card, or it wanted me to do something else." - "I was giving it a job, because it's my rabbit, my tool, and it was giving me tasks." (it2_P4_part1)*

The dialog analysed in full in the previous section is from iteration 2, and only one of a series of similar interactions where sometimes she succeeds and sometimes she fails to make the rabbit useful for her. In iteration 3, we encounter the same pattern. Her dissatisfaction becomes visible in the decreasing number of interactions (from iteration 2 to 3) which showed her distancing:

> *"It did not meet my needs. It frustrated me. It asked me questions that just were not relevant or important, you know, not timely." (it3_P4_part1)*

> *"And a lot of times towards the (end?) I became quite indifferent to it, because I did not feel it was helping me."(it3_P4_part2)*

An interesting observation could be made: she did not in any significant way change her approach. She did not learn from prior interactions or adapt to the robot's dialogs. She sticked to her practices and, doing so, infallibly re-produced frustrating experiences which confirmed and reinforced her negative impression. P4 reacted positively to the two recommendations she happened to hear on the robot's initiative, but never took the initiative herself to explore its functionalities.

Interestingly, the conflict user does not always and from the start refuse to play the "conversation game" or to enter into social interaction, even into a relationship (contrary to the minimalist user). In iteration 2, P4 started out talking much, and as the case study (section 4.3) shows, she continued doing so.

Companion Design: It is hard to envision a companion design that would satisfy user requirements that focus exclusively on functionality. The "conflict user" makes it clear that companion robots may not be the right kind of technology for everybody. P4, in the interviews, says that she would have preferred some other device - a simple cube, or a screen - with some buttons to serve her purpose, which was only to quickly record and sum her physical acitivity periods. This user style reminds us of the fact that there can be no "one size fits all" technology in the realm of assistive companions.

5.3   User Style "Compliance"

Our prototype user with this style is P5. If P5 had participated from the start of the field study, many changes and improvements in the interaction skills of the rabbit would probably not have been made, because this was a "model user" who interacted with the robot exactly in the way as the designers had intended. He did not initiate many interactions himself but introduced hiw own topics frequently and with a high success rate. What is striking in the data from this participant is the smoothness and fluidity that he achieves. To code and represent this perceived rhythmic coordination

[40], one would have to use micro-observational methods, for example to measure (typically in tenth of seconds or less) the gaps and overlaps between turns - methods that were outside the scope and possibilities of the present study. Given the limited flexibility in the rabbit's interaction, fluidity has to be the user's achievement. The compliant user adapts to the timing, rhythm, and conversation style of the robot. Responses are suitable to the dialog and given in the best time slot for the dialog manager to proceed. Where an input is not understood by the rabbit and a request for repetition given, the user does not take this "personally" (as the conflict user does) and complies calmly with the request. The user understands the limitations of the system and works with them. For example: the RFID cards for the amount of activity only went up to 60 minutes, while P5 often wanted to record much longer stretches (up to four hours). He repeated the AddtoLog sequence the required number of times without showing any sign of impatience. All functions and dialogs of the rabbit were activated at one time or the other. The drawback of this style seems to be that, in order to achieve fluidity and full functionality, the user had better be pragmatic and understand and operate the robot as a machine - which contradicts the goal of having a social-relational companion.

Companion Design: the field study setup seemed to be almost perfectly designed for this user style. The focus of the compliant user is on utility. The companion would have to offer a wider range of services to satisfy these users' needs, drawing on the affordances of an embodied "screen-free" and, ultimately, speech operated device in the home. Such services could be information tailored exactly to the situation and current needs of the user, which requires advanced situation awareness and knowledge. P5 mentions, just as an example, the departure time of the next bus as a desirable service.

5.4   User Style "Playfulness"

The playful user is similar to the compliant user in many respects, but goes one step further. Compliance ensures that interactions are smooth, that the functionality is fully deployed, and that the user succeeds in taking the initiative and changing the topic. But, contrary to the compliant user, the playful user draws pleasure from these interactions. The playful user is much more initiative than the compliant user, and likes to "show off" the robot to guests and family members. He happens to like the appearance and behaviour of the robot and actually develops a warm relationship with it. P6 comments, in the interview:

> "I was very taken by the fun of the whole enterprise. Which surpised me a bit ..."

> "My wife and I became very fond of it. We liked the idea of personalizing it. the rabbit is as good as a person as anything else. And we were charmed by it."

Although the social character of the interaction plays an important role, the playful user would not do without useful functions and services. However, these services are different and more personal, based on the social relationship. For example, P6 could imagine that the companion would be better in reminding him of things to do or priorities to set than a human:

"I think that this is a more user friendly way of being reminded than someone appearing to nag you and getting the blame of being a nag ... "

Interestingly, P6 also confirmed that the companion had some influence on his behaviour with regard to the scenario of monitoring and encouraging physical activity. The playful user, then, would also be the one who benefits most from the assistive functionality of the companion.

Companion Design: Appearance and interaction style play a role in making the companion attractive and a social relationship possible. Obviously, the same look cannot satisfy all users, so that a variety of forms and media to choose from would have to be catered for (e.g. zoomorphic vs. humanoid vs. abstract; coloured lights, voices, gestures). Utility concerns here have to aim at personalized services that the users can easily install and configure themselves. Their relationship with the companion would ensure that they are ready to invest some effort into adapting the companion to their needs.

5.5   Resume: Tinas and Butlers in the Plural

The field study showed that a companion finally is and becomes what its user makes of it. The attitudes, expectations, and creative practices of users are as important in the human-companion relationship as are the capabilities of the device. Users and companions both shape the relationship, and the users contribute according to their individuality and personality.

The "Tina" persona is close to what has here been called the "compliant" user style. We hypothesise that designers have a tendency to create such compliant personae in order to highlight the functionality (instead of the breakdowns and shortcomings) of a system. At the same time, the compliant persona is a dangerous simplification, because it avoids the challenges with which other user styles face the system and thus inhibits innovation in research and design.

The aim of this chapter was to show that there cannot be a single "persona" for a one-size-fits-all companion. If the technology is to provide social affordances for different kinds of relationships, it will be necessary to define several personae that capture the variance of user styles, and to push research toward systems that are adaptive or adaptable to different user styles, including alternative technologies. We have shown that the study of long-term human-robot interactions in the wild can contribute insights into the relevant parameters that distinguish these styles.

Acknowledgments. The data collection for this chapter has received funding from the European Community's Seventh Framework Programme [FP7/2007-2013] under grant agreement no. 231868, project SERA - Social Engagement with Robots and Agents. The data analysis has been funded by the Austrian Ministry for Transport, Innovation and Technology (BMVIT) under the programme "FEMtech Women in Research and Technology" grant nr. 821855, project C4U.

References

1. Gassner, R., Steinmuller, K.: Scenario "Tina and her Butler". In: Trappl, R. (ed.) Your Virtual Butler. LNCS (LNAI), vol. 7407. Springer, Heidelberg (2013)
2. Cooper, A.: The Inmates are Running the Asylum. SAMS, New York (1999)
3. Graf, B., Reiser, U., Hägele, M., Mauz, K., Klein, P.: Robotic Home Assistant Care-O-bot® 3 - Product Vision and Innovation Platform. In: IEEE / Robotics and Automation Society: IEEE Workshop on Advanced Robotics and its Social Impacts, ARSO 2009: Workshop Proceedings, Tokyo, Japan, November 23-25, pp. 139–144. IEEE, Piscataway (2009)
4. Wada, K., Shibata, T.: Living with seal robots - Its sociopsychological and physiological influences on the elderly at a care house. IEEE Transactions on Robotics 23(5), 972–980 (2007)
5. Kidd, C.D.: Designing for Long-Term Human-Robot Interaction and Application to Weight Loss. PhD Thesis, School of Architecture and Planning, MIT, Cambridge, MA (2008)
6. Sung, J.-Y., Guo, L., Grinter, R.E., Christensen, H.I.: "My Roomba Is Rambo": Intimate Home Appliances. In: Krumm, J., Abowd, G.D., Seneviratne, A., Strang, T. (eds.) UbiComp 2007. LNCS, vol. 4717, pp. 145–162. Springer, Heidelberg (2007)
7. Creer, S., Cunningham, S., Hawley, M., Wallis, P.: Design decisions for an interactive domestic robot: describing the SERA project set-up. Social Engagement with Robots and Agents. Special Issue, Applied Artificial Intelligence 25(6), 445–473 (2011)
8. Prochaska, J., Velicer, W.: The transtheoretical model of behaviour change. American Journal of Health Promotion 12, 38–48 (1997)
9. Bickmore, T., Picard, R.W.: Establishing and Maintaining Long-Term Human-Computer Relationships. ACM Transactions on Computer Human Interaction (ToCHI) 59(1), 21–30 (2005)
10. Bickmore, T., Schulman, D., Langxuan, Y.: Maintaining Engagement in Long-Term Interventions with Relational Agents. Applied Artificial Intelligence 24(6), 648–666 (2010)
11. Klamer, T., BenAllouch, S.: Acceptance and use of a social robot by elderly users in a domestic environment. In: 4th International ICST Conference on Pervasive Computing Technologies for Healthcare 2010, Munich (2010)
12. Klamer, T., BenAllouch, S.: Zoomorphic robots used by elderly people at home. In: Proceedings of the 27th International Conference on Human Factors in Computing Systems. ACM International Conference on Human Factors in Computing Systems (CHI 2010). ACM Press, Atlanta (2010)
13. von der Pütten, A., Krämer, N.C., Eimler, S.: Living with a Robot Companion - Empirical Study on the Interaction with an Artificial Health Advisor. In: Proc. 13th International Conference on Multimodal Interaction ICMI, Alicante (2011)
14. Payr, S.: Ritual or Routine: Communication in Long-Term Relationships with Companions. In: Trappl, R. (ed.) Proceedings EMCSR 2010, Vienna (2010)
15. Payr, S.: Closing and Closure in Human-Companion Interactions: Analyzing Video Data from a Field Study. Paper Read at 19th IEEE International Symposium in Robot and Human Interactive Communication (RO-MAN), Viareggio, September 12-15 (2010)
16. Heylen, D., op den Akker, R., Mark ter, M., Petta, P., Rank, S., Reidsma, D., Zwiers, J.: On the Nature of Engineering Social Artificial Companions. Social Engagement with Robots and Agents. Special Issue, Applied Artificial Intelligence 25(6), 549–574 (2011)
17. Wallis, P.: A Robot in the Kitchen. In: Proc. ACL 2010, Uppsala (2010)
18. Wallis, P.: From Data to Design. Social Engagement with Robots and Agents. Special Issue, Applied Artificial Intelligence 25(6) (2011)
19. Wallis, P., Maier, V., Creer, S., Cunningham, S.: Conversation in Context: what should a robot companion say? In: Trappl, R. (ed.) Proceedings of EMCSR 2010, Vienna (2010)

20. Goodwin, C.: Video and the analysis of embodied human interaction. In: Kissmann, U.T. (ed.) Video Interaction Analysis, pp. 21–40. Peter Lang, Frankfurt/Main (2009)
21. Allen, J.F.: Mixed-initiative interaction. IEEE Intelligent Systems, 14–16 (1999)
22. Allen, J.F., Byron, D.K., Dzikovska, M.: Towards Conversational Human-Computer Interaction. AI Magazine (2001)
23. Fischer, K.: What Computer Talk Is and Isn't. AQ-Verlag, Saarbrücken (2006)
24. Byron, D.K.: The OSU Quake 2004 corpus of two-party situated problem-solving dialogs. Tech. Report OSU-CISRC-805-TR57. Ohio State University, Columbus (2005)
25. Byron, D.K., Fosler-Lussier, E.: The OSU Quake 2004 corpus of two-party situated problem-solving dialogs. In: Proceedings of the 15th Language Resources and Evaluation Conference (LREC 2006), Genoa (2006)
26. Ferguson, G., Allen, J.F., Miller, B.: TRAINS-95: Towards a mixed-initiative planning assistant. In: Drabble, B. (ed.) Proc. 3rd Conference on Artificial Intelligence Planning Systems AIPS-96, Edinburgh, pp. 70–77 (1995)
27. Chu-Carroll, J., Brown, M.K.: Tracking Initiative in Collaborative Dialog Interactions. In: Proceedings of the 35th Annual Meeting of the Association for Computational Linguistics (ACL/EACL 1997), Madrid, pp. 262–270 (1997)
28. Brindöpke, C., Häger, J., Johanntokrax, M., Phade, A., Schwalbe, M., Wrede, B.: Darf ich Dich Marvin nennen? Instruktionsdialoge in einem WoZ-Szenario. Szenario-Design und Asuwertung. In: SFB-Report Situierte künstliche Kommunikatoren 95/16. Bielefeld: Universität Bielefeld (1995)
29. Ferguson, G., Allen, J.F.: TRIPS: An Integrated Intelligent Problem-Solving Assistant. In: Proc. AAAI 1998, Madison, WI, pp. 567–573 (1998)
30. Wallis, P.: Revisiting the DARPA Communicator Data using Conversation Analysis. Interaction Studies 9(3), 434–457 (2008)
31. Payr, S.: So Let's See: Taking and Keeping the Initiative in Collaborative Dialogues. In: Pelachaud, C., Martin, J.-C., André, E., Chollet, G., Karpouzis, K., Pelé, D. (eds.) IVA 2007. LNCS (LNAI), vol. 4722, pp. 175–182. Springer, Heidelberg (2007)
32. Maynard, D.W.: Placement of topic changes in conversation. Semiotica 30(3/4), 263–290 (1980)
33. Okamoto, D.G., Smith-Lovin, L.: Changing the Subject: Gender, Status, and the Dynamics of Topic Change. American Sociological Review 66(6), 852–873 (2001)
34. Schegloff, E.A.: On the Organization of Sequences as a Source of "Coherence" in Talk-in-Interaction. In: Dorval, B. (ed.) Conversational Organization and its Development, pp. 51–77. Ablex, Norwood (1990)
35. Hutchby, I.: Conversation and Technology. From the Telephone to the Internet. Polity Press, Cambridge (2001)
36. De Angeli, A., Carpenter, R.: Stupid computer! Abuse and social identities. Paper Read at The Interact 2005 Abuse Workshop, September 2005, Rome (2005)
37. De Angeli, A.: On verbal abuse towards chatterbots. In: De Angeli, A., Brahnam, S., Wallis, P., Dix, A. (eds.) CHI 2006 Workshop: Misuse and Abuse of Interactive Technologies, pp. 21–24 (2006), http://www.agentabuse.org/papers.htm
38. Beach, W.A.: Conversation Analysis: "Okay" as a Clue for Understanding Consequentiality. In: Sigman, S.J. (ed.) The Consequentiality of Communication, pp. 121–162. Lawrence Erlbaum Ass., Hillsdale (1995)
39. Howe, M.: Collaboration on Topic Change in Conversation. In: Ichihashi, K., Linn, M.S. (eds.) Kansas Working Papers in Linguistics, pp. 1–14. University of Kansas (1991)
40. Collins, R.: Interaction Ritual Chains. Princeton University Press, Princeton (2004)
41. Kidd, C.D., Taggart, W., Turkle, S.: A sociable Robot to Encourage Social Interaction among the Elderly. In: Proceedings of the International Conference on Robotics and Automation, ICRA 2006, Orlando, Florida, May 15-19, pp. 3972–3976. IEEE (2006)

What Issue Should Your Virtual Butler Solve Next?

Stefan Rank

Austrian Research Institute for Artificial Intelligence (OFAI)
Freyung 6/6/7, 1010 Vienna, Austria
stefan.rank@ofai.at

Abstract. In this chapter, a scenario-based analysis of the guiding vision of a virtual butler is presented. After introducing the concept of scenario-based analysis for comparing agent-based technology design, we use the characterization of the scenario hinted at in the vision document to discuss several technological issues that arise from it. By disregarding non-technical issues, we arrive at problems (or rather challenges) of technology in a wide sense that could be steps in the direction of the virtual butler. The order of presentation of these challenges is based on a subjective estimation of the complexity involved in arriving at the competence required for a virtual butler.

1   Introduction

Throughout this chapter, we refer to a document that describes the interaction with a virtual butler as a guiding vision for research on this topic, reprinted in the introduction to this volume. For the convenience of the reader, we provide a short summary of this text:

> The vision document follows a day in the life of almost 70-year-old Tina, a very active lady in the year 2020. The reader experiences how she gets interviewed about her youth via video call by her granddaughter, how she waters the flowers for her neighbor Dorothy who is on vacation, how she first enjoys a shared fitness training session with a friend and then invites her to her home for coffee. During all these activities, Tina is supported by her virtual butler James who manages incoming calls, schedules her appointments, and accompanies her in a bracelet when she leaves the house. The interview about the 'old times' frames a description of the technological advances that led to an improved lifestyle, while the visit to her neighbor's house introduces another virtual butler, Djinn, and thus demonstrates the personalization of these agents. Additionally, the text presents the active, working life of Tina and her participation in social activities, as well as more details on the training and maintenance of virtual butlers.

A virtual butler as described qualitatively in this guiding vision is essentially an intelligent affective agent. While intelligent agents are an area of artificial intelligence that researches on developing entities that are autonomous, persist over time, and can act in and adapt to their environment, affective agents specifically target domains in which emotional and related phenomena are important. Current research uses the

R. Trappl (Ed.): Your Virtual Butler, LNAI 7407, pp. 179–186, 2013.

terms embodied conversational agent [1], intelligent virtual agent [2], or autonomous personality agent [3] to refer to different variants of intelligent affective agents with more or less well-defined uses. The virtual butler can be seen as a fully developed end-product of all the different research strands surrounding this field, i.e. a complete agent application.

This chapter will first present the idea of the scenario-based method to get a more detailed insight into the technical requirements of a specific agent application. Then an analysis of the described scenario, as if it were a technical specification, will serve as the basis to come up with a subjectively ordered list of issues that separate the vision from reality.

Note that we disregard issues of trust and other social requirements of a virtual butler; these are covered in more detail in other chapters. Further, potential flaws of the underlying goals of the virtual butler as described are ignored. Thus, even if the steps are followed, they are far from a recipe for success and we might arrive at a different endpoint than originally thought; even if all the issues mentioned were solved overnight, the resulting technological possibility might still not be viable or desirable.

2   Scenario-Based Analysis

We originally introduced scenarios in the EU-project Humaine[1] as a tool for comparison of affective agent architectures by making criteria applicable to different agent applications explicit [4,3]. To be able to relate different approaches that meet specific sets of requirements, we developed a context-dependent analysis based on scenario descriptions. These descriptions explicate purpose of and motivation for building a system, detailing the desired interactions while maintaining a clear separation from implementation aspects.

Sloman [5] makes a similar argument concerning planning and evaluation of research[2], arguing for a focus on robotic scenarios. Scenarios are points in the niche space[3] for agents: the possible purposes and environments of use. However, scenarios are also valuable for the design phase of a new agent application, since they are relevant for the requirements analysis step of the (idealized) process of systems engineering.

As scenario-based design and evaluation is an established concept in usability [7,8], we need to point out the differences to the present concept: in usability specific user stories allow for iterative refinement of the actual requirements of a system. A scenario in usability is a prototyping tool that handles one user achieving one specific goal and thereby focuses on specific functionalities and a certain depth of the system. The analogy we use for (affective) agent architectures consists in regarding human behaviour as the system - a scenario is then the part that an agent architecture should be able to reproduce.

---

[1] http://emotion-research.net/

[2] See [6] for a scenario template proposed in the CoSy project.

[3] In evolutionary biology the role of an organism in an ecological system to which it is adapted is called its ecological niche.

The basic characteristics of an application scenario are the motivation for building the system, its purpose, and the details of a possible deployment. Motivation and purpose are most useful for the comparison of different systems rather than for the design phase. However, while we can idealistically assume that the motivation for building *Tina's butler* is to improve living conditions and active participation in a modern society (rather than the more straightforward motivation for building most commercial service systems, i.e. money), it is not evident what the actual purpose of the system is. A clearly defined purpose is crucial in order to evaluate if an agent is performing well. Let's assume that the (ill-defined and overly broad) purpose of the butler is to either help with or completely take over those tasks of its user that are either impossible to perform for her or that she does not enjoy doing.

Most interesting from a technology standpoint are the details of deployment. A crucial point is the characterization of the system's *interaction qualities*: this includes the user interface as well as the interaction between the agents and their environment. The *user interface* can be regarded as a special case on the spectrum of agent-environment interaction that ranges from sequential binary decisions and sensations (e.g., in the iterated prisoner's dilemma) to the complexity of human interaction in the real world. User interfaces can be as reduced as in turn-based dialog systems or as complex as in some robotic applications. *Interactions* can be described informally as typical scenario scripts that illustrate the possible activities, including tool use and social relations, as well as the utilization of second-order resources, complemented by negative scripts of interactions that fall outside a given scenario. A more formal description of interaction qualities could include all agent tasks possible; agent-local performance measures (e.g., maximum response time for user requests); the *average number of conflicting long-term or short-term tasks*; and further qualitative behavioural criteria such as coherence, variety, or believability in virtual character applications. Even though hard to quantify, the latter often form an essential part of scenario descriptions. Another part is the characterization of the *environment as presented to the agent*. This comprises the intrinsic limitations, dynamics, and regularities of the interactions, including properties such as being time-stepped or asynchronous (cf. also the 'PEAS' characterization of agents in [9]). The scenario should also specify the *number of agents* and *agent types* (including interacting humans) in terms of typical and hard or practical limits.

3   Tina's Butler Interpreted as Scenario

If we take the description of Tina and her butler James as a typical script of what the system is supposed to do, we can try to derive the intended interaction qualities. The environment of the agent is in this case the real world (sensed in real-time with unspecified sensors) and additionally a range of (electronic) interaction channels that are not available directly to humans. The core system seems to consist of only one agent type, the virtual butler, but see the section below on synchronous operation at multiple locations for a qualification. The agent interacts with humans and other agents of the same type but is trained to have a unique personality. The main user interface is anthropomorphic. Specific performance measures are impossible to derive from a qualitative description as it only highlights certain features and their typical quality, but considering the combination of all the features described is and assuming a seamless integration points towards the expected performance. Note also that the text does not contain any negative examples, i.e. competences that fall outside the capabilities of the virtual butler. Based on the activities described in the text the following is a list of technological issues, subjectively ordered based on perceived severity.

3.1   Language Competence – From Domain-Specific to General

The most obvious capability of the butler from a user's perspective is that it is able to 'understand users', apparently in completely unrestricted conversations. It also uses generated speech to express itself. This already is an extremely demanding requirement compared to today's domain-specific speech recognition and language understanding.

In addition, the butler not only understands conversations of other humans but it can anticipate what its user wants to say at a particular moment, allowing it to give the user a prompt and thus work as an extended memory with a speech-based real-time query interface. In the text, the agent anticipates a name that Tina did not remember, and in addition, it has the ability to decide in real-time that this was an actual memory fault (rather than, e.g., an intentional figure of speech), that it is currently appropriate to pro-actively prompt, and how to prompt. The agent can also derive appointments and plan changes based on promises overheard. While this is not directly stated in the text, we can safely assume, given the other abilities in the scenario, that these promises are automatically picked up without explicit notification. One could argue that the ability to discern real promises and polite promises is necessarily included in general conversation understanding anyway. However, overall, the natural language technology required for the open domain conversation and the additional features described in the guiding vision is still technology of a distant future—merely the step from domain-specific language understanding to unrestricted domains is currently unsolved—with 2020 being a rather optimistic timeframe.

3.2   Synchronous Operation at Multiple Locations

James is presented as a single agent, but it interacts with a very diverse environment. The agent communicates not only with its owner but also with other people (directly through speech as well as through other channels), but the agent is not limited to one communication at a time as it can be at different locations at the same time (e.g. at home talking to guests while also away with the owner). The agent itself is mobile, i.e. it can be interacted with using different devices (e.g. Tina's bracelet) and modalities as well as using different interface representations.

These characteristics imply one of two options: either that the agent has to be constructed with a quite different form of *embodiment* and *situatedness* than humans have; or that it is actually a collection of semi-independent agents, i.e. a distributed multi-agent system [10]. Many feats of human intelligence rely on the benefits that human situatedness in a relatively regular physical environment provides. It provides a scaffolding [11] that allows for the use of locally effective, indexical structures as a basis for more complex competences and it is the basis for the functionally meaningful regularities that restrict the complexity of agent-environment interactions, i.e. an agent's *lifeworld* [12]. While the lifeworlds of humans are far from understood concerning their implication for control structures, a single-agent virtual butler would have to deal with a lifeworld of considerably increased complexity.

The latter option on the other hand, i.e. that the virtual butler is actually better described as a multi-agent system, points to a challenge for coordination techniques (in addition to those described below in the last subsection).

3.3   Domain Knowledge, Including Specialized Knowledge

The virtual butler combines knowledge in many different domains: it not only talks with its owner and manages the household technology, it negotiates offers (one assumes: in diverse areas of commerce), it also functions as a mobility and travel agent, it plans and re-arranges trips if necessary based on information about the weather or about delays. In addition, the butler *offers advice with many problems of daily life*.

In the terms of Minsky [13], the agent is expected to have common-sense knowledge and reasoning competence in a broad range of different 'realms', superior to the competence of average, or even most, humans. Many different artificial intelligence projects over the last years have attempted to capture common-sense knowledge in a form directly usable by machines, e.g. [14] and [15]. The coverage of these projects is not yet satisfactory and, furthermore, most of them focus mostly on the collection of declarative knowledge with little consideration of the usage of knowledge in interactive applications, especially in real-time (see below).

3.4   Tightly Integrated Personalization across Domains

Personalization is one of the features of James (and Djinn) that is mentioned repeatedly. The knowledge and consideration of personal preferences is not only restricted to one domain as in current systems but encompasses several domains. The agent can further recognize the current condition of the user 'by the pitch of her voice'. While this is presented only as a potentially false impression in the text, we can, based on the described capability of understanding normal conversations, assume that it is an actual requirement.

The agent knows and respects preferences of guests (in the text we learn that the coffee prepared by James for Tina's friend is just as she likes it), i.e. it has an elaborate user model, not only of its owner but also of other human agents. It remembers and recognizes users. The interaction with the user is personalized: it respects preferences of the user regarding interaction style but also regarding time management, i.e. what kind of interaction is appropriate at different times and in different moods. The agent manages personal privacy, i.e. it knows about what information to disclose to whom. It takes care of security and authentication in diverse communications. As a small concession to the personalization requirement the text hints at the rather long training period that is needed. Long-term user models that accompany a user across different applications and tasks and that are easily inspected by the user herself to provide for the necessary control and privacy are currently a guiding vision for research in the field of user modeling [16].

These capabilities taken together require the competence to resolve conflicts between different personalization needs[4]; a problem that is often a challenge for the human herself. Note that this problem gives rise to the one point in the text that mentions an imperfection: Dorothy's Djinn decides to clean up immediately, following its owner's preferences, at the expense of annoying Tina.

3.5   Affective Interaction, Empathy, Politeness, Relationship Maintenance

Never directly stated, but implicit in the previous requirements, is the competence of interacting with humans on a near equal level. This involves knowledge of affective components of interaction, an understanding of empathy, politeness, and the complexities of social relations. In short, the agent has to understand, and maintain, its social lifeworld [17]. A big range of emotional competences such as the detection of norm violations is a prerequisite. These competences are an active research topic in psychology, in a descriptive fashion. As a problem of control, they are a target of research for affective agents where the current focus is on replicating single components, e.g. [18,19,20]. An integrated approach to a social lifeworld for artificial agents that is applicable in real-world scenarios as described for the virtual butler is still in its infancy.

3.6   Real-Time Behaviour Competence Surpassing the Average Human

A further, even more general requirement can be assumed from the text: the agent needs to apply all of the above competences in real-time interactions. As exemplified at the beginning of the guiding vision, Tina merely needs to 'adjust herself' which prompts James to activate a pending video call. The agent thus needs to be able to interpret mere movements correctly in context, deriving the intention of the user[5]. This, however, is not restricted to what humans are capable of. Since the agent also communicates with other agents of its kind, taking care of payments and information exchange; since it also monitors several other devices, including potentially time-critical ones such as the 'Vitals Monitor' of its owner, the agent exemplifies a veritable advancement in real-time control architectures, not only compared to current state of the art in technology but also compared to what (single) humans are capable of.

3.7   Autonomous Coordination of the Different Competences and Multiple Concerns

But even if we disregard the particular complexities of real-time control, the range of concerns and competences that the agent has to coordinate is still vast. If we take

---

[4] On the other hand a broader approach to personalization involving more information sources can also create beneficial synergies: consider current personalization techniques that fail because they miss information like "what I just bought was not for me, but for someone else".

[5] Unless this is simply a command gesture which would imply that the human is the one who was trained.

into account that a single agent is probably not sufficient as an analogy for James, the coordination task is akin to the management and coordination of a small corporation.

James takes care of the different (automatic) payments of daily life; it communicates with other agents of its kind; it monitors the vital functions of the owner and her 'optimal training level'; it manages appointments and dynamically considers planning opportunities ('you could water the flowers for Dorothy') thus pro-actively performing time management while integrating the plans of others as relevant to the user; it coordinates different appliances and synchronizes the personal information therein; it controls household technology; it negotiates offers.

Thus, James is not restricted to a small set of tasks. It has to manage a multitude of different short-term and long-term tasks and concerns that will often conflict. Further, all of these tasks are active research topics of their own and, as mentioned previously, the butler has to fulfill them in a way superior to what a single human assistant would be capable of. While this may sound like an insurmountable problem, we think that exactly this last challenge may provide for a key solution that can also be leveraged to further research on the other challenges presented. In [3], we claimed that this coordination of behaviour is the central problem for any intelligent autonomous agent and, for this reason, we have put this issue last in this chapter. The virtual butler is but one of the many application scenarios that advancements in the area of behaviour coordination would bring closer to reality.

4   Conclusion

Looking back at the purpose of the virtual butler that we hypothesized about at the beginning of the previous section—to help with or completely take over those tasks of its user that are either impossible to perform for her or that she does not enjoy doing—we have to reconsider: The competences hinted at in the guiding vision cover both more and less. But mostly, the virtual butler completes tasks that would be impossible to perform for the user in that quality, e.g. that fast or with considering that much information. The crucial requirement for this is the integration of all the competences described, which is a central topic of behaviour coordination. So, while most of the descriptions in this chapter may sound rather pessimistic, important scientific advances in the mentioned fields are happening today and the potential synergies between these fields, as fostered by guiding visions such as the virtual butler, are exciting, to say the least.

While many of the issues brought up in this chapter are probably obvious for researchers working in this area, the intention of listing them, and of listing them in a particular order, was to provide for provocative talking points of what constitutes the most pressing or the hardest issues to be tackled in the next years. The challenges presented are certainly not independent. Progress in common-sense knowledge and reasoning will have an impact on open domain natural language technology. Real-time behaviour and behaviour coordination in general are closely related. Advances in affective interaction are definitely a prerequisite for further progress in general language competence. Even more interesting than the problem of ordering these issues is therefore the question, if any of them crucially depend on progress in other areas or if can they be worked on separately at all? A fascinating question that we have to leave unanswered, for now.

References

1. Cassell, J.: Embodied Conversational Agents: Representation and Intelligence in User Interface. Special Issue on Intelligent User Interfaces, AI Magazine 22(4), 67–83 (2001)
2. Luck, M., Aylett, R.: Applying Artificial Intelligence to Virtual Reality: Intelligent Virtual Environments. Applied Artificial Intelligence 14(1), 3–32 (2000)
3. Rank, S.: Behaviour Coordination for Models of Affective Behaviour. Dissertation, Vienna University of Technology, carried out at the Austrian Research Institute for Artificial Intelligence (OFAI) (2009)
4. Rank, S., Petta, P.: Comparability is key to assess affective architectures. In: Trappl, R. (ed.) Cybernetics and Systems 2006, Proceedings of the Eighteenth Meeting on Cybernetics and Systems Research, pp. 643–648 (2006)
5. Sloman, A.: AI in a new millennium - obstacles and opportunities. School of Computer Science, University of Birmingham, UK (2005)
6. Sloman, A., Wyatt, J.: COSY scenario template (2006), http://www.cs.bham.ac.uk/research/projects/cosy/scenarios/scenario-template.txt
7. Nielsen, J.: Usability engineering. Academic Press (1993)
8. Cooper, A.: The inmates are running the asylum. SAMS Publishing (1999)
9. Russell, S., Norvig, P.: Artificial intelligence - a modern approach. Pearson Education Inc., Upper Saddle River (2003)
10. Weiss, G.: Multiagent Systems - A Modern Approach to Distributed Artificial Intelligence. MIT Press, Cambridge (1999)
11. Clark, A.: Being There: Putting Brain, Body and World Together Again. MIT Press/Bradford Books, Cambridge, London (1997)
12. Agre, P.E., Horswill, I.: Lifeworld Analysis. Journal of Artificial Intelligence Research 6, 111–145 (1997)
13. Minsky, M.: The emotion machine. Simon & Schuster, New York (2006)
14. Panton, K., Matuszek, C., Lenat, D., Schneider, D., Witbrock, M., Siegel, N., Shepard, B.: Common Sense Reasoning – From Cyc to Intelligent Assistant. In: Cai, Y., Abascal, J. (eds.) Ambient Intelligence in Everyday Life. LNCS (LNAI), vol. 3864, pp. 1–31. Springer, Heidelberg (2006)
15. Lieberman, H., Liu, H., Singh, P., Barry, B.: Beating common sense into interactive applications. AI Magazine, Winter 2004 25(4), 63–76 (2004)
16. Kay, J.: Lifelong Learner Modeling for Lifelong Personalized Pervasive Learning. IEEE Transactions on Learning Technologies 1(4), 215–228 (2008)
17. Rank, S., Petta, P.: Motivating dramatic interactions. In: Canamero, L. (ed.) Agents that Want and Like: Motivational and Emotional Roots of Cognition and Action, AISB Proceedings, pp. 102–107 (2005)
18. Wang, N., Johnson, W.L., Mayer, R.E., Rizzo, P., Shaw, E., Collins, H.: The politeness effect: Pedagogical agents and learning outcomes. International Journal of Human-Computer Studies 66(2), 98–112 (2008)
19. Paiva, A., Dias, J., Sobral, D., Aylett, R., Sobreperez, P., Woods, S., Zoll, C., Hall, L.: Caring for agents and agents that care: building empathic relations with synthetic agents. In: Proceedings of the Third International Joint Conference on Autonomous Agents and Multiagent Systems, AAMAS 2004, pp. 194–201 (2004)
20. Skowron, M., Rank, S., Paltoglou, G., Ahn, J., Gobron, S.: No peanuts! Affective Cues for the Virtual Bartender. In: Guesgen, H., McCarthy, P., Murray, C. (eds.) Proceedings of the 24th International FLAIRS Conference (FLAIRS-24), Palm Beach, FL, USA. Affective Computing Special Track, AAAI Press, Menlo Park, CA (2011)

Author Index